UNIVERSITY OF NORTH CAROLINA AT CHAPEL HILL
DEPARTMENT OF ROMANCE LANGUAGES

NORTH CAROLINA STUDIES
IN THE ROMANCE LANGUAGES AND LITERATURES

Founder: URBAN TIGNER HOLMES

Editor: FRANK A. DOMÍNGUEZ

Distributed by:

UNIVERSITY OF NORTH CAROLINA PRESS

CHAPEL HILL
North Carolina 27515-2288
U.S.A.

NORTH CAROLINA STUDIES IN THE
ROMANCE LANGUAGES AND LITERATURES
Number 289

READING THE *EXEMPLUM* RIGHT:
FIXING THE MEANING OF
EL CONDE LUCANOR

READING THE *EXEMPLUM* RIGHT: FIXING THE MEANING OF *EL CONDE LUCANOR*

BY
JONATHAN BURGOYNE

CHAPEL HILL

NORTH CAROLINA STUDIES IN THE ROMANCE
LANGUAGES AND LITERATURES
U.N.C. DEPARTMENT OF ROMANCE LANGUAGES

2007

Library of Congress Cataloging-in-Publication Data

Burgoyne, Jonathan, 1967-
　　Reading the exemplum right: fixing the meaning of El Conde Lucanor / Jonathan Burgoyne.
　　p. cm. – (North Carolina Studies in the Romance Languages and Literatures ; no. 289).
　　Includes bibliographical references and index.
　　ISBN 0-8078-9293-9 (softcover)
　　1. Juan Manuel, Infante of Castile, 1282-1347. Conde Lucanor. I. Title. II. Series.

PQ6402.B87 2007
863'.1–dc22　　　　　　　　　　　　　　　　　　　　　　　　　　　　　2007023194

Cover design: Heidi Perov

© 2007. Department of Romance Languages. The University of North Carolina at Chapel Hill.

ISBN 0-8078-9293-9

DEPÓSITO LEGAL: V. 3.718 - 2007

ARTES GRÁFICAS SOLER, S. L. - LA OLIVERETA, 28 - 46018 VALENCIA
www.graficas-soler.com

CONTENTS

	Page
ACKNOWLEDGEMENTS	7
INTRODUCTION	9
PART I: READING *EL CONDE LUCANOR* RIGHT	31
CHAPTER 1: ETHICAL AMBIGUITY IN *EL CONDE LUCANOR*	42
CHAPTER 2: JUAN MANUEL'S EXEMPLARY ART	74
CHAPTER 3: THE *EXEMPLUM* IN ACTION	99
PART II: FIXING THE MEANING OF *EL CONDE LUCANOR*	119
CHAPTER 4: THE IDEOLOGICAL READING OF *EL CONDE LUCANOR*	124
CHAPTER 5: THE LATE MEDIEVAL AND EARLY MODERN AUDIENCES OF *EL CONDE LUCANOR*	169
CONCLUSIONS: THE MODERN CRITICAL RECEPTION OF *EL CONDE LUCANOR*	195
BIBLIOGRAPHY	223
INDEX	231

ACKNOWLEDGEMENTS

My fascination with the Spanish short prose narrative, and particularly Juan Manuel's masterpiece, *El Conde Lucanor*, intensified during my graduate studies, and after completing my dissertation on the short stories of Juan Manuel, Juan Timoneda, and Miguel Cervantes, I returned to Spanish medieval literature with a desire to study the manuscripts of *El Conde Lucanor* directly. I was especially motivated by John Dagenais's book, *The Ethics of Reading in Manuscript Culture: Glossing the Libro de buen amor* (1994). This ground-breaking study has encouraged many hispanomedievalists to refocus their attention on the material manuscript situation of works that are so often only accessed through modern critical editions. I am in debt to Professor Dagenais's work, and this book is, in many ways, a tribute to the important contributions he has made to the field of medieval studies.

I cannot acknowledge here all of the scholars whose work informs my book, but like many studies that engage the variant manuscript performances of a particular piece of medieval literature, this book builds on the foundations laid by Paul Zumthor and Bernard Cerquiglini; especially Zumthor's *Essai de poétique médiévale* (1972) and Cerquiglini's *Éloge de la variante: histoire critique de la philologie* (1989) . Many other important scholars working in the so-called "new" philology have served as guides for my research, such as Howard Block, Lee Patterson and Stephen Nichols, all of whom contributed seminal essays to the special issue of *Speculum* on "The New Philology" (vol. 65, 1990).

I am also in debt to the generosity and friendship of Laurence de Looze, George Greenia, Aníbal Biglieri, and Joseph Snow. While working on this book, I had the pleasure of inviting Laurence de Looze to lecture at The Pennsylvania State University. Recently, Professor De Looze has published what will surely be one of the most important studies on *El Conde Lucanor* to date, *Manuscript Diversity, Meaning, and Variance in Juan Manuel's El Conde Lucanor* (2006). I am thankful for his encouragement, constructive criticism, collegial spirit, and most of all for his friendship. I would also like to thank George Greenia and the reviewers who collaborate with *La corónica* for providing such insightful comments and helpful criticisms on my articles. The reviewers of this book were also extremely helpful and generous with their comments, and I thank them for their efforts.

Several years ago at a conference in Burgos, I had the good fortune of participating in a seminar with Aníbal Biglieri. Professor Biglieri is an authority on Juan Manuel, and over the years I have benefited from his expertise in many engaging conversations at the Kentucky Foreign Language Conference, as well as at his home in Lexington. His hospitality, friendship and sound advice are sincerely appreciated.

I must also thank the staff of the Sala Cervantes at the Biblioteca Nacional in Madrid for their assistance, as well as the excellent librarians at the Real Academia de la Historia, and the Real Academia Española. Among my most pleasant and rewarding experiences from working at the Biblioteca Nacional was discussing my research with Professor Joseph Snow. He has long been a model of excellence for many scholars, and I consider myself fortunate for having been able to take advantage of his impressive knowledge of Spanish medieval literature.

This book would not have been possible without the support from research grants funded by The Catholic University of America, The Pennsylvania State University and the Program for Cultural Cooperation between Spain's Ministry of Culture and North American Universities. Finally, these acknowledgments would not be complete without thanking my wife and family for their loving support, and I dedicate these pages to the Angulo family who afforded me the space and time to write this book in the relaxing old Mediterranean fishing village of La Mata.

INTRODUCTION

Since the earliest print edition in 1575 of Don Juan Manuel's most important work, *El Conde Lucanor* (hereafter *CL*), completed in 1335, many scholars and editors have been preoccupied with bringing this fourteenth-century collection of short stories, maxims and medieval Christian doctrine to the attention of a larger international audience. They have been particularly interested in the first of five parts in Juan Manuel's book, also known as the *Libro de los enxiemplos del Conde Lucanor et de Patronio*, made up of fifty one short illustrative narratives, each framed by a conversation between a powerful nobleman, Count Lucanor, and his adviser, Patronio, who solves the Count's myriad political troubles and spiritual concerns through the use of various *exempla*.[1] One reoccurring observation found in the introductions of early editions and critical commentaries points to the lack of critical attention paid to this aristocratic Castilian author, but these early reviews seem to contradict the manuscript witnesses of Juan Manuel's earliest reception. With five late medieval and early modern manuscripts surviving, medievalists imagine that the *CL* was widely read among the literate elite of its time, yet its first editor, Gonzalo Argote de Molina, laments in his introduction that it was relatively unknown in Spain by the sixteenth century:[2]

---

[1] The remaining four parts, each framed by the continuing dialogue between the Count and Patronio, are made up of a collection of axioms (parts II-IV) and a concluding treatise on faith and the sacraments which has a "sermon-like" structure according to Paolo Cherchi, one of the most important critics who has studied in detail this often ignored conclusion to Juan Manuel's book (373).

[2] Daniel Devoto traces some of the earliest recorded references to the *CL*, as

> Juzgaua ser cosa indigna que un príncipe tan discreto y cortesano, y de la mejor lengua de aquel tiempo anduuiesse en tan pocas manos (A4r, It seemed to me improper that [the work of] such a discreet and courtly prince, whose use of language was the best of his time should be handled by so few).[3]

With a second edition of the *CL* published in Madrid in 1642, Juan Manuel became one of the more popular medieval authors among intellectuals and literary circles of the Spanish Golden Age.[4] The famous seventeenth-century playwright, Pedro Calderón de la Barca, was inspired by Juan Manuel's work and used its title for one of his plays, while the Jesuit author Baltasar Gracián saw fit to cite Juan Manuel several times in his *Agudeza, y arte de ingenio* as an example of style, rhetoric, and ethics. Not only does Gracián point to the *CL* for examples of literary and rhetorical devices, he even recasts some of Patronio's *exempla*, creating his own versions of Juan Manuel's tales as he read them in Argote de Molina's edition.[5] It is also quite conceivable that Cervantes had the *CL* in mind, among other early-modern Spanish collections of short prose narratives such as Joan Timoneda's *El patrañuelo* (1567), when he remarked in his introduction to the *Novelas ejemplares* (1613) that he was the first to write original *novelas* in the Castilian language (1: 52).

---

well as the history of various lost manuscripts in his excellent critical introduction and bibliography, concluding that "the manuscript copies of Juan Manuel's work appear to have been abundant" ["*las copias manuscritas de esta obra de Don Juan Manuel parecen haber sido abundantes*"] (292).

[3] Whenever possible, English translations of the first part of *El Conde Lucanor* will be cited from John E. Keller and L. Clark Keatings's edition, *The Book of Count Lucanor and Patronio*. Unless noted otherwise, all other English translations are my own. Quotations from the original Spanish text are taken from José Manuel Blecua's edition. I have chosen Blecua's edition because it is based on manuscript S, and as such it will serve as a base text for later comparisons with other manuscript witnesses of the *CL*.

[4] While Francisco López Estrada points out that Juan Manuel was the most famous medieval author of the Spanish Golden Age (*Introducción a la literatura medieval* 428), María Rosa Lida de Malkiel claims in her now classic essay, "Tres notas sobre don Juan Manuel," that the *CL* was the *only* medieval work of a Spanish author known in Spain during the sixteenth and seventeenth centuries (164).

[5] In *Agudeza, y arte de ingenio* as it appears in *Obras de Lorenzo Gracián*, vol. 2, see "Discurso XXIII La agudeza paradoxa" (130), "Discurso XXVII Las crisis irrisorias" (158-159), and "Discurso XXXV De los conceptos por ficción" (208). Erasmo Buceta opined in 1924 that Gracian's admiration for Juan Manuel demonstrates the blending of renaissance and medieval elements in the "spirit" of the Spanish Golden Age (66).

This book is divided into two general studies of the *CL*. The first is a literary analysis of the text, and the second is a study of the reception of the *CL* as it can be determined by its manuscript witnesses. A central thesis of the first part of this book is that Juan Manuel was one of the earliest European authors to appropriate the ideological power and cultural authority of narrative in the form of the *exemplum*, especially the tradition of the sermon *exemplum* popularized throughout Western Europe in large part due to the mission of the Dominican and Franciscan orders, and the impulse to educate the faithful promoted by the Fourth Lateran Council (1215).[6] The association just made between the narrative form of the *exemplum* and ideology is borrowed from Larry Scanlon's study of Chaucer's place in the history of the form. More than "a narrative enactment of cultural authority," as Scanlon redefines the *exemplum* (34), Juan Manuel's collection of exemplary tales moves beyond the appropriation of cultural authority by providing instruction for any reader with a basic medieval education in grammar, logic, and rhetoric, on how to enact the same discursive maneuver for a myriad of personal, ethical, and spiritual needs. Juan Manuel teaches this lesson to those who can follow the rhetorical mode of thinking that structures his collection of stories, and exposes the inherently ambivalent nature of the *exemplum* as a narrative sign.

My reading of the *CL* in chapter 1 uncovers this ambivalence by exposing the ethical ambiguity that is created when exemplary behaviors applied to similar situations are compared and contrasted. My comparative reading process is, in fact, prompted by manuscript reading aids that identify the author's narrative design and divisions, pointing the reader to the beginning of a critical reading practice that recognized divisible parts in search for a work's complete meaning. Building on my conclusions from the previous chapter, in chapter 2 I follow Juan Manuel's meta-rhetorical message in selected tales from Part I, and maxims from Parts II to IV, that expose the *exemplum* as an ambivalent sign whose meaning is entirely contingent upon its reader. In chapter 3 I focus my literary analysis on two tales from Part I (*ejemplos* 3 and 33), as well as a concluding *exemplum*

---

[6] Derek Lomax's essay "The Lateran Reforms and Spanish Literature" is still one of the best studies of the impact of this important council in the Iberian peninsula. His comments on the sermon *exemplum* and its influence on lay authors are particularly relevant here.

from Part V that put the power of the *exemplum* on display for the reader in concrete political, ethical and soteriological contexts.

The second part of the book shows how Juan Manuel's first audiences read his *exempla* right in two ways. First, by employing the *exempla* in new contexts, accurately recognizing that Juan Manuel's tales invite new applications; and second, by fixing a conservative interpretation for an amazingly complex, even paradoxical work that invites numerous interpretations and applications. I often describe this reading tradition as "the right reading," intentionally playing with the double meaning of "right" (i.e. "correct" and "ideologically conservative"), and I will discuss my choice of words like "fix" and "right" further on, but for now I must state that I do not use the verb to imply that any particular reading is broken or incorrect, nor that there is any one sufficient reading of the *CL*; on the contrary, I would like to argue that there can be more than one correct reading, and that the author himself anticipates various types of readers and uses for his tales. I use the verb "to fix" here as "to establish" or "to stabilize," since I believe that the late medieval and early modern reception of the *CL* established a meaning that would become conventional over time.

There is also a shift in method in the second part of this book which deals more properly with manuscript studies, or "materialist philology." I borrow this name of a new philology from Siegfried Wenzel, whose approach to manuscript studies, especially medieval anthologies, may best describe the various approaches some medievalists have employed in order to reconstruct medieval responses and readings based on the physical evidence found in hand-made books. A materialist philology, as Wenzel defines it, "postulates the possibility that a given manuscript, having been organized along certain principles, may well present its text(s) according to its own agenda," and that "[f]ar from being a transparent or neutral vehicle, the codex can have a typological identity that affects the way we read and understand the texts it presents" (2). I would add to this that the medieval manuscript not only affects our reading of it, but it also anticipates its original audience's reading practices, or *modus legendi*. Traces of those practices, and early medieval responses to a work can often be found marked in the books themselves, in reading aids, marginal notes, pointing fingers, deletions, corrections, and glosses, all of which remind us that each medieval book recreates its own discreet history and reception.

I have divided my manuscript study of reception into two general categories; the ideological reading of the *CL* that aligned the work with the audiences' expectations (chapter 4), and a sketch of the audience itself (chapter 5). Such a clear distinction between the reading imposed on the text and the audience does not exist as such in the manuscripts themselves; rather, they are both present at the same time, but for the sake of organization, I have attempted to separate the interpretation from the audience that reshaped and recruited the *CL* for various uses. Nevertheless, an overlap is unavoidable, since all of the manuscript witnesses of the *CL* reveal both categories simultaneously.

In my conclusion I will examine the first print edition of the *CL* and revisit one of the manuscript witnesses briefly in order to point to the construction of the author as an essential part of a reception that would become conventional, even orthodox, and can be traced in the history of critical editions, commentaries, and our modern critical debate over the significance and didactic content of Juan Manuel's most canonized work.

I must make a final concession before moving on with regard to what I refer to above as the "right" reading and conventional understanding of the *CL* today. In chapter 4 I cite María Rosa Menocal's excellent essay on "openness" in the *CL* in which she succinctly summarizes a very long critical tradition of reading Juan Manuel's work as essentially closed, with a meaning that can only be understood within the socio-political frame of fourteenth-century Castilla, or even limited to Juan Manuel's biography: "[I]t is openly and positively and unambiguously didactic" –according to Menocal's review– "it is a limpid guide to help meet the needs, duties and difficulties of a Castilian nobleman in the time when Castilla is beginning to establish its various hegemonies in the peninsula" (475).

Here Menocal alludes to some of the most omnipresent topics in the critical bibliography on the *CL*; it is transparently didactic, completely untroubled by ambiguity or contradiction, and essentially referential to Juan Manuel's political life experiences and culture. Although Menocal's rehearsal of Manuelian criticism is accurate, in my opinion, most of the critics working today on Juan Manuel and the *CL* have abandoned the simplistic open / closed dichotomy of this reading. I do not intend, nor is it necessary for my argument, to set up this critical tradition as a kind of straw man, since I am not immediately concerned with refuting it. This critical reception is certainly valid, but it is also only one response –historically and ideologically constructed within the development of hispanomedievalism and Spanish philology– to one semantic level in a work which is far more innovative and complex. I would even suggest that Juan Manuel's work is more representative of the skeptical and uncertain fourteenth-century philosophical and political environment, closer even to the work of Juan Ruiz than many scholars have led us to believe, especially in its treatment of the contingency of language and narrative.[7] Rather than undermining this critical reception, my study in the following chapters attempts to simply indicate where this reading begins, how it was fashioned and continued, and perhaps more daringly I will suggest that, in fact, the conventional meaning of the *CL* is as much the result of its medieval reception as it is the author's design.

Although the debate over Juan Manuel's work as either "open" or "closed" does continue, most recent scholarship on the *CL* recognizes threads of contradiction, gaps or aporia, even ambiguity and paradox in Juan Manuel's tales. Many scholars are beginning to appreciate "openness" in the *CL*, while at the same time acknowledging an authorial attempt at closure. Dayle Seidenspinner-Núñez, to cite one scholar, finds the meaning of Juan Manuel's work to be "closed" due to the author's use of "carefully contrived stages of mediation and constrictive guidelines" –a reading reminiscent of Aníbal Biglieri, whom I cite in chapter 3 (*Hacia una poética* 262). In the same essay, Seidenspinner-Nuñez uncovers similarities between the *CL* and *Libro de buen amor*; the most significant for my own study is the critic's observation of contradictions in both Juan Ruiz and Juan Manuel's didactic message:

> In both 'didactic' authors, then, we observe a shift from faith based on received authority [. . .] to informed understanding based on lived experience as an appropriate basis for human actions, and a new emphasis on pragmatism, individual will, and personal responsibility. Yet the didactic framework of both works is fraught with internal contradictions. (254)

---

[7] In his chapter on fourteenth-century Nominalism, Armand Maurer summarizes fourteenth-century thought as tending "toward division and decline," and that "[s]kepticism in philosophy permeated the atmosphere" (255-256).

As I will argue in the first part of this book, the troubling contradictions and paradoxes are in fact designed to teach and train the reader on the rhetorical power of the *exemplum* itself, but literary criticism does not have to be a zero-sum game. The fact that other readers with different *entendimientos* can also read the tales as a "limpid guide" to help with their ethical and political dilemmas, or as entertaining short stories that mark the beginning of a modern national literary tradition, is a tribute to Juan Manuel's innovation and artistry.

To cite only a few more examples of this critical trend, I would remind the reader of Aníbal Biglieri's insightful book in which he acknowledges the potential for "play" in the text, but concludes that it is ultimately a closed work (214). Recently, Fernando Gómez Redondo has written in his impressively exhaustive *Historia de la prosa medieval castellana* that Juan Manuel demonstrates "una singular unidad de conciencia literaria y pensamiento político" (1: 1095, "a singular unity of literary consciousness and political thought"), that his literature is a direct reflection of his political life (1: 1093-1094), and that he did not write a single line that did not have a political and social purpose: "no escribe una sola línea que no tenga un propósito político y social" (1: 1095). While Biglieri intelligently cautions against reading the *CL* as autobiographical in any way, scholars such as Gómez Redondo and Alan Deyermond, along with many others, continue to read Juan Manuel's work as ultimately referential to his life and socio-political environment.[8] The echoes of the orthodox readings that Menocal alludes to are clearly audible today, and I hope to trace it further in the following chapters, beginning with its earliest detectable expression.

The *CL* has come down to us in five manuscript forms and one early print edition, which make up the material evidence of its earliest reception (among other less familiar early-modern copies that I have examined). One of my objectives has been to reconstruct those early readings, to clarify how we have arrived at our conventional critical understanding of the *CL* today, and finally suggest a hypothesis about the history of our modern reception of medieval literature in general. I would argue that we have inherited more

---

[8] See Deyermond's "Cuentística y política en Juan Manuel: *El Conde Lucanor*," in which the renowned scholar concludes that, over all, Juan Manuel's fiction ultimately relates back to the author's political life experiences (234).

than old, corrupted copies of the *CL* that are for us modern critics mere letters in *stemmata codicum*, or footnotes in critical editions. We have also inherited readings of the works we edit, found implicit and explicit in the codices that bind them, and can still be heard today.

To what extent these early readers established the meaning of the *CL* in the late medieval and early modern era, and how their readings may linger with us today will be an underlying question of the entire book. Having alluded to a history of reception of the *CL*, Hans Robert Jauss's essay, "Literary History As a Challenge to Literary Theory" is worth recalling here, since our modern critical response to the *CL* is a fascinating case in point of how a medieval work's earliest response mediates its meaning and artistic capital through time:

> The relationship of literature and reader has aesthetic as well as historical implications. The aesthetic implication lies in the fact that the first reception of a work by the reader includes a test of its aesthetic value in comparison with works already read. The obvious historical implication of this is that the understanding of the first reader will be sustained and enriched in a chain of receptions from generation to generation; in this way the historical significance of a work will be decided and its aesthetic value made evident. (*Toward an Aesthetic of Reception* 20)

The reception of the *CL* tests this theory, and corroborates it. I would only add that Juan Manuel's earliest readers responded more to the moral content of the *CL*, rather than its aesthetic value, precisely because they did associate it with "works already read," or an entire corpus and tradition of works, particularly the *exemplum* as it appeared in numerous collections, both in Latin and vernacular languages. This early reception and association with a specific orthodox and catechistic tradition guided the future readings of the *CL*, much in the way Jauss describes the history of reception above, but more than enriching its response, "the first reader" of the *CL* channeled and contained the reception of Juan Manuel's stories, ultimately fixing the conventional meaning it still has today. An early example of this established reception is witnessed in the first print edition of the *CL* which contains an official reading and approbation by doctor Heredia of the Holy Inquisition, stating that it is a

"Catholic work" with "all manner of profitable advice": "Parece me obra cathólica [. . .] a manera todo de consejos prouechosos (A3ʳ).

As a book that takes on the topic of medieval reading practices as mediators of meaning, the present study also addresses what John Dagenais has called "lecturature," or reading as the "dominant literary mode of the Middle Ages" (*The Ethics of Reading* 24). I do attempt to trace lecturature as an event in both parts of the book, but not to the exclusion of literature or the author, as Dagenais has ardently proposed. In the first part of my study, which ultimately returns to the author and his design, I follow the traces of medieval reading customs inscribed in the very structure of the *CL*, and in the second part I examine the manuscript evidence that testifies to real medieval readings and applications of Patronio's lessons. Many of Dagenais's views put forth in his book are born out by the manuscripts of the *CL*, while others will be challenged. In particular, Dagenais's argument that medieval readers engaged in a kind of ethical decision-making process with the text that required their active participation in filling in meanings, and adapting the work to individual lives by glossing a "negatively charged" text will be tested in the case of the *CL* (*Ethics of Reading* 38).

The manuscript situation of the *CL* does in fact demonstrate a reading tradition that filled in, and stabilized a meaning for the text. Part of this ethical reading of the *CL* can be studied in the very composition of some of the manuscripts, as well as the more telltale and idiosyncratic traces of scribal readings they contain. Juan Manuel's tales were read ethically in the sense that they were viewed as belonging to a literary tradition that dealt more with human behavior than art, and they were acted upon by real individual readers. The *CL* was not read so much as recruited, recast and employed, or put into action by professional medieval readers for practical uses. Each codex and early print edition, even the early modern manuscript copies, are purposeful rewritings of the *CL*, recycling it in various forms for specific audiences and needs. One of the most significant consequences of these performances of Juan Manuel's stories is that they set an orthodox reading of the *CL* as doctrine that became conventional. How those readings have survived to the present is a question that this book will attempt to answer, but the answers point to new questions about how medieval readings remain with us today that I have alluded to in the quotation from Jauss above, forming a hypothesis that needs to be tested on many more medieval works in order to determine its usefulness. Nevertheless, I believe this book is a good first step toward reevaluating how medieval readers whisper to us still in our modern critical debates and editions of works that more often than not come to us already read, with meanings fixed by medieval minds.

I have also written this book on the *CL* and its late medieval reception with a larger audience of literary scholars and historians in mind; in particular, I hope to reach across disciplines to those working outside the field of hispanomedievalism. Furthermore, I hope that this book will also be of interest to those working on the subject of book making in the later Middle Ages, especially with regard to the often inaccurately named miscellany, since three of the five manuscript witnesses of the *CL* are, in fact, late medieval anthologies whose design programs shed a great deal of light on how the *CL* was read in fifteenth-century Spain. As a study of the reception of one canonical medieval author, it also follows that this book would be profitable to researchers investigating medieval reading practices in general, and the ways in which medieval textuality anticipates medieval reading customs. Finally, I expect that my book will help literary historians understand more about one of the most important literary forms of the later Middle Ages, the *exemplum*.

Since Larry Scanlon, Jean-Claude Schmitt, Jacques Le Goff, Claude Bremond, Fritz Kemmler, Jean Welter, Joseph Mosher, and many others who have studied the medieval *exemplum*'s impact on lay authors writing in vernacular languages tend to overlook Juan Manuel, I hope to introduce the author to a larger audience of literary critics, medievalists and historians of the later Middle Ages. Although the oversight is surprising, my study of Juan Manuel's appropriation of the *exemplum* tradition is very much in debt to the scholars mentioned above, among others, Judson Boyce Allen, whose study of the ethical poetics of the later Middle Ages is mandatory reading for anyone interested in medieval reading practices and the *exemplum*.

As the title suggests, this book is also about reading in the Middle Ages, and more particularly, medieval readings of the *exemplum* as they appear in the various manuscript performances of the *CL*. My focus on the *exemplum*, rather than the short story for example, is justified since the author identifies Patronio's tales as *enxiemplos*, and they are employed rhetorically to illustrate an argument, behavior, or moral, in keeping with classical and homiletic traditions. Any survey of the critical definitions of the *exemplum* as a literary form and / or rhetorical device, from the *Rhetorica ad Herenium* to Joseph Mosher and Jean Welter's classic studies, or Claude Bremond, Jacques Le Goff and Jean-Claude Schmitt's more recent work, would suffice to demonstrate through comparison that the tales framed by the discourse between the Count and his adviser are, for all intents and purposes, *exempla*.⁹

"The history of the *exemplum* in Spain is long and complicated," as John England has observed ("*¿Et non el día del lodo?*" 69), so much so that a complete review of this important literary history, even limited to the Iberian peninsula, would take up more space than is proper in an introduction.¹⁰ In fact, it is quite difficult to pin down one definitive definition of the form, perhaps because of its

---

⁹ As one of the most important Latin treatises on rhetoric in the Middle Ages, the pseudo-Ciceronian *Rhetorica ad Herennium* is often cited for its definition of the *exemplum* which associates it with an historical event and person invoked to persuade an audience through comparison: "Exemplum est alicuius facti aut dicti praeteriti cum certi auctoris nomine propositio. Id sumitur isdem de causis quibus similitudo" (382). Modern definitions are equally concerned with classifying the *exemplum*'s various generic forms, while they all insist on its rhetorical use as proof of an argument, as in Welter's classic definition: "Par le mot *exemplum*, on entendait, au sens large du terme, un récit ou une historiette, une fable ou une parabole, une moralité ou une description pouvant servir de preuve à l'appui d'un exposé doctrinal, religieux ou moral" (1). Bremond, Le Goff and Schmitt pay greater attention to detail, offering four categories for classifying an *exemplum*, as well as an outline of its formal and ideological characteristics (41-42), but their final definition limits the *exemplum* to "a short story": "un récit bref donné comme véridique et destiné à être insérté dans un discours (en général un sermon) pour convaincre un auditoire par une leçon salutaire" (37). As a final example, Frederic Tubach provides an excellent definition that handles the *exemplum*'s various forms, its rhetorical function, and association with orthodox doctrine. Indirectly, Tubach's definition also points out the importance of the rhetor's interpretation of the narrative in order to determine its signification: "Divergent as this material may be in its content and origin, the *exemplum* is an attempt to discover in each narrative event, character, situation or act a paradigmatic sign that would either substantiate religious beliefs and Church dogma or delineate social ills and human foibles" (523). The idea of the *exemplum* as a paradigmatic sign will be taken up again in the following chapters on Juan Manuel's use of *exempla* in the *CL*.

¹⁰ John Keller has written a very helpful and concise summary of the history of the *exemplum* in Spain in his introduction to *Motif-Index of Mediaeval Spanish Exempla*, reminding his readers that "[t]he development of the *exemplum* in Spain followed much the same course as in neighboring countries," and more particularly that "[t]he *exemplum* in Spain was common property of the Church and the laity and it was employed in books of pious instruction, in doctrinal treatises, in sermons, in extra-clerical works to be read as guides to ethical and successful living, and finally and most importantly to the development of literature, as a source of recreational reading" (ix).

ancient history and perennial appearances throughout time, and in almost all cultures, including our own postmodern world. An interesting case in point of the conventional use of the *exemplum* in recent times for "moral education" may be best observed in William Bennett's *The Book of Virtues*, whose introduction advocates for shamelessly employing the coercive powers of narrative to indoctrinate America's youth, and to undo "some of the distortions of the age in which we now live" (14). This is a blatant example, I believe, of how political and social reactionaries have often turned to this type of narrative because of the illusion it creates of benevolent conservatism, and transparent didacticism.

Returning to the Middle Ages, the heterogeneous nature of the *exemplum* is striking, ranging from a vague rhetorical case in point, to a specific Biblical character or citation, a general model of behavior, a real historic event or person, fable, precious stone, herb, personal anecdote, or short story. John Lyons, like many of the scholars mentioned above, detects a tension that can be sensed in the critical definitions of the form. According to Lyons' survey of the concept of example, a conflict arises from the desire to define the *exemplum* as either an essentially literary form, or part of a rhetorical device. Summarizing Erasmus, Lyons explains how even a personal opinion can be an example:

> [A]n example is not a self-contained and inherently definable type of discourse. Instead, example is the term used for the function of a unit of discourse within a whole. This concept runs decidedly against the tendency of some to see example as being necessarily embodied in a genre like the narrative, for even an opinion, according to Erasmus, can be an example. (17)[11]

All these authors concur, however, that by the end of the thirteenth, and for most of the fourteenth century, the *exemplum* was one of the most popular forms of literature in Europe, in Latin and vernacular languages, in oral or written form, and that the *exemplum* by this time took the shape of "many sorts of texts," as Fritz Kemmler concludes (67). I will have further occasion to refer to

---

[11] Lyons' work on the *exemplum* is of particular interest for those readers studying the decline of the authority of the *exemplum* "as a source of knowledge" from the early Renaissance to the seventeenth-century (238), and the historical links that connect the *exemplum* with the early modern novella collection.

these studies of the *exemplum* in more detail, but for now it is worth recalling Thomas Fredrick Crane's book on Jacques de Vitry in which he addresses the topic of vernacular *exempla* collections for "the edification of the general reader" (ciii), particularly in Spain during the later Middle Ages: "The best and most extensive of these [*exempla*] collections in the vernacular are found in Spain, a land early distinguished for its fondness for moral stories" (ciii). The *CL* is one of the most outstanding examples of this trend.

Juan Manuel wrote his book in an age "unloved by literary criticism," according to Roger Chartier's view of the fourteenth century, and the *CL* may well be one of the best and earliest expressions of the three literary innovations of the fourteenth century that Chartier outlines concisely in a foreword to Jacqueline Cerquiglini-Toulet's *The Color of Melancholy*; namely, the modern notions of author, literature, and the book (xiii-xv). Juan Manuel is often remembered for his distinctive, non-medieval reluctance to cite authorities, except his own works, and his passion for collecting and correcting his entire *opus*, binding it into one manuscript (now lost), and pleading with his readers to refer to his authorized volume if they should encounter mistakes in different copies. Evidence of these early-modern characteristics in Juan Manuel's attitude toward his work are typically found in a famous passage from the prologue of the *CL*:

> Et porque don Iohan vio et sabe que en los libros contesçe muchos yerros en los trasladar, porque las letras semejan unas a otras, cuydando por la una letra que es otra, en escriviéndolo, múdasse toda la razón et por aventura confóndesse, et los que después fallan aquello escripto, ponen la culpa al que fizo el libro; et porque don Iohan se reçeló desto, ruega a los que leyeren qualquier libro que fuere trasladado del que él compuso, o de los libros que él fizo, que si fallaren alguna palabra mal puesta, que no pongan la culpa a él, fasta que bean el libro mismo que don Iohan fizo, que es emendado, en muchos logares, de su letra (45-46, And because Don Juan saw and knew that in copying books many errors occur, because letters resemble one another, and it is thought that one letter is another, and in writing the entire meaning is changed and by chance confused; and people who later on find it so written, blame the one who wrote the book; and because Don Juan was fearful of this, he beseeches people who read any book whatever which was copied from what he com-

posed or wrote, that if they read an ill-couched word, they place not the blame on him, until they read the very copy which Don Juan wrote, which has been corrected in many places in his own hand [39]).

Juan Manuel's acute sense of authorship certainly deserves all the critical attention it has received, and in his brief prologue one finds not only Chartier's profile of the fourteenth-century author, but also a view of the modern book as "a means for presenting the work and the author in their full individuality" (xv). Like many late medieval authors, Juan Manuel surprises us with flashes of modernity, but I would like to resist placing him at the beginning of a new era, or at the starting point of a national vernacular literary history; instead, I believe Juan Manuel's literary creativity shines best in its own light of the late thirteenth and early fourteenth centuries.

In traditional Spanish literary historiography, Juan Manuel stands at the beginning of the history of Castilian prose, along with his uncle Alfonso X, "El Sabio," and other works of the thirteenth and fourteenth centuries, such as king Sancho IV's *Castigos e documentos*, and the anonymous *Libro del caballero Zifar*, but the *CL* may be better understood as a mature expression of the transformation of the Latin *exemplum* tradition into the vernacular, described by Bremond, Le Goff and Schmitt as the form became more familiar among lay audiences.[12] By the end of the Middle Ages, according to these three scholars, *exempla* were also collected for private reading: "ne sont plus offerts seulement à l'audition collective du sermon, mais à la lecture individuelle de 'moralités'" (64). Placed in the literary context of the *exemplum* as a fully-formed manifestation of medieval art, rather than a kind of modern short story in embryonic form –to paraphrase Salvatore Battaglia's views on the medieval *exemplum* (70)– the *CL* stands at the zenith of a medieval literary tradition, rather than at the beginning of a modern one.[13]

---

[12] These scholars clarify the important transformation in form and function of the *exemplum* in the fourteenth century, fusing with other popular narrative forms, breaking away from its conventional place in sermons, and taking on a new lay readership witnessed in the works of Chaucer and Boccaccio, among others (*L"Exemplum'*, 64-65). The absence of Juan Manuel in their list of early examples of this transformation is discouraging.

[13] For further research on the medieval *exemplum*, see the extensive web-based bibliography, *Bibliographie européenne des exempla* prepared by the Groupe d'Anthropologie Historique de l'Occident Médiéval (Centre de Recherches Historiques de Paris).

María Rosa Lida de Malkiel was one of the first scholars to point out the place of the *exemplum* in Juan Manuel's work in her classic essay, "Tres notas sobre don Juan Manuel." Since that time there has been a modest amount of scholarly interest in exploring Juan Manuel's use of *exempla*, with some noteworthy examples from hispanomedievalists such as Germán Orduna, María Jesús Lacarra, Paolo Cherchi, Carlos Alvar, Fernando Degiovani, and Eloísa Palafox. There are also significant general studies on the impact of the homiletic tradition in medieval Spanish literature, such as Derek Lomax's essay on the Fourth Lateran Council, and Francisco Rico's *La predicación y literatura en la España medieval*, as well as taxonomic explorations of the Spanish short prose narrative,[14] and motif classifications, the most important of which is John E. Keller's *Motif-index of Mediaeval Spanish Exempla*.

Much of this scholarship on the *exemplum* in Spain and Juan Manuel's use of the form tends to concentrate on identifying sources and appraising narrative innovations.[15] María Rosa Lida de Malkiel located Dominican origins for three of Juan Manuel's tales (157-158), and Carlos Alvar has argued that Juan Manuel may have drawn his *exempla* from the fourteenth-century Franciscan preacher Servasanctus, whose *Liber de exemplis naturalibus*, according to Alvar, was extraordinarily popular throughout Spain ("Contribución" 193-194). But the exact sources that may have inspired Juan Manuel's literary creations, as Germán Orduna concludes, are almost impossible to pin down ("El exemplo" 119-120). This does not mean, however, that we cannot engage in educated conjecture about his literary influences based on Juan Manuel's early education and intellectual environment.

Many of the critics cited above acknowledge that Juan Manuel would have had the best possible education available to a fourteenth-century Castilian nobleman.[16] The author also expresses in

---

[14] On this extremely complicated and rich research topic, María Jesús Lacarra (*Cuentística*) and Juan Paredes Núñez (*Formas narrativas breves en la literatura románica medieval*) are especially useful.

[15] Much of the criticism on Juan Manuel is still preoccupied with the author's creative adaptation of traditional narrative material. Reinaldo Ayerbe-Chaux's *El Conde Lucanor: Materia tradicional y originalidad creadora* is one of the most exhaustive studies on this subject.

[16] Many have studied the question of Juan Manuel's education, and most all scholars concur that he would have benefited greatly from the intellectual environment of Sancho IV's court. He certainly knew Latin, and was conversant in Arabic.

his early works –the *Crónica abreviada* and *Libro de la caza*, both composed before 1329– an admiration for the literary endeavors sponsored by his famous uncle, king Alfonso X.[17] Furthermore, Juan Manuel was a favorite cousin of Alfonso's son, Sancho IV, who followed the example of his father by patronizing important works of didactic literature such as the *Castigos e documentos del rey don Sancho IV* and the *Lucidario*, as well as a Castilian translation of Brunetto Latini's *Li livres dou trésor* (*El libro del tesoro*) which Juan Manuel may have studied as a manual of rhetoric (Kinkade, "Sancho IV" 1048).[18]

Like the *Castigos e documentos*, there are many other significant literary works that make use of *exempla* for the edification and entertainment of the aristocratic elite that were likely available to Juan Manuel during his youth and early adulthood. This was an historically tense period of conflicts of interest between the monarchy and Castilian aristocracy which has become associated with the political and ideological campaign to consolidate royal power, described by some historians as *el molinismo*, named after Sancho's wife Doña María de Molina, one of the most powerful and persuasive queens of Castilla who defended the interests of her son Fernando and grandson Alfonso against the political ambitions of neighboring monarchs and the alliances of powerful noblemen, including Juan Manuel.[19] In collaboration with the court during this time, the

---

John Keller estimates in his introduction to *The Book of Count Lucanor* that Juan Manuel was "sophisticated, polished, and educated quite probably beyond most of his contemporaries" (1), and in his *Libro infinido* (chapter 36), Juan Manuel himself defends his literary interests against anonymous gossips he criticizes for wasting their time on gambling and other decadent pastimes.

[17] For further study on Juan Manuel's attitude toward his famous uncle, see Manuel Alvar, "Alfonso X contemplado por Don Juan Manuel," and Diego Catalán, "Don Juan Manuel ante el modelo alfonsí."

[18] In the same essay cited above, Kinkade concludes that all three works (*Castigos*, *Lucidario*, and *Libro del Tesoro*) were direct influences on Juan Manuel's literary career (1039). The third book in Latini's *Book of the Treasure* could have served as a concise treatise on rhetoric written for an aristocratic audience charged with governance, since Latini clearly places rhetoric at the service of politics: "You should know that rhetoric comes under the science of governing a city, according to what Aristotle says in his book [. . .], just as the art of making bridles and saddles is under the art of chivalry" (281).

[19] Fernando Gómez Redondo outlines the ideological and political makeup of *el molinismo* in *Historia de la prosa medieval castellana* (1: 861-63). Leonardo Funes has described *el molinismo* as "ideología monárquica o regalismo" ("monarchical ideology or royalism") that "aspired to consolidate power in the person of the king to the detriment of the upper nobility": "aspiraba a una concentración del poder

cathedral school of Toledo, under the direction of archbishop Gonzalo García Gudiel, was an influential center of learning which would have informed Juan Manuel's early education. Germán Orduna has convincingly demonstrated that the time of Sancho IV's reign, and well into the first half of the fourteenth century, was not the cultural wasteland that many historians believe. On the contrary, it witnessed the production of many important works of Spanish medieval literature ("La élite intelectual" 59). John Keller recalls that even the most canonical work of the Spanish Middle Ages, the *Poema de mio Cid*, as we know it today is the product of this era (*The Book of Count Lucanor* 3).

The cultural and literary contexts that surrounded Juan Manuel were as eclectic as one would expect from a region as diverse as the Iberian peninsula, including works such as *Barlaam e Josaphat*, the Alphonsine *Estoria de Espanna*, the *Libro de los cien capítulos*, and the *Libro del Caballero Zifar* with its version of *Flores de filosofía* –often cited as the *Castigos del Rey Mentón*– itself a popular collection of medieval chivalric moral and ethical doctrine, according to Hugo Bizzarri, that was widely disseminated throughout the peninsula (48). One could add to the list such works as the *Disciplina Clericalis*, "the very foundation of all *exempla* collections," according to Keller (*Motif-Index* ix), and the collections of Eastern framed narratives such as those found in *Calila e Dimna* and *El libro de los engaños*. Juan Manuel was also familiar with the mirror of princes genre, one of the most famous of which he cites in his *Libro infinido*, namely, *De regimine principum*.[20] All of these works could have contributed to Juan Manuel's unique literary creation, putting the *exemplum* to use in the field of political philosophy, following the example of the *Castigos e documentos*.

Although the author of the *anteprólogo* makes clear that the *enxemplos* included in Sancho's *Castigos* would make profitable reading for any audience ("a toda pressona de qualquier estado o condición que sea" [29]), they are particularly important for the instruction of young princes who will have to take on the responsibili-

---

político en la persona del rey en perjuicio de la alta nobleza" ("Ruptura" online posting).

[20] See José Manuel Blecua's edition of Juan Manuel's complete works (1: 159). Giles of Rome's work was glossed and translated into Castilian by Juan García de Castrojeriz, probably at the request of king Alfonso XI between 1340 and 1344 (Beneyto Pérez edition, 1: xxvi-xxvii).

ties of the crown ("a los reyes e prinçipes que han de gouernar reynos e gentes" [32]). It is also tempting to see a parallel between Sancho's conventional estimation of traditional wisdom handed down through the ages as a vehicle for salvation and honors ("[e] aprenderá muy buenas costunbres e condiçiones para beuir en este mundo onrradamente e sin pecado, en manera que se saluará si quisiere" [29]), and Juan Manuel's intention to write *exempla* in the *CL* for the benefit of his readers' souls, bodies and estates:

> Este libro fizo don Iohan, fijo del muy noble infante don Manuel, deseando que los omnes fiziessen en este mundo tales obras que les fuessen aprovechosas de las onras et de las faziendas et de sus estados, et fuessen más allegados a la carrera porque pudiessen salvar las almas. Et puso en él los enxiemplos más aprovechosos que él sopo de las cosas que acaesçieron, porque los omnes puedan fazer esto que dicho es (45, This book was written by Don Juan Manuel, son of the noble Prince Don Manuel, with the wish that all men should accomplish in this world such deeds as would be advantageous to their honor, their possessions, and their stations, and so that they would adhere to the career in which they could save their souls. And in it he sets down the most profitable tales which he knew concerning things that happened, so that men can do what has been mentioned above [39]).

But exact sources are not necessary to appreciate Juan Manuel's use of *exempla*, as Germán Orduna concludes, since most of the literate elite were familiar with the narrative material contained in these works whether or not they actually read them privately. Orduna introduces a refreshing perspective on the topic of literary sources in Juan Manuel's writings, and the whole matter of source studies in general, by reminding us that much of the literary material found in the works surveyed above would have been familiar to many of Juan Manuel's contemporaries without having direct access to written sources: "Los contemporáneos de don Juan," Orduna states, "habían oído o leído muchas veces esos relatos, sentencias, normas morales y símiles, que don Juan usa como materia propia" ("Exemplo" 125, Juan Manuel's contemporaries had very often heard of or read these stories, sentences, mores and similes that Don Juan uses as his own material).

Juan Manuel describes the oral mode of literary transmission that common sense tells us was the most ordinary and successful vehicle for disseminating maxims, fables, legends and short stories, as it still is today. In the *Libro de los estados*, Juan Manuel recommends that a fatigued emperor listen to stories to help him fall asleep and learn a good lesson at the same time. The passage creates a vivid literary contact with the past that many of us who still keep a book by our bedside can relate to: "si non puede dormir, deve mandar que leyan ante él algunas buenas estorias, de que tome buenos exemplos" (180, If the Emperor cannot sleep, he should order that good stories be read to him, from which he can learn good examples). Putting aside the written sources of Juan Manuel's tales, one of the social institutions that was most prolific in disseminating stories in the Middle Ages was the Church through the sermon *exemplum*.

James Murphy argues that the "homiletic revolution," begun in the thirteenth century (*Rhetoric in the Middle Ages* 310), produced a body of rhetorical and literary materials that far outweighed the entire Classical age: "A staggering total of discourses was involved, when one considers the thousands of churches active over many hundreds of years. The entire oratorical output of pagan Greece and Rome was minuscule by comparison" (297). When one takes into consideration Juan Manuel's personal relationship with the Dominican order and access to regular private masses,[21] it is not hard to imagine how he could have learned the rhetorical use of *exempla* to persuade and prove a point, following the example of the popular *divisio extra* sermons which were commonly preached in the vernacular, and made successful use of illustrative narratives from a wide range of sources.[22]

An important point to make here about the *exemplum* within the medieval homiletic tradition is that it could serve as a model of rhetoric, more than just a literary source. Like most any member of European society, and part of the corporate tradition of preaching in that society, Juan Manuel, even more than the average Castilian, would have been able to witness and learn from the coercive

---

[21] María Rosa Lida de Malkiel identifies three of Juan Manuel's personal contacts with the Dominican order, one of the most significant was Fray Ramón Masquefa who served Juan Manuel on delicate diplomatic missions (156).

[22] Deyermond goes so far as to suggest that the popularity of the "modern" *divisio extra* sermon and the very foundation of the mendicant orders provided the impetus to create collections of tales in the Iberian peninsula during the reign of Alfonso X ("The Sermon," 134).

rhetoric of the medieval sermon which by his time had been codified in a myriad of *artes praedicandi*, and put on display for hundreds of thousands of faithful in thousands of sermons preached during the later Middle Ages alone. The influence of preaching on literature may be impossible to measure empirically, but its indisputable omnipresence in the medieval world makes it equally impossible to dismiss its impact on vernacular literatures.

In the Iberian peninsula, Francisco Rico has written a brief study of that influence, listing the literary techniques, styles, and modes of expression in Spanish medieval literature derived from homiletic practices. The sermon as an object of parody in works such as the *Libro de buen amor*, in particular the prose prologue, is now common knowledge, but Rico goes further by uncovering the imprint of preaching on Spanish medieval literature among authors who do not explicitly call attention to the sermon genre, ironically or otherwise (*La predicación* 21-23). Rico cites several important elements of the medieval sermon that can be found in the works of lay authors, such as the representation of daily life and the use of the first person to speak directly to the audience regarding things seen, heard or read by the speaker himself. In addition to the *exemplum*, Rico describes the use of sermon-like divisions in vernacular works, as well as the combination of verse and prose.

Impressively, all these elements, or "rasgos," can be found in the *CL*. Juan Manuel's "yo" appears repeatedly to sanction each of Patronio's tales and compose a concluding aphorism in verse to summarize his lessons. The glimpses into daily life seen in the dialogue between the Count and Patronio have been so frequently commented on by critics that the "realism" of the *CL* has become almost cliché. The rigid divisions that structure Juan Manuel's tales has received comparatively less critical attention, but they are an important point of departure for the following analysis of Juan Manuel's appropriation of the sermon *exemplum* tradition.

Juan Manuel's use of *exempla* and other sermon-like techniques seems to trouble some scholars who prefer to place Juan Manuel at the beginning of a purely "literary" history, while others are more comfortable with the blending of literary and homiletic traditions, as in the case of Francisco Rico and Alan Deyermond. Deyermond staunchly defends the literariness of the *CL* ("The Sermon" 134), but also acknowledges that "[t]he *exemplum* is fundamental to Juan Manuel's technique at almost all stages of his literary career" ("The

Sermon" 135).[23] While important scholars such as Reinaldo Ayerbe-Chaux have gone great lengths in dissecting Juan Manuel's artistic innovations and creativity in reworking the materials and traditions handed down to him, others have continued to demonstrate Juan Manuel's use of the rhetoric of preaching in his writings.

Fernando Degiovanni has contributed an excellent study on the fifth book of the *CL*, clarifying Juan Manuel's familiarity with rhetoric and the precepts of the medieval art of preaching, concluding that the fifth part of the *CL* structurally corresponds to the sermon genre (10). Paolo Cherchi, in his study of obscurity and linguistic ambiguity that Juan Manuel explores in Parts II to IV, points out the importance of the *exemplum* and the "sermon-like" structure of the first and fifth parts of the *CL* respectively, arriving at an important conclusion regarding the place of rhetoric in Juan Manuel's masterpiece:

> The *exempla* of the first part, as well as the sermon-like discourse of the fifth part, aptly use the *stylus gravis*. The first part deals mostly with the problem of living up to the expectations of the 'estado'; the fifth part is concerned with the problem of eternal salvation. Rhetorical education seems to constitute the link between the two: rhetorical education as the proper means to understand both goals and to giving them a formulation worthy of their social and religious values. (373-374)

These two critics, along with the recent work of Eloísa Palafox, shift the focus of study on the *CL* from form to rhetoric and narrative strategy, much like Larry Scanlon deals with Chaucer. Like the work of Palafox, my study of Juan Manuel's appropriation of the ideological power and cultural authority associated with the *exemplum* is indebted to Larry Scanlon's insights into the history of the form and its "ecclesiological dimension" (58).

Scanlon insists on treating the *exemplum* as a method or vehicle for expanding the Church's influence into every sector of medieval society (58), resisting the "modernist" tendency "to separate narrative form entirely from ideological function" (28). It is the rhetorical function and ideological power of the *exemplum* that Chaucer

---

[23] Francisco Rico is very clear on this topic, resisting any attempt to draw impermeable lines between the sermon as a uniquely medieval genre, and other forms of vernacular literature (*La predicación* 19).

co-opts, according to Scanlon, following in the footsteps of authors such as Dante and Boccaccio (118). It was Boccaccio, according to Scanlon, that produced "the definitive lay appropriation of the public *exemplum*" (118), but I would argue that this milestone should be attributed first to Juan Manuel. Be this as it may, I find Scanlon's approach to the *exemplum* among lay authors to be the most helpful for understanding Juan Manuel's work, and like the medieval authors and commentators Scanlon studies, the following analysis of the *exemplum* in the *CL* will be more interested in uncovering its rhetorical potential, rather than its formal characteristics and sources. "Medieval discussions of the *exemplum*" –Scanlon concludes– "were much more interested in its function than its form. This often neglected fact demonstrates two things: medieval culture was keenly interested in using narrative, but it was less interested in discussing it" (27). I believe that Juan Manuel intended to instruct his audience on how to use narrative, while entertaining his readers at the same time.

I would agree, finally, with Paolo Cherchi that Juan Manuel has a rhetorical lesson to teach his readers that involves the strategic appropriation of the authority of the *exemplum*. The *infante* teaches, through his master rhetorician Patronio, how the coercive power of exemplification can be put to use beyond the pulpit, and indeed beyond the bindings of his book. In order to teach this lesson in rhetoric, Juan Manuel exposes the inherent ambivalence of the *exemplum* by putting it to the test on the apparently paradoxical question of how to harmonize salvation with politics, wealth and honors with eternal life, God with the World.

PART I

READING *EL CONDE LUCANOR* RIGHT

As I state in the introduction, my study of the *CL* in the following chapters grows out of a medieval reading of the work found in the manuscripts themselves. I will anticipate some of my conclusions here by adding that the medieval reception of the *CL* that I examine in detail in the second part of this book also corroborates some of the basic scholarly conclusions about the structure of Juan Manuel's tales (in particular the artistic autonomy of their narrative parts), as well as a nagging suspicion among many readers that there is an awkward, often unsatisfying argumentative development from the Count's problems posed to his adviser, to Patronio's exemplary tales, and finally Juan Manuel's concluding maxims. Ian Macpherson hints at this uneasy dissatisfaction in "Dios y el Mundo," when he concluded that "although the problems which preoccupy Don Juan Manuel are real for him and cause him concern, the rounded answer which he provides for them is for the modern reader just a little too self-satisfied" (38).

In the following chapter I take as a point of departure the common-sense notion that authors write for familiar audiences, consciously or unconsciously taking into consideration their contemporary modes of reception. Not every author, and especially not every medieval author, writes for all audiences of all times, but for the readers and the reading practices of their own moment in history with which they are inherently familiar. It follows that the closer we can get to a work's original reception, the closer we may get to understanding more precisely how, and why it was written.

Following these ideas, I would agree with many reader-response theorists that, in varying degrees, a work anticipates its mode of reception. The advantage of working with medieval hand-made books, however, is that they often provide material evidence of reading customs that allows us to avoid imagining an implied reader.[1] With evidence of real-life readings, we can bring the medieval horizon of expectation surrounding the *CL* into greater focus. Rather than relying on a modern aesthetic response to the surprising otherness of a medieval work in order to reconstruct its original reception, as Jauss proposes ("Alterity and Modernity" 182), or imagining the "social and cultural conventions of a particular public for which the particular text is specifically intended," borrowing from Wolfgang Iser's concept of "expectation norms" (89), we can let the physical traces of discreet medieval readings be our guide.

The most important of these traces for my reading of the *CL* in the following chapter that points to how the *CL* was read in the fifteenth century, and how it was written by Juan Manuel in the fourteenth, is found in the margins of manuscript M. Like much of the idiosyncratic codicological elements of the manuscripts containing the *CL*, the marginal reading aids inscribed by the same hand that drew flourishes, enlarged initials, and paraph symbols in red ink have gone unnoticed by most scholars, with some noticeable exceptions, such as Laurence de Looze and John Dagenais who have both described this striking marginalia.[2]

In *The Ethics of Reading in Manuscript Culture*, John Dagenais calls attention to the marginal notes in red ink systematically placed to highlight each of Juan Manuel's tales, dividing them into *capítulos* and *enxenplos*, as an example of *divisio textus*, but since his book deals specifically with reading the *Libro de buen amor* in the Middle Ages, he does not develop his observations into a more detailed study of the *CL*. I will return to this marginalia in chapter 5, where I argue that manuscript M, along with manuscript P, provides some of the most robust evidence of reading the *CL* in the fifteenth century.

As mentioned above, the same hand that indexed Juan Manuel's

---

[1] I use the term "implied reader" (as opposed to a real reader) according to one of its most familiar definitions: "the audience presupposed by a text; a real reader's second self (shaped in accordance with the implied author's values and cultural norms)" (Prince, 43).

[2] For "paraph" as a punctuation symbol, see Parkes, *Pause and Effect* (305). I am grateful to Laurence de Looze for sharing with me a manuscript copy of his forthcoming book on the *CL*.

tales for future readers with the abbreviated word "c<apítul>o" and "enxenplo" in the margins, decorated the author's *viessos* with enlarged red paraph symbols, and fenced off the end of Patronio's tales from Juan Manuel's proverbs with red chain borders to separate one material from the other.[3] Without rehearsing the conclusions of chapter 5, it will be helpful to contemplate the significance of this omnipresent medieval mode of thinking, reading and writing visible in M.

For the following chapter, the most important observation to make about the reading aid in M is that the note "enxenplo" always appears in the margin exactly across from the line of text where Patronio introduces his illustrative tale that will help the Count decide how to act, or what to believe. An important and interesting aspect of these red notes is that they are systematically inscribed as part of the plan and layout of the book, and they are entirely subordinate to the *CL* text; they highlight for the reader an inscribed division that the author invariably marks with a formulaic introduction that can be located easily by most any reader, and in the case of manuscript M, they were indeed found and indexed. In a sense, the notes are a special kind of medieval paratext; an unofficial / scribal "message" that does, however, draw authority from the author's work.[4]

Patronio's tales are always separated from the frame narrative that is the Count's question for Patronio with a statement very similar to the following, cited from the fourth story, "De lo que dixo un

---

[3] Angular brackets < > indicate abbreviated letters that I have resolved.

[4] I am borrowing here from Gérard Genette's definition of "paratext," and particularly what he defines as an "official" paratext, being a "message" from the author or publisher (*Paratexts* 10). Genette insists that "something is *not* a paratext unless the author or one of his associates accepts responsibility for it, although the degree of responsibility may vary [my emphasis]" (9). In the Middle Ages, bookmakers, scribes, illuminators, correctors, and all the other professionals involved in manufacturing books are easily imagined as "associates." The scribal notes in M do fit, however, Genette's broader definition of paratext, found in *Palimpsests*, which include "marginal" and "infrapaginal" notes that provide the text with commentary, "official or not" (3). The most helpful insight Genette offers on the paratext for understanding its function in manuscript M is that "the paratextual is always subordinate to 'its' text" (*Paratexts* 12). As paratexts, the notes in M cannot be fully appreciated without their text; they point to and comment on the structure of the *CL*. Since many of Genette's ideas on paratexts are productive in the context of medieval books, it is all the more disappointing to find that this important scholar has fallen into the fallacy of the "primitive" Middle Ages, when he writes that medieval texts "circulated in an almost raw condition," and that manuscripts are "devoid of any formula of presentation" (*Paratexts* 3).

genovés a su alma cuando se ovo a morir" ("What a Genoese Said to His Soul When He Was about to Die"): "Señor conde Lucanor –dixo Patronio–, para que vós fagades en este fecho lo que vos más cunple, plazerme ýa mucho que sopiésedes lo que contesçió a un genués" (75, "Sir Count Lucanor, said Patronio, in order for you to do what is most suitable, I should like you to hear what happened to a certain Genoese" [55]). In every tale of the first part of the *CL* Juan Manuel uses almost the exact same language to introduce Patronio's *exempla*. Any random selection of tales will demonstrate this point.

In *Ejemplo* 10 the author marks the beginning of Patronio's tale with the familiar syntax: "Señor conde Lucanor –dixo Patronio–, para que vos conortedes quando tal cosa vos acaesçiere, sería muy bien que sopiésedes lo que acaesçió a dos omnes que fueron muy ricos" (93, "Sir Count Lucanor, said Patronio, in order to comfort you in these moods I should like you to hear what happened to two very rich men" [66]). *Ejemplo* 22 has the same language: "Señor conde Lucanor –dixo Patronio–, para que desto vos podades guardar, plazerme ýa mucho que sopiésedes lo que conteçió al león et al toro" (136, "Sir Count Lucanor, said Patronio, in order for you to protect yourself, I should very much like you to hear what happened to the lion and the bull" [95]), and in the ninth tale Patronio asks the Count to listen to another *exemplum* with almost the exact same introduction: "Señor conde Lucanor –dixo Patronio–, este fecho es muy grande et muy peligroso, et para que meior entendades lo que vos cumplía de fazer, plazerme ýa que sopiéssedes lo que contesçió en Túnez a dos cavalleros que bivían con el infante don Enrique" (90, "Count Lucanor, said Patronio, this is a very dangerous situation, and so that you may better understand what you ought to do, I should like you to hear what happened in Tunis to two gentlemen who lived with Prince Don Enrique" [64]).

All of the stories in Part I of the *CL* are divided with practically identical statements as those cited above, with very little variation, as in the fifth story, "De lo que contesçió a un raposo con un cuervo que tenié un pedaço de queso en el pico" ("What Happened to a Fox and a Crow Who Had a Piece of Cheese in His Beak"). Here Juan Manuel adds a bit more detail, anticipating Patronio's conclusion and advice for the Count, but the formula is quickly recognized since it is essentially the same as all the others: "Señor conde Lucanor, sabet que este omne vos quiere engañar, dándovos a entender que el vuestro poder et el vuestro estado es mayor de quanto es la verdat. Et para que vos podades guardar deste engaño que vos quiere fazer, plazerme ýa que sopiésedes lo que contesçió a un cuervo con un raposo" (79, "Sir Count, I think this man is trying to deceive you by making you think your power and standing is greater than they are. And if you are to guard against the trick that he intends to play on you, I should like you to hear what happened to a crow and a fox" [57]). But the introductory statements that separate Patronio's tales represent only one division in a collection that is rigidly, and repetitively structured.

The layout and decoration of the *CL* as it appears in M contains more evidence of reading the divisions in Juan Manuel's tales; more particularly, the beginning of each new story and conclusion with Juan Manuel's proverbs. As in the case of Patronio's *exempla*, Juan Manuel makes use of formulaic language to begin his narratives. Each new tale begins with Juan Manuel's own version of "Once upon a time," as in *ejemplo* 2: "Otra vez acaesçió que el conde Lucanor fablava con Patronio su consejero" (61, "Another time Count Lucanor happened to be talking to his adviser" [47]). Similarly, the third tale begins with "Un día se apartó el conde Lucanor con Patronio, su consejero, et díxol así" (67, "One day Count Lucanor took his adviser Patronio aside and spoke to him as follows" [50]), and the next story begins with "Un día fablava el conde Lucanor con Patronio, su consejero" (75, "One day Count Lucanor was talking to Patronio, his adviser" [55]), and so on, and so on. The beginning of each new story as they appear in M have a red "capítulo" note in the margin with a roman numeral–no titles for the stories were written in this manuscript–and at the end of every tale Juan Manuel's proverbs are indented and marked with a red flourish, further aiding the reader in locating the various parts of each tale. Just as with Patronio's *exempla*, the scribe could identify these parts because Juan Manuel mapped them with a textual pattern that any reader could follow.

One might argue that this formulaic language indicates an oral component in Juan Manuel's tales,[5] but as Paul Zumthor has shown, formulaic language is often found "in certain written texts that are designed to be read to oneself" ("The Text and the Voice"

---

[5] John England in his now classic study on the structure of the *CL* notes the traces of an oral transmission in Juan Manuel's tales ("*¿Et non el día del lodo?*" 84).

MS M (Biblioteca Nacional 4236), folio 27 verso, displays the page layout of the *CL* with indented *viessos*, enlarged decorated paraph symbol, and marginal notes.

81-82). The mode of composition that Zumthor defines as "litany" may be one of the most useful for understanding Juan Manuel's use of formulaic language in the *CL*. Litany, according to Zumthor, is a medieval mode of composition that displays "an indefinite repetition of an identical syntactic and in part lexical structure with some of the words being altered upon each repetition so as to delineate a progression" (84). I would add that Juan Manuel's use of litany delineates the separate, perhaps even independent narrative parts of which his tales are constructed, as well as the narrative progression from the Count's question to Juan Manuel's maxim.

There are abundant examples of Juan Manuel's use of formulas that create and sustain an expectation on the part of the reader, anticipating his or her desire to identify parts and contemplate their relationship to each other, to each individual tale, and indeed the entire collection of tales they belong to and construct. Each story can be divided into four narrative parts; the Count's question, Patronio's *exemplum*, Patronio's advice, and Juan Manuel's proverbs, each marked by a formulaic statement, one of the most conspicuous of which is the coda used to introduce the concluding *viessos*, cited here from *ejemplo* 1: "Et entendiendo don Iohan que estos exiemplos eran muy buenos, fízolos escribir en este libro, et fizo estos viessos en que se pone la sentençia de los exiemplos" (60, "And Don Juan, thinking this a good story, had it included in this book, and wrote these verses to express the moral" [47]). Not only were these divisions apparent to the reader of manuscript M, they were not overlooked by Juan Manuel's modern editors. Most of these critics read the textual cues as indicators of new paragraphs–where more often than not there are no actual paragraph separations in the manuscripts themselves–and set apart the concluding verses which are not indented from the rest of the text in manuscript S, the most commonly accepted best text for editing Juan Manuel's work. Nevertheless, these divisions are as easy to locate in the manuscript witnesses as they are in any modern edition, thanks to Juan Manuel's reliable use of language.

Even though textual critics editing the *CL* have followed Juan Manuel's divisions, the repetitive language used to structure his tales has often been overlooked by literary scholars. Until now, the author's formulaic style of writing seems to have been dismissed as a vestige of primitive narrative techniques, especially with regard to the basic narrative frame Juan Manuel repeats in every tale. Reinaldo Ayerbe-Chaux alludes to this modern prejudice in his edition of the *CL*, and reminds his readers that the structure of Juan Manuel's stories deserves more critical attention (18-20).[6] I would argue that the author's use of repetitive textual cues to mark the beginning, middle and end of his narratives is a deliberate and refined use of language that calls attention to patently homologous parts, the discursive ties that bind parts into whole narratives, and finally each narrative into a whole book. Put another way, the repetitive, almost rhythmic structure of the *CL* is an expression–and a signal for the audience–of Juan Manuel's modal approach to narrative and exemplification.

The red marginal reading aid systematically marked in manuscript M preserves for us a discrete late medieval response to Juan Manuel's style of writing, and ultimately the mode of thinking that structures each tale. The notes are evidence of reading the *CL* at the level of its *forma tractatus*. Applying Judson Boyce Allen's excellent study of medieval modes of thinking and writing to the scribal notes in M, I would conclude that they betray "a critical concern for that unity of a work which is achieved by the ordering of its parts" (Allen 72). I will return to Allen's discussion of *divisio, forma tractatus* and the *exemplum* in chapter 5 where I examine in greater detail the content and structure of manuscript M.

Before moving on to a study of the *CL* that also attempts to follow Juan Manuel's divisions, it is interesting to recall that one of the most forceful medieval applications of division as a rhetorical device is witnessed in the medieval sermon, which made extensive use of *divisio* to elucidate a biblical text or *thema*, employing *exempla* and *auctoritates* as divisions and subdivisions of the larger whole sermon, following the medieval dialectic method of preaching.[7] Henri-Jean Martin also reminds us that the medieval "fondness for

---

[6] Germán Orduna also warns against reading Patronio's *exempla* out of the context of their narrative frames, as many critics, even editors have done in the past ("El exemplo" 140). Pedro Barcia's study of the *CL* demonstrates the traditional preference for Juan Manuel's *exempla* as the most "flavorful" and artistically valuable ("más sabrosa y valiosa") part of each story, since they have an "independent life of their own": "puede cobrar vida independiente pues al arrancarla de su marco su factura queda impecablemente orgánica" (27).

[7] James Murphy shows that by the beginning of the thirteenth century a new *modus* of "thematic preaching" based on "divisions and amplifications" appeared "fully developed" in authors such as Thomas of Salisbury, Richard of Thetford, and Alexander of Ashby (276).

subdivision and articulation" was prevalent in the preaching of the Dominican Order (151); an order that Juan Manuel was personally fond of, dedicating the last chapter of his *Libro de los estados* to a brief history and apology of the mendicant friars. It is tempting to compare the divisions of Juan Manuel's tales–the prologue, the Count's questions, the *exempla*, Patronio's advice, and Juan Manuel's proverbs–with the various parts of a medieval sermon, and as I have mentioned above, other critics have noticed "sermon-like" techniques in the *CL*. Juan Manuel's use of *divisio* may be yet another example of this influence, but what is certain is that the author deliberately and repeatedly employs formulaic division to create homologous narrative parts that should make sense within each whole story.

By conspicuously dividing his narratives with almost identical textual markers, Juan Manuel anticipates the critical reading practices of his time which considered divisions as "the basis of any possible serious consideration of a text's wholeness, subject, or meaning," according to Allen (126). The scribe of manuscript M marked the beginning of a critical reading of the *CL* for future readers that begins with recognizing homologous parts, then must move on to understanding the "wholeness" of each narrative, and possibly even the entire collection with its over-arching didactic message. Julian Weiss has outlined this medieval reading practice in *The Poet's Art*, and he describes it as essentially a "comparative approach" (147), beginning with *divisio*, then moving on to a comparison of parts, "searching for contradictions or inconsistencies, and finding solutions to the problems posed" (*quaestio*), and concluding with "a meditation on the written word," or *lectio* (146-49).[8] My own study of the *CL* attempts to follow the scribe's instructions on how to read Patronio's *exempla*, but it must be made clear again that those instructions were laid out by the author himself; they were merely noted by the scribe who conveniently highlighted them.

Following a medieval reading strategy that the marginal notes in M outline uncovers new lessons in the *CL*. Rather than arriving at a conclusion for the collection's central ethical / spiritual conun-

---

[8] Among other sources, Weiss refers to Hugh of St. Victor, who states in book 3 and 5 of the *Didascalicon de Studio Legendi* (chapters 9 and 12, respectively), that *divisio* is the first step of any critical reading process: "Modus legendi in dividendo constat" (Sancto Victore 58, 129).

drum–how to save one's soul and win honors on earth–the array of narrative parts leads the reader away from one univocal meaning for each *exempla*, and indeed the entire collection of tales, to what Laurence de Looze describes as a "multiplicity of meanings" ("Subversion" 342), even paradox, that exposes another, perhaps even more useful lesson on how to employ the power of the *exemplum* beyond the confines of any book. Juan Manuel acknowledges the potential for different interpretations of his book in the prologue where he speaks of the different sorts of *entendimientos*, or capacities for understanding and learning that each reader may, or may not have, "porque [a] muchos omnes las cosas sotiles non les caben en los entendimientos, porque non las entienden bien" (49, "because many men do not catch subtle meanings, because they do not understand them well" [40]).

While the author assures his audience that his tales are at the very least pleasant to read because of their "palabras falagueras et apuestas" (51, "charming and elegant words" [41]), he also describes his method of writing with *exempla*; a method he compares to the physician's use of sugar-coated pills, introducing helpful medicines into the patient's body, whether he like it or not: "et aunque ellos non lo dese[e]n, aprovecharse an dellas, así commo el fígado et los otros miembros dichos se aprovechan de las melezinas que son mezcladas con las cosas de que se ellos pagan" (51, "And even though they do not wish to read the profitable elements which they will find in it and may not desire them, they will be helped by them, just as the liver and the other aforesaid organs profit by the medicines which are mixed with the things they like" [41]). Aside from the familiar *topos* of the sugar-coated medicine, it is very suggestive to compare Juan Manuel's ideas on how a tale can please different readers with some of the earliest theories on the use of *exempla* in preaching.

One of the first expressions of the *exemplum*'s usefulness when preaching to an audience with varying degrees of education, as James Murphy states in *Rhetoric in the Middle Ages*, is found in Alexander of Ashby's *De modo praedicandi*. The qualities of the *exemplum* Alexander emphasizes are strikingly similar to those suggested by Juan Manuel in his prologue, especially with regard to readers with unequal learning capabilities, and how the simple-minded will appreciate the "palabras falagueras et apuestas" (charming words), while others may indeed be able to learn the "cosas porvechosas" (profitable elements) in his book. Citing *De modo praedicandi*, Murphy points to Alexander's comments on how to employ a "charming allegory" or a "pleasant story (*exemplum*) so that the learned may savor the profundity of the allegory while the humble may profit from the lightness of the story" (313).[9] By the time Juan Manuel was writing the *CL*, the use of the *exemplum* in preaching to diverse audiences was standard practice, and it is not impossible that Juan Manuel learned of the *exemplum*'s polysemic qualities from his Dominican contacts, or perhaps through simple hands-on experience listening to sermons and "pleasant stories." Regardless of Juan Manuel's sources, it is clear from the prologue that Juan Manuel understands that his tales may have various meanings for different readers. Furthermore, the prologue demonstrates that the author is aware of a rhetorical strategy behind his writing with *enxiemplos*; his book is designed as a means of indoctrination, or inoculation. It is Juan Manuel's "medicinal" use of narrative, his mode of exemplification which is essentially a coercive rhetorical strategy, that is one of the more "subtle meanings" of the *CL* that the careful reader, with adequate *entendimiento*, can learn for his or her own use.

---

[9] Murphy also cites the original Latin text, Latin MS, Oxford Magd. Coll. 168, fol. 129r: "Secundus aliqua dulce exponere allegoriam et aliquod iocondere enarrare exemplum ut eruditos delecte allegorie profunditas et simplices edificer exempli levitas ut habeant itaque qui secum reportent" (313).

Chapter 1

ETHICAL AMBIGUITY IN *EL CONDE LUCANOR* [1]

IN chapter four of the *Libro infinido*, Juan Manuel explains to his son Fernando the differences between a king and a tyrant, but it is not Juan Manuel's intention to write a treatise on the nature of monarchs.[2] This chapter, like most of the book, is designed to help the reader make informed decisions, and put ideas into action, and in this case, the problem is how to act as the subject of a good or evil lord. Juan Manuel's comments regarding tyrants are of particular interest because of his notoriously turbulent relationship with Alfonso XI, and his words betray not only a concern for his son but a sense of personal frustration as well. One can imagine the discomfort his readers must have felt when deliberating on how to apply these cynical words of warning to his own life:[3] "Ca fasca tan graue cosa es veuir omne en tierra de su sennor e auerse a guardar dél, commo meter la mano en el fuego e non se quemar" (33-34, "It is as difficult a matter for a man to live in the land of his lord and have to protect himself from him at the same time, as it is to place one's hand in a fire without getting burned"). This from a man who

---

[1] A version of this chapter was published in *La corónica* under the title "Ideology in Action: The Consequences of Paradox in *El Conde Lucanor* (Part I)." I am grateful to the editor, George Greenia and the readers of this important journal for their constructive criticism and encouragement.

[2] On the matter of monarchs and tyrants, Juan Manuel directs his son in this same book (chapter 4) to Giles of Rome's *De regimine principum* (*Obras completas* 1: 159).

[3] Writing within the literary tradition of educational books for princes, Juan Manuel's implied reader in the *Libro infinido* is male and aristocratic, but this type of literature was considered beneficial for any reader, and there is no reason to assume that the original audience of this type of literature did not include women.

knew all too well the tribulations of a *rico omne* in fourteenth-century Castilla.[4]

In this passage, the reader is struck by a powerful simile in which one of the elements of likeness (i.e., placing one's hand in a fire without getting burned) is a self-contradictory idea. The entire simile becomes a figure of thought, and more particularly a paradox, when the reader is forced to reconsider the context which the apparently absurd statement describes. Although this statement is not a semantic antinomy of the Liar paradox type, it qualifies as a paradox because of its capacity to surprise the reader with a comparison of seemingly contradictory ideas that refocuses attention on the context in which it is used. In order to search for a possible solution to this quandary, it is worth citing the context from the *Libro infinido* at greater length. As mentioned above, the passage deals with the problems of living with a tyrant, who is also one's sovereign lord:

> Et si por auentura entendiere que non es de las maneras [e] de las condiçiones que deuen seer los buenos reys, e que es de la manera de los tirannos, commo quier que el rey sea tal, pues el rey e[s] señor natural, deuel seruir quanto pudiere. Et deuese guardar quanto pudiere del fazer enojo [. . .]; pero si el pleito llegare a bagar que una voç diga que ha reçelo del su cuerpo, en ninguna manera non se meta en su poder e escuse la su vista. Et non crea que por berse con el rey en canpo, nin con muchas conpannas, que en ninguna guisa puede ser guardado de muerte, si el rey fazerlo quisiere. Otrosí conuiene que se guarde de dia e de noche en las posadas que posare. Otrosí de se poner en poder de villa, nin de omne de [qui] non fie muy conplidamente: ca los más de los omnes mucho fazen por ganarse con los reyes. Et bien cred que para ser el guardado, que es mucho mester que guarde a Dios; ca si el guarda a Dios, guardara Dios a el [. . .]. Otrosí ha mester para esto muy grant entendimiento; ca fascas tan graue cosa es veuir omne en tierra de su sennor e auerse a guardar del, commo meter la mano en el fuego e non se quemar. Et non a cosa en el mundo quel pueda guardar si Dios et la su verdat e la su lealtat non lo guarda. Et esto guardado, deue fazer quanto pudiere por auer grant poder de fortalezas e de vasallos e de

---

[4] Kenneth R. Scholberg calls attention to Juan Manuel's figurative use of fire "almost always to express difficulty or impossibility" in the *CL*, as well as the *Libro de los estados* and *Libro infinido* (151).

parientes e de amigos para se defender si mester fuere (32-34, And if by chance you find that he does not have the manners and customs that a good king should have, and that he has the manner of a tyrant, since the king is still your natural lord you must serve him the best you can. And you must take care as best you can to not offend him [. . .]; but if you should hear a rumor that the king is angry with you and wishes you harm, by no means should you let yourself be placed in his charge, and you should avoid being in his presence. Nor should you believe that, finding yourself with the king in the field, or with many companies of men, by any means can you defend yourself from death if the king wishes it. You should also be on guard day and night in the places where you stay. You should be careful not be taken in by any town or man that you do not completely trust, since the majority of men will do anything to win the favor of the king. And you must firmly believe that in order for you to be well-protected, it is absolutely necessary that you trust in God; for if you trust in God, God will protect you [. . .]. Furthermore, in all of these things one must have great understanding, since it is as difficult a matter for a man to live in the land of his lord and have to protect himself from him at the same time, as it is to place one's hand in a fire without getting burned. And there is nothing in the world that you can keep safe if you are not faithful to God and his truth. Safeguarding all these things, you should take care to have great strength in fortresses, vassals, relatives and friends in order to defend yourself just in case).

The king, whether he be a just lord or a tyrant, is as a God on earth, demanding complete obedience, and in this aspect of feudal ideology lies the potential for conflict, especially during a period of cultural crisis when dominant theoretical norms that govern social institutions are constantly being tested by alternative and antagonistic practices. The hypothetical situation becomes more perilous if one cannot avoid falling into disrepute with the king, and from this point on the unfortunate nobleman must adopt an almost paranoid attitude in his dealings with the king and all other men who are not of the utmost trustworthiness.

The situation seems hopeless from a political and pragmatic point of view, and the author's only recourse is to invoke faith and the will of God to guarantee success. This is a rhetorical maneuver that invokes an orthodox doctrine and removes complete control of the situation from the subject, placing it half way between the faithful living under the rule of a tyrant, and Divine Providence. The recommended course of action that will guarantee that all other actions are proper and advantageous is to remain faithful, but the paradox that immediately follows casts serious doubt on the possibility of being able to do all that the author recommends: "Furthermore, *in all of these things* one must have great understanding." The demonstrative adjective "esto" ("all of this," or "all these things") can refer to all the advice given up to this point in the text; staying on guard day and night, always looking over one's shoulder, distrusting almost everyone, as well as remaining faithful to God. The paradox is not very encouraging, and the final instructions move back to more pragmatic advice on the material things a nobleman should have in order to survive in this dangerously tense relationship. One must be faithful, but it helps to have some strong fortresses and a good army, just in case. This may be a somewhat cynical interpretation of the text, but another example of this paradox from the *Libro de los estados* can corroborate it.

In the following passage, the young prince and his teacher Julio continue a discussion about the dangers an emperor must face, and Julio assures the prince that this *estado* provides as many opportunities for salvation as any other, perhaps even more:[5]

> Et lo mismo vos digo agora en el estado de los enperadores, qui si quisieran, bien pueden perder las almas et aun los cuerpos; mas, si quisieren, non ay estado en que mejor las pueden salvar. Et si queredes saber cómmo lo pueden fazer, yo vos lo diré en pocas palabras: çierto es que muchos enperadores fueron sanctos, pues el que fuere enperador sepa la manera en que visco et las obras que fizo aquel enperador que fue sancto, et faga lo que el otro fazía, et será salvo et aun sancto (167-168, And now I will tell you the same thing about the Emperor's *estado*; that if they choose, they too can lose their body and soul; but if they wish, there is no better estate in which they can save their souls. And if you want to know how they can do so, I will explain it to you in a few words: it is true that many emperors were saints, therefore he who would be emperor should learn from the manners and deeds of the emperor that was a saint, and do what he did, and he will be safe as well as a saint).

---

[5] As Luciana de Stéfano explains, the term *estado* can have a number of meanings in different contexts (330-31). In the chapters dealing with the election, confirmation, and duties of the emperor, it seems to refer to a specific political position in society, with a specific set of responsibilities.

Julio's explanation of how an emperor can save his soul does not do justice to the seriousness of the matter, especially since this is the estate into which the *infante* may have to enter.[6] Rather than go into detail, he prefers to explain himself "in a few words," and the solution is easier said than done, even in a society where saints and miracles were much more imaginable than today. This passage echoes the same discussion in chapter 48 in which Julio rephrases the paradox, in an equally troublesome fashion, by stating that the very same deeds that can save the emperor can also cost him his soul, and that there is no way out of this situation unless he could survive without food, drink and money: "Et aun en las cosas del mundo, en aquellas cosas mismas que puede fazer su pro et lo que deve, en aquellas mismas puede fazer su daño para el cuerpo et para el alma. Ca vós savedes muy bien que non puede omne bevir sin comer et sin bever et sin dinero" (151-152, "And even in the matters of this world, in the very same things that you should do and that benefit you, those same things can harm your body and soul. Since you know very well that a man cannot live without food, drink and money").

Following Julio's logic, it seems that only through a miracle, earned with actions that can save and / or condemn, can the emperor be protected from these paradoxes. Those who are saved are those who can win God's intervention, as Julio explains in chapter 47: "Los que fizieron en este mundo tales obras en serviçio de Dios, que meresçieron que Dios feziese miraglos por ellos" (*Libro de los estados* 149, "Those who have done such deeds in this world in God's service, that they deserved that God perform miracles for them"). Although he repeatedly claims that the emperor, like anyone else in their respective *estados*, can be saved, the philosopher also acknowledges the almost insurmountable difficulties of this task, and it appears that an emperor must, for all intents and purposes, become a saint in order to save himself. The prince is noticeably concerned about his chances, and his replay betrays incredulity regarding the advice he has just been given: "Julio –dixo el infante–, bien sé yo que los enperadores salvarse pueden; mas entiendo yo tantos peligros en los sus fechos et en la vida que an de fazer et en

---

[6] In chapter 47 the prince states that he may enter into this *estado*, and that he is deeply concerned about his salvation. As the conversation continues into the next chapter, Julio claims that this *estado* is indeed the one God has chosen for him.

el mundo, que tengo que es muy grave de se salvar. Ca çierto es que muy grave cosa es estar omne en el fuego et non se quemar" (168, "Julio–said the prince–I know very well that an emperor can be saved; but I know that there are so many dangers in the duties and the life that he has to lead in the world, that I believe it is very difficult for him to be saved. Indeed, it is a very difficult thing for a man to be in a fire and not get burned").

Clearly, the prince is troubled by his teacher's lesson, and Julio must acknowledge that his advice is almost impossible to follow, as his pupil complains. Furthermore, Julio cannot satisfactorily solve the paradox, in spite of his many efforts. As seen in the *Libro infinido*, a course of action based on faith is again offered up to the prince as the only way out of the oxymoronic state of being in the world, like being in a fire, without getting burned:

> Señor infante –dixo Julio–, todo esto que vós dezides es verdat. Mas, bien así commo dezides que es grave cosa estar omne en el fuego et non se quemar, bien así es muy grant meresçimiento el que está en el mundo aviendo muy grant poder para fazer lo que quisiere et conplir su voluntad, et non lo dexan por mengua de poder nin de riquezas nin por miedo, et dexarlo por non fazer pesar a Dios, et fazer mucho bien, et non tomar deleite, nin sobervia nin loçanía, por el poder que ha. Ca vós sabedes, señor, que en el evangelio non loa Dios al pobre, mas loa al pobre de voluntad (168, Sir prince–said Julio–all that you say is true. But, even as you say it is hard for a man to be in a fire and not get burned, even so it is meritorious that he who is in the world with great power to do as he pleases and carry out his wishes, and does not deny these things for lack of power or wealth or fear, and denies them so as to not offend God, and do good deeds, and not take pleasure, nor pride nor flattery, because of the power he has. Since you know, sire, that in Scripture God does not praise the poor man, rather the man who chooses to be poor).

Julio's answer does not deny the emperor's paradoxical situation of being in the world and saving his soul at the same time, instead he can only match one truism with another: since the task is so difficult, the reward is great. He does not reject the truth of the paradox, and by not doing so the tensions it creates are left unresolved. Julio can only insinuate that the emperor should retreat from the exercise of power and do good deeds, since this is most pleasing to

God who favors those who give up privileges by choice. The imaginary solution to the emperor's double bind is a kind of religious flanking maneuver. Julio can only circumvent the paradox with a circuitous argument that does not address it head on. He alludes to a hagiographic tale that might convince the prince, comparing again the chances of salvation with saints and miracles, but he does not want to go into detail (168). The *infante*, along with the reader, are left to contemplate the image of a saintly man blissfully petting his cat as Julio's best answer for his pupil (168).[7] Julio sums up the whole matter with the tautological conclusion that all emperors can save themselves if they simply act properly: "si viviere[n] como deve[n]" (169, "if they live as they should").[8]

While the similes cited in detail above may indeed teach a social and political lesson for Juan Manuel, his son, and other fourteenth-century aristocratic readers, they also provide fascinating insights into Juan Manuel's use of paradox to textualize his perception of real conflict in his own socio-political setting. As a rhetorical device, paradox also opens fissures in these texts that demand greater reader participation by moving the final interpretation of a seemingly irreducible contradiction outside of the text. It is a device Juan Manuel will employ again—with similar consequences for the reader—to conclude his collection of *exemplos* in the first part of the *CL*.

A close examination of the ideological conflicts that arise from tracing the array of homologous narrative parts in search of the "wholeness" of each narrative and the entire collection discloses a deep ethical ambiguity and semantic ambivalence in a text that has

---

[7] The image of the man petting his cat is similar to that of the old woman weaving in the sun which Juan Manuel uses in Part V of the *CL* as a model of blind faith and obedience to the teachings of the Catholic Church. Carlos Alvar believes this kind of *exemplum*, like others that illustrate the pure faith of the ignorant, was a commonplace in medieval sermons ("Contribución" 192).

[8] By tautological I do not mean redundant; rather, I use the term to imply something similar to its meaning in logic, where it describes a statement that is always true no matter if its simpler statements are true or false. Here, the statement "if they live as they should," like "do good, avoid evil," is more of a self-evident statement that is always true, but it does not help the character or the reader decide what is proper and what is not, what is good and what is evil. In fact, these kinds of statements seem to avoid answering crucial questions about behavior. I will show in chapter 3 how Juan Manuel points out in Part V of the *CL* that these statements are useless: "grant verdat et poco seso" (308, "a great truth, but not very helpful advice").

been traditionally viewed as conservative, or even reactionary, in terms of its didacticism and the ideological worldview fashioned within it.

Scholars studying the *CL* have traditionally focused their attention on questions of form, source studies, and the author's artistic creativity in re-working a body of tales drawn from well-known classical and eastern traditions. Daniel Devoto, María Jesús Lacarra, Joaquín Casalduero, Reinaldo Ayerbe-Chaux, John England, María Rosa Lida de Malkiel, María Dolores Nieto, and James Burke, among many other respected scholars, have contributed important studies on these topics, but other critics have also studied the *CL*, along with Juan Manuel's other writings, through the lenses of biography, the author's didactic intentions, and ideology. Ian Macpherson, Julio Rodríguez-Puértolas, Luciana de Stéfano, Peter Dunn, José Antonio Maravall, Andrés Giménez Soler, Marta Ana Diz, and Germán Orduna, among many others, have concurred on the notion that Juan Manuel's opus evokes and defends a highly idealized model of medieval Castilian estate society as the author understood and wrote about it in works such as the *Libro de los estados* and the *Libro del cavallero et del escudero*.[9]

According to the author's intentions outlined in the prologue of the *CL*, Juan Manuel creates a collection of tales that, through the contemplation of practical situations and "real-life" problems, will aid his readers in the ethical decision-making process necessary to navigate two seemingly contradictory paths: winning salvation while increasing their wealth and honors on earth:

> Este libro fizo don Iohan, fijo del muy noble infante don Manuel, deseando que los omnes fiziessen en este mundo tales obras que les fuessen aprovechosas de las onras et de las faziendas et de sus estados, et fuessen más allegados a la carrera porque pudiessen salvar las almas. Et puso en él los enxiemplos más provechosos que él sopo de las cosas que acaesçieron, porque los omnes puedan fazer esto que dicho es (45, This book was written by Don Juan Manuel, son of the noble Prince Don Manuel, with the wish that all men should accomplish in this world such deeds as would be advantageous to their honor, their

---

[9] María Rosa Lida de Malkiel is one of the first scholars to point out the Dominican influence behind Juan Manuel's ardent defense of the rigid tripartite medieval estate society ("Tres notas" 97-98).

possessions, and their stations, and so that they would adhere to the career in which they could save their souls. And in it he sets down the most profitable tales which he knew concerning things that happened, so that men can do what has been mentioned above [39]).

Exemplo 3, "Del salto que fizo el rey Richalte de Inglaterra en la mar contra los moros" ("How King Richard of England Leapt into the Sea against the Moors"), is often cited as one of Juan Manuel's most convincing examples of how to balance the two "paths," and at the same time legitimates the dominant ideology of the medieval estate society. This story, including Patronio's hermeneutic reading of it, suggests that a knight can save his soul and increase his honor by executing the divinely-ordained mission of his estate.

Juan Manuel collected these illustrative tales during a period of extraordinary political and social unrest in which Castilla experienced the erosion of its social institutions, increased urbanization, the emergence of a middle class, and a growing dependency on a monied economy, all of which had a profound impact on the aristocracy's role in society, especially during the second decade of the fourteenth century.[10] In response to this crisis, many scholars argue that Juan Manuel's tales evoke the tradition and authority of estate ideology in order to promote social stability, and the identity of the aristocracy within that society during a time of social and political destabilization.

The *Libro infinido* dramatizes the instability of this estate society and the extent that a nobleman had to stay on guard, especially in his dealings with the king, while attempting to balance personal interests with honor and duty. Juan Manuel describes this situation to his son as a constant state of battle readiness. The boundaries of Castilian society and its political etiquette mapped out in the *Libro infinido* are much more subjective than one would expect, and they often depend on the reader's ability to imagine a hypothetical situation in which one might have to break the rules of conduct, and actually make war on his king. As seen in the passages cited earlier from the *Libro infinido* and *Libro de los estados*, Juan Manuel's advice to his son seems to slip from the ideological center of estate so-

---

[10] Julio Valdeón Baruque contributed an excellent essay for *Juan Manuel Studies* on the political and economic situation of the aristocracy during this period.

ciety to its margins and back again, in a never-ending struggle for political survival in an exceptionally violent socio-political field. On one hand, the king must be obeyed, whether he is a tyrant or not, but on the other hand there may arise certain situations in which a subject might have to step outside of his proper place in society and act in defense of his own private interests.

In this historical struggle Juan Manuel wore many different masks, at times inventing official positions for himself by force, often against the wishes of his queen, Doña María de Molina, during the minority of Alfonso XI; on other occasions he functioned as the self-appointed regent of the king for the city of Ávila. With blatant disregard for correct behavior according to his station, Juan Manuel had his own royal seal of regent made so he could exercise this office, since he could not acquire it from the queen herself. On other occasions he had to wage war against Christian nobles, in particular the queen's son Felipe, to protect his claim to the city of Ávila, for example, or to aid his ally Don Juan "el Tuerto" in taking the city of Zamora from Felipe and his allies.[11] In other instances he was a model knight, fighting for his king and God against the Moors.[12]

It is in historical episodes such as these outlined above where one observes the real consequences of Juan Manuel's attempts at reinventing himself for political advantage or survival. In these texts the reader glimpses the shadow of Juan Manuel in the process of acting in history. This is the ideologically unstable historical moment that resonates throughout the *CL*, expressed in the Count's questions, worries, ethical dilemmas, and political quagmires, as well as in Patronio's exemplary tales, pronouncements and advice.

As a product of and response to this moment, the *CL* does not ratify a theoretical feudal worldview that may never have been consolidated in Castilian social structure.[13] Instead, Juan Manuel's col-

---

[11] For a description of these events, see the *Gran crónica de Alfonso XI*, 1: 323-27.

[12] See H. Tracy Sturcken's essay for a study of Juan Manuel's assassination of Diego García, and the *Gran crónica de Alfonso XI* for an interesting comparison of two narratives describing Juan Manuel's comportment on the battlefield. In one episode he is an exemplary knight (1: 388), while at the Battle of the Río Salado he is a paragon of cowardice (2: 426-27).

[13] Claudio Sánchez Albornoz has argued that the experience of the Reconquest paralyzed the development of feudalism in medieval Spain (2: 7-16), and José Luis Romero has suggested that the Castilian feudal estate society, as a real social practice rather than a theory, began to fall apart at the same time the aristocracy was

lection of tales creates a literary arena of conflicting exemplary behaviors in which alternative ethical decisions and actions can be legitimated by individual readers. More particularly, Juan Manuel draws the ethical conflict identified as *Dios y el Mundo* into his collection and obscures it, primarily through the use of paradox and exemplary actions that are irreconcilable when compared to each other and the homologous contexts to which they correspond. As seen in the *Libro infinido* and the *Libro de los estados*, the paradox of placing one's hand in a flame without being burned cannot satisfactorily solve the ethical dilemma of those who must act in the World, and be judged by God according to their actions.

The consequences of this paradox preclude reading the *CL* as merely a laconic expression of the promotion and legitimization of the interests of the Count and the class he represents.[14] The final interpretation of the collection is forced outside the text by the paradox and conflicts confronted by a reader who is searching for the book's "wholeness" following the modal narrative progression in each tale. It is the reader who must meditate on Patronio's advice given in each story, comparing it with the Count's questions, Juan Manuel's proverbs, and the ethical frame of the entire collection, before he or she can apply what has been learned to his or her own life. In this respect Juan Manuel's book provides an example of the "ethics" of reading in the Middle Ages, according to John Dagenais, in which those who read are caught up in a "process of judgment and choice" regarding the application of the text to their own individual circumstances (16).

The author of the *anteprólogo* understands that the collection demands this kind of reading where the text becomes action, when he writes that each reader will be able to find in the *exemplos* circumstances similar to his own: "Et sería maravilla si de cualquier cosa que acaezca a cualquier omne, non fallare en este libro su semejança que acaesçió a otro" (45, "And it would be a wonder if in

---

attempting to stabilize it for their own political and economic interests (306-307). José Antonio Maravall corroborates Romero's view of this crisis, and situates it within the lifetime of Juan Manuel, who, according to Maravall, documents the decay of the estate society with "fina intuición histórica" (467, "a keen historical intuition").

[14] Eloísa Palafox has written an excellent study of Juan Manuel's appropriation of the rhetorical strategy of the *exemplum* for his personal political agenda. I would argue that Juan Manuel puts the rhetorical power of the *exemplum* on display for any reader able to discern it and put it to use in his or her own life.

this book there will not be found something which has happened to someone else" [39]). A logical conclusion here is that the text has the potential to program real behavior, a generic characteristic of the *exempla* since they are always presented as models of behavior, but in this case attention is drawn to the process of interpretation and application. The notion that the reader must determine how to put the text into action confounds the didacticism of the collection by subverting Patronio's and Don Juan's exclusive authority to interpret each *exemplo*.

If the implied reading process is followed and advice is put into action, then the text successfully participates in the fashioning of ideology itself, if ideology is understood, as Louis Althusser suggests, in terms of "material practices" which "exist in the material action of a subject acting according to his belief" (17). In this sense, Part I of the *CL* is a literary model of the strategies of ideology at work, since it can materialize and legitimate action at the same time. What the reader encounters in Part I of the *CL* is a discursive array of symbolic actions that often collide with each other, creating tension, ambiguity, and antinomy. One of the consequences of this conflictive ethical field pulled into the framework of the collection is that the reader is coerced into performing his or her own critical act of reading. This reading process is begun when the tensions and antinomies of the text break through the surface of its conventional structure designed to contain the meaning of the entire collection by masking its contents with the appearances of tradition and orthodoxy associated with the *exemplum* as a "narrative enactment of cultural authority" (Scanlon 34). It is not impossible that a medieval critic, following an interpretive practice that begins with identifying divisions–conveniently marked in one manuscript–, then searching for the "full shape and significance" of a text in the ordinance of its parts (Allen 138), could have grasped the paradox and aporia that arise from Juan Manuel's mode of exemplification outlined in the Count's troubles, Patronio's advice and Juan Manuel's maxims.

Faced with unsatisfactory or "self-satisfied" solutions to many of the Count's persistent ethical dilemmas, equivocating advice and contradiction, a retrospective reading of the entire book exposes Juan Manuel's method of exemplification itself as a way out of the paradox of living in the world without getting burned. As I have already stated, Ian Macpherson concludes in "Dios y el Mundo–The Didacticism of *El Conde Lucanor*" that the fundamental dilemma presented in the prologue of the *CL* is worked out in an unsatisfactory manner for the modern reader (38). In the last two decades, some scholars, such as Laurence de Looze, Dayle Seidenspinner-Núñez, Mariano Baquero Goyanes, and María Rosa Menocal, have been paying more attention to this aspect of the book, pointing out that the text has a "multiplicity of meaning" that has traditionally gone unnoticed (De Looze, "Subversion" 342).[15] Like the prince in the *Libro de los estados*, the Count himself is aware of these tensions and uncertainties, as demonstrated by the Count's confusion in *exemplo* 50, and his plea for one simple piece of advice, since there are so many things to remember:

> [V]os ruego que me digades quál es la mejor cosa que omne puede aver en sí. Et esto vos pregunto porque bien entiendo que muchas cosas a mester el omne para saber acertar en lo mejor et fazerlo, ca por entender omne la cosa et non obrar della bien, non tengo que meiora mucho en su fazienda. Et porque las cosas son tantas, querría saber a lo menos una, porque siempre me acordasse della para la guardar (257, I beg you to tell me what is the best quality a man may have. And I ask you this because I clearly understand that a man needs many things to enable him to do what is best and to know how to do it, since for a man to understand something and not perform it well, will not, I think, add to his reputation. And since there are so many things, I should like to know at least one which I may remember in order to carry it out [181]).

Contrary to the notion that only the modern reader is dissatisfied with Patronio's advice, the Count's intellectual fatigue suggests that Juan Manuel may have anticipated his original readers' frustration with the adviser as well. Furthermore, the *Libro infinido* and *Libro de los estados* at the very least demonstrate the serious challenges Juan Manuel faced when attempting to articulate a troubling paradoxical problem, and in those texts one also encounters wor-

---

[15] Laurence de Looze believes that this ambiguity brings *El Conde Lucanor* "closer" to the *Libro de buen amor* ("Subversion" 342), and Dayle Seidenspinner-Núñez argues that both Juan Manuel and Juan Ruiz, as "'didactic' authors" display an "emphasis on pragmatism" (254). Mariano Baquero Goyanes writes that *El Conde Lucanor* causes confusion because of the multiplicity of advice and relativism, or "perspectivismo de opinión" (33), created in the collection, and María Rosa Menocal demonstrates how the very frame structure of the tales produces moral relativism (479).

ried and dissatisfied counselors and pupils. This evidence suggests that not only the modern reader can sense tensions in the text; a medieval critical reader who may have been even more attuned to the progression of narrative parts in Juan Manuel's mode of exemplification could certainly have appreciated the Count's desire for clarity since "las cosas son tantas." The principal source of conflict within each tale–and among them when compared to each other–is uncovered by following the medieval writing and reading custom that highlights homologous and repetitive narrative parts and formulaic divisions. A pair of tales compared and contrasted with each other can set this reading practice in motion, exposing Juan Manuel's method of exemplification more than any one particular lesson we can easily remember.

Exemplo 26, "De lo que contesció al árvol de la Mentira" ("What Happened to the Tree of Lies") presents an allegorical tale that inverts the image of God's universe, according to Peter Dunn, by replacing the Tree of Knowledge at its center with the Tree of Deceit (238). The question that frames this tale is, in essence, the same as many of the other stories throughout the *CL*: how to know if one is being deceived, how to recognize lies, and how to protect oneself from them. The Count comes to Patronio with a common problem. He has enemies that are slandering him and causing him great loss, and he does not want to use these same tactics to defend himself: "Et aun creed que si yo quisiesse obrar por aquella manera, que por aventura lo sabría fazer tan bien commo ellos; mas porque yo sé que la mentira es de mala manera, nunca me pagué della" (158, "And you may well believe that, if I were willing to act as they do, perhaps I would be as good a liar as they are, but because I believe lying is a bad business, I have never done it" [110]). The solution to this problem repeated throughout the collection, however, is not always the same, as will be seen when this *exemplo* is compared with the first.

Patronio's allegorical tale, based on the folk motif of the deceitful division of the harvest, explains how La Verdad (Truth) and La Mentira (Deceit) plant a tree together. La Mentira convinces La Verdad to take the roots as her part of the tree while La Mentira takes the part above ground. La Verdad agrees, since it is not in her nature to distrust, and lives underground with her share, while people from all around gather to learn from La Mentira under the shade of her tree. Meanwhile, La Verdad must eat the roots to survive, killing the tree which topples over on La Mentira and all her disciples.

Patronio advises through the use of his allegory that the Count do nothing directly to solve his problem; rather, he should be patient, even self deprecating, like La Verdad, and selflessly endure his hardship:

> Por ende, si aquellos vuestros contrarios usan de llas [sic] sabidurías et de los engaños de la mentira, guardatvos dellos cuanto pudierdes et non querades seer su conpañero en aquella arte, nin ayades envidia de la su buena andança que an por usar del arte de la mentira, ca cierto seed que poco les durará, et non pueden aver buena fin; et cuando cuydaren seer más bien andantes, estonçe les fallecerá, assí commo fallesció el árbol de la Mentira a los que cuydavan estar muy bien andantes a su sombra (162, Wherefore, if your antagonists use the skills and tricks of Falsehood, guard yourself as best you can against them and do not try to equal them in their art. Be not envious of the debonair manner which they have, because they use the art of Falsehood, for it will not last them long and they will come to no good, even though they think they are in a most agreeable posture, for it will fail them just as the tree of Falsehood failed those who imagined themselves well off in its shade [112]).

With its evocation of the sacred symbol of the Cross, this tale recalls *Genesis* and the Christian cosmology explaining God's universe. According to Patronio's application of this allegory, the Count must accept his place in that universe and suffer the lies of his enemies, waiting for God's divine judgment.

There are numerous other tales dealing with deceit in the *CL* that propagandize this moral and political philosophy, but there are others that display an alternative course of action for the same type of problem. An alternative is presented in the first *exemplo* of the collection, "De lo que contesció a un rey con un su privado" ("What Happened to a King and His Favorite"). Here again, the basic problems are lies and deceit.

The Count believes that a powerful gentleman will turn over to him all his property upon leaving his country, but as Patronio explains with the help of his *exemplo*, in fact the Count is being deceived by his friend; furthermore, Patronio will imply that the malicious lies of the Count's enemies are at the heart of this matter, linking the tale thematically with many others that deal with the same problem, including *exemplo* 26. The solution illustrated in this tale, however, is ethically opposed to that of *exemplo* 26. Instead of passively allowing oneself to be deceived and relying on faith in God's ordained social order and justice, this tale suggests that one should use deception in order to defend against it. This is in fact how the counselor in Patronio's *exemplum* saves himself from his enemies who have planted the seeds of doubt in the mind of his king in the first place, provoking him to test the loyalty of his favorite adviser, who in turn deceives his king by not telling him that he knows he is being tested, pretending to want to join him when he abandons his kingdom.

Patronio's reading of the story states that the Count should not allow himself to be fooled, but by comparison with his *exemplum*, which duplicates the Count's situation, the implied course of action is to fight fire with fire–a strategy distinctly pro-active when compared to the passivist approach taken in *exemplo* 26. In this tale, as in many others, role playing is linked with lying and deceit. In fact, Patronio's advice to the Count is to play a role, made complete with a costume "such as is worn by wonderers who beg alms" (46), in order to deceive the king and make him believe that he wants to join him in his journey. This kind of play acting is directly linked to pernicious lies, as in *exemplo* 32–Juan Manuel's version of The Emperor's New Clothes story–where charlatans deceive the king and his men with make-believe stitching and wonderment at their work. The moment in which the reader understands the damage done by lying is when the king himself accepts his role and pretends to see the cloth as well.[16]

The essential problem in *exemplo* 1 is different only in detail when compared to *exemplo* 26: how to recognize lies. In this case it may be a friend who is trying to test the Count, but nevertheless the trouble is the same, since the king is lying to his counselor about his plans to abandon his kingdom, and Patronio believes that the Count's "friend" is doing the same. Ian Macpherson identifies this

---

[16] James Burke associates play acting with the idea of role reversals in the *CL*. He argues that the various framing agents repeated throughout the collection structure the text through inversions of reality in order to highlight desirable social values, so the inverted role is "diametrically opposed" to the desirable value ("Frame and Structure" 269). In this way, role playing is seen as a subversive behavior, like lying.

recurring Manuelian theme of testing friendship in the *CL* as one that is preoccupied with protection from deception ("Amor and Don Juan Manuel" 175-6), but his comments on one tale in particular, *exemplo* 5, are of interest here since Macpherson detects the potential for an alternative reading of one of Patronio's *exempla* as an apology for trickery. Macpherson shows that Patronio draws a different moral for a tale, the "essence" of which "is that the fox (cunning and hypocrisy) wins the day against the crow (vanity and gullibility)" ("Amor" 175). Macpherson clarifies that this is *not* the lesson Patronio wishes to teach the Count–he advises him to be cautious and to not be taken in by deceit–but the critic makes an important observation by pointing out that Patronio's *exemplum* can have an alternate, even opposite reading that actually favors the use of trickery: "[I]t is tempting to conclude"–Macpherson speculates–"that Juan Manuel is here illustrating a case in which flattery and cunning pay off–in this tale the gullible man is no match for the crafty man" ("Amor" 175).

As I have already stated, Patronio's tale in the first *exemplo* also raises a suspicion that the test itself stems from the lies of the Count's enemies: "ca todo aquello quel rey le dixiera, non fuera porque el rey oviese voluntad de los fazer, sinon que algunos quel querían mal avían puesto al rey quel dixiese aquellas razones por le provar" (57-58, "For everything that the king had said was not said because he meant to carry out his plans, but because someone who wished his master ill had urged the king to say these things in order to test him" [45]). In fact, the course of action Patronio suggests is to play act like the counselor in his tale: "Et conviene que en tal manera fabledes con él, que entienda que queredes toda su pro et su onra, et que non avedes cobdiçia de ninguna cosa de lo suyo" (59, "You must, therefore make him think that your sole desire is his advantage and honor and that you have no desire to possess anything of his" [46]).

Patronio is for all intents and purposes advising the Count to lie, since the Count makes it clear from the beginning that he is indeed interested in the opportunity to take advantage of his friend's offer: "Et pues esto quiere, seméjame muy grand onra et grant aprovechamiento para mí; et vós dezitme et consejadme lo que vos paresçe en este fecho" (53, "Now since this is his wish, and since this would be greatly to my advantage and honor, advise me as to what I must do" [43]). The idea that the Count is only concerned for his friend's well being and honor is not all together true, and if he tells his friend, following the example of Patronio's story, that he wants to join him, that would most certainly be a lie. As in every tale, the Count follows Patronio's advice with success, according to the standard conclusion marked with a formulaic statement such as the one found in Juan Manuel's introductory tale: "El conde se falló por bien aconsejado del consejo de Patronio, su consejero, et fízolo commo él le consejara, et fallóse ende bien" (60, "The count thought himself well advised by his counselor, and he did as he was told and profited by it" [46]). So one can imagine that in this case the Count does indeed lie to his friend, something that he claims he would not do even to his enemies in *exemplo* 26.

These two *exemplos* can serve as representatives of generally conflicting ethical behaviors, actions or *carreras*–actions based on faith and the divine order of things (God), and actions based on deceit and political acumen (World)–that Juan Manuel attempts to harmonize by framing them within Part I of the *CL*. The book itself operates as an agent of redress in this conflicting discourse by affording to each tale the same degree of authority when Juan Manuel's persona repeatedly appears to conclude each *exemplo* and stamp his seal of approval with his ubiquitous *viessos*. Even though these behaviors appear to be self-contradictory since they are applied to essentially the same problem, the reader is told that each approach is equally legitimate, inscribing in the text itself the paradox that the collection proposes to solve. Interestingly, Juan Manuel's first story contains the traces of this conflict in its "double" proverbial conclusion: "And Don Juan, thinking this a good story, had it included in this book, and wrote these verses to express the moral: Be not deceived that any man will freely spare / What is his own, if harm alone will be his share. And these verses also: By friend's advice and pious deeds, / Your troubles end, your will's achieved" (47). Keller and Keating's translation of the original Spanish smooths over the tensions between these two *viessos*. Blecua's edition of the *CL* reads: "Non vos engañedes, nin creades que, endonado, / faze ningún omne por otro su daño de grado. Et los otros dizen assí: Por la piadat de Dios et por buen consejo, / sale omne de coyta et cunple su deseo" (60). Rather than relying on "deeds," the original Spanish is clear in its invocation of faith in "God's mercy" ("la piadat de Dios"). In the very first tale, then, the reader can detect the friction between God and World. After all, the Count in this tale employs "good advice" and trickery, more than religious devotion to avoid his enemies' trap.

But these antinomies do not simply create an ambiguously open text. Juan Manuel frames within the first part of his book a series of actions for very similar life situations that when compared to one another obfuscate any univocal didactic message; instead, once the reader learns to resonate to these conflicts, the *CL* can be read as a work that teaches the reader how to adopt Juan Manuel's appropriation of the authority associated with the *exemplum* for individual needs and ethical choices. In this way, by providing the reader with a rhetorical strategy that makes use of *exempla*, Juan Manuel's book does indeed aid its readers in performing "such deeds as would be advantageous to their honor, their possessions, and their stations," as well as actions that, if authorized by an illustrative narrative, will benefit their souls.

Once the reading process outlined above is begun, focusing primarily on the array of constitutive narrative parts and the discursive logic that binds them together, the tensions created by contradictory exemplary actions inevitably reorients the expectations for each tale, moving them further away from one "best quality a man may have," to a deeper appreciation of Juan Manuel's narrative technique. A case in point are *exemplos* 4 and 16. In each of these tales the Count is at peace, and his dilemma is whether or not he should take advantage of opportunities to increase his wealth and honors. Fernán González's famous reply to Nuño Laynez in *exemplo* 16, "Murió el omne, mas non murió el su nombre" (117, "Dead the man's name but not dead his fame" [82]), along with Patronio's advice, demand that the Count never rest on his laurels, but should always act in order to win eternal fame: "nunca por viçio nin por folgura dexaredes de fazer tales cosas, porque, aun desque vos murieredes, siempre viva la fama de los vuestros fechos" (117, "You will never fail through ease or idleness to do such deeds that even after your death the fame of your actions may live on" [82]).

On the other hand, in *exemplo* 4, the sick Genoese tells his soul that it should be grateful for all of God's blessings, and Patronio's advice is that the Count should also be thankful and never risk losing his good fortune on dangerous and costly adventures: "Et vós, señor conde Lucanor, pues, loado a Dios, estades en paz et con bien et con onra, tengo que non faredes buen recabdo en abenturar esto" (77, "And you, Sir Count Lucanor, since, praise be to God, you are at peace and enjoying wealth and honor, I think you would be ill advised to seek adventures" [56]). In some tales, for example *exemplo* 49, "De lo que contesçió al que echaron en la ysla desnuyo quandol tomaron el señoría que teníe" ("What Happened to the Man Whom They Cast out Naked on an Island When They Took away from Him the Kingdom He Ruled"), Patronio's story repeats the commonplace that fame and wealth on earth are fleeting: "et que por los estados et honras deste mundo, que son vanas et falleçederas, que non querades perder aquello que es çierto que a de durar para siempre sin fin" (256, "In exchange for the holdings and honors of this world, which are empty and perishable, you will not want to lose that which is certain and must endure forever without end" [180]), yet in other *exemplos* fame is of great value. I will study other tales in more detail in the following chapters, but let the following survey of concluding aphorisms suffice for now to demonstrate the consistency of the tension between these contradictory ethical postures. Such a comparison is easy to carry out in many of the manuscripts that set Juan Manuel's *viessos* off from the body of text, as in the case of manuscript M where they are indented and decorated with flourishes.

On one hand, there are the tales that advise in favor of a Christian ethic, legitimized by tradition and ordered by dogmas of salvation, in which man passively accepts his place in God's universe and endures all hardships:

> El que en Dios non pone su esperança / morrá mala muerte, abrá mala andança (*exemplo* 45, Who does not on the Lord rely, / Will badly live and badly die); Por este mundo falleçedero, / non pierdas el que es duradero (*exemplo* 49, Do not exchange God's endless day / For this brief one, however gay); Por quexa non vos fagan ferir, ca siempre vençe quien sabe sofrir (*exemplo* 15, Waging war no evil cures; / He conquers most who most endures); Sufre las cosas en quanto divieres, / estraña las otras en quanto pudieres (*exemplo* 29, Accept such ills as you can bear, / Repel the rest with utmost care); Por pobreza nunca desmayedes, / pues otros más pobres que vós ve[r]edes (*exemplo* 10, It matters not how poor you are, / For other men are poorer far); Non te quexes por lo que Dios fiziere, / ca por tu bien sería quando Él quisiere (*exemplo* 18, What God hath wrought is all for thee, / Be patient, then, his will to see).

On the other hand, there are tales and proverbs that subvert the order of this rigid worldview, testing the boundaries of God's will, and moving from the ideological center of traditional Christian authority to the margin, where social structure and the divine order of things are challenged by a pragmatic ethic in which man acts independently, in pursuit of his own personal interests:

> En lo que tu pro pudieres fallar, / nunca te fagas mucho por rogar (*exemplo* 17, If you're seeking personal profit, / When it's offered do not scoff it); Si por viçio et por folgura la buena fama perdemos, / la vida poco dura, denostados fincaremos (*exemplo* 16, If idle ways destroy our fame, / Our life, though short, will bear the blame); Si muy grand tu pro puedes fazer, / nol des vagar, que se pueda perder (*exemplo* 31, Seek fortune now, if you know how, / For if you wait, t'will be too late); Aquesto tenet çierto, que es verdat provada: / que onra et gran vicio non an una morada (*exemplo* 37, Learn this truth and learn it well: / That sloth with honor cannot dwell); Si Dios te guisare de aver sigurança / puña de ganar la complida bien andança (*exemplo* 33, If God to thee is ever kind, / Then thou must keep Him on thy mind).[17]

These are only a few examples, but the reader could go through the entire collection and uncover many more sources of this kind of tension among the conflicting opinions, beliefs, and behaviors that can be understood broadly as "ideologemes," or more specifically as exemplary ethical actions that are informed by conventional belief systems.[18]

The tales cited above, along with other *exemplos* in the collection, are more nuanced in detail than this argument may suggest;

---

[17] Keller and Keating take enormous poetic license to create rhyme in their translations of Juan Manuel's verses, in most cases their translations are excellent, but in others, as in the proverb for *exemplo* 33, the original meaning is more than slightly altered. The original Spanish *viessos* for this tale is significantly more subversive than the English translation conveys. A less poetic, but more literal translation might be: "If God is to protect you, / fight to win the (or his) full blessing (or good fortune)." A simple English proverb catches the meaning well: God helps those who help themselves.

[18] The term ideologeme is borrowed from Fredric Jameson who defines it as an utterance of a "larger class discourse" (87). In this discourse, the ideologeme can function as "a pseudoidea–a conceptual or belief system, an abstract value, an opinion or prejudice," and is "susceptible to both a conceptual description and a narrative manifestation all at once" (87).

nevertheless, they do display an ethical alignment that when compared to each other can create ambiguity and ideological tension. I would describe this ambiguity as a disjunctive ethical ambiguity because the tales can be organized in two systems of behavior and beliefs that are mutually exclusive. At this level of interpretation, the ambiguity is essentially ethical, instead of semantic, because it deals with exemplary human action and decisions.[19] There are, however, some tales that do not clearly express a single ethical behavior. Some stories allow for more latitude of interpretation and, therefore, action. *Exemplo* 43, "De lo que contesçió al Bien et al Mal, et al cuerdo con el loco" ("What Happened to Good and Evil and the Wise Man and the Madman"), may be the best expression of the conflicts that have been studied thus far in separate tales. *Exemplo* 43 is essentially two tales in one, displaying two possible courses of action for the Count's problem.

In this *exemplo*, the Count has two neighbors; he has a good relationship with one of them, and they help each other when they can, but sometimes his neighbor offends him: "et non sé qué pecado o qué ocasión es que muchas vezes me faze algunos yerros et algunas escatimas de que tomo muy grand enojo" (223, "And I can't say for what devilish reason or cause he often hurts me and cheats me to my great annoyance" [157]). Likewise, the other neighbor bothers him from time to time, but the Count does not have a friendly relationship with him: "et el otro non es omne con quien aya grandes debdos nin grand amor" (223, "But the second is not a man with whom I have close ties, nor for whom I feel deep affec-

---

[19] My idea of a disjunctive ethical ambiguity borrows from Shlomith Rimmon's *The Concept of Ambiguity–the Example of James*. Rather than a narrative ambiguity, my focus here is on exemplary behaviors, but Rimmon's comments on narrative ambiguity are helpful because there is a finite number of exemplary behaviors in the *CL* presented in a highly structured form, all of which ultimately limits the possibility of infinite subjective interpretations of the tales. These two ethical systems are also mutually exclusive: one cannot be passive and active at the same time in the same situation. The characteristics of what I have called disjunctive ethical ambiguity meet many of Rimmon's prerequisites for defining ambiguity; more particularly, it is a contradiction that is delineated and contained by the text: "[A]mbiguity is a fact in the text–a double system of mutually exclusive clues" (12). Furthermore, an ambiguous text is "characterized by a highly determined form, limiting the text's plurality by its organization of the data into two opposed systems which leave little or no room for further 'play'" (13). Finally, the ethical systems of behavior represented in the *CL* are not compatible with each other, especially when we see them applied to similar problems; thus actions, rather than the meaning of a particular word for example, are "mutually exclusive, thus calling for disjunction and choice" (22).

tion" [157]). The Count asks Patronio how he should treat each of these men. His counselor answers him with the second allegorical tale of the collection.

The story of the unequal division of the crop between Good and Evil expands on the concept of Good conquering Evil with truth begun in *exemplo* 26. Here, as seen in many other *exemplos*, passive acceptance of one's place in the world (rather than the use of deceptive role playing, or even violence) undoes the evil of trickery and deceit. In Patronio's tale of Good and Evil unequally dividing all their possessions in halves, Evil must beg his counterpart to let his son nurse from his partner's half of the woman they share. Good explains that he was always aware of his companion's trickery when they divided the woman, but he agreed to take the "inferior" parts of their possessions without complaint: "Amigo, non cuydes que yo tampoco sabía que non entendía quáles partes escogiestes vós sienpre et quáles diestes a mí; pero nunca vos demandé yo nada de las vuestras partes, et pasé muy lazdradamiente con las partes que me vós dávades" (225-226, "Friend, don't think that I was so simple that I didn't recognize the kind of parts you always picked and the kind you gave me while I never asked of you anything from your share and I got along wretchedly with what you gave me" [159]). El Bien continues his chastisement and states that he will not let Evil now break their contract unless he proclaims to the townspeople that Good conquered Evil by being good; by accepting his plight without complaint: "Amigos, sabet que con bien vençe el Vien al Mal" (226, "Friends, know that Good conquers Evil [by being good]" [159]).[20]

As in *exemplo* 26, Good conquers Evil by passively accepting injustices, showing that those who choose to remain faithful will win in the end. *Exemplo* 43 takes the moral of *exemplo* 26 one step further by revealing that this passivism is indeed a strategy, rather than a transparently naïve lifestyle. By forcing Evil to admit that Good had beaten him, the idea of ethical behavior as strategy is brought to the surface of the plot much more so than in *exemplo* 26. In *exemplo* 43, Good is truly calculating and punitive, as wit-

---

[20] Here Keller and Keating have left out an important detail in the original Spanish that deserves attention. The Spanish text states that Good conquers Evil "with good," or "by being good" ("*con bien* vençe el Vien al Mal" [my emphasis]). John England has another translation of the statement: "My friends, I say to you that through good, Good conquers Evil" (259).

nessed in his dialogue with Evil once the child is born and he needs the other half of their woman: "pues si agora Dios vos traxo a lugar que avedes mester algo de lo mío, non vos marabilledes si vos lo non quiero dar, et acordatvos de lo que me feziestes, et soffrid esto por lo al" (226, "And since God has now placed you in a predicament where you need something of mine, don't be surprised if I refuse to give it to you. Remember what you did to me, and take what is coming to you" [159]). Once Evil promises to do whatever is demanded of him, Good devises what seems to be the most satisfying revenge: "Desque el Bien esto vio, tovo quel fiziera Dios mucho bien en traerlo a lugar que viesse el Mal que non podía guaresçer sinon por la vondat del Bien, et tovo que esto le era muy grand emienda" (226, "And when Good understood this, he realized that God had favored him greatly in putting him in a position where Evil could not live without his kindness, and he regarded this as a great victory" [159]).

This punitive quality is lacking in the Truth character from *exemplo* 26 who is naïve almost to a fault: "porque non ay en ella muchas maestrías et es cosa de grand fiança et de grand creençia, fiosse en la Mentira, su compaña, et creó que era verdat lo quel dizía, et tovo que la Mentira le conseiava que tomasse muy buena parte" (159, "[B]ecause she is a naive and trusting creature, she trusted Falsehood, her companion, and believed her and thought Falsehood was advising her to choose the better part" [110]). In both cases, however, the moral is the same: those who faithfully endure the difficulties of their stations in life, those who can "sofrir," will know God's justice. Patronio's second tale, on the other hand, exemplifies an alternative course of action that undermines his allegory's central lesson.

The second story Patronio tells in *exemplo* 43 describes the plight of a man who owns a bathhouse. Every day a madman chases off his clients by beating them, and burning them with boiling water. One morning, the owner waits at the bathhouse for his uninvited guest, and when he arrives, the owner gives him the thrashing of his life, solving his problem forever.

Patronio offers each of these *exemplos* as exemplary actions for the Count to consider with regard to his own situation, just as the reader outside the text must do. With the Count's friend, Patronio suggests that he be like El Bien. The Count should always fulfill his side of their bargains, and he should forgive him his offenses, but always making sure that this neighbor understands that the Count does so out of duty and friendship, and from a position of power: "et aunque vos faga algunos enoios, datles passada et acorredle sienpre al su mester, pero siempre lo fazed dándol a entender que lo fazedes por los debdos et por el amor quel avedes, mas non por vencimiento" (227, "[A]nd even if he annoys you somewhat, forgive him and always help him when he needs it; but always do so while making him understand that you are doing so because of the ties and affection that you have for him and not because you are afraid or annoyed" [160]). This last piece of advice, to some extent, subverts the concept of respectfully suffering while waiting for divine justice in the way *exemplo* 26 suggests, but the posture is still based on an acceptance of one's responsibilities and social standing. In the case of the Count with his neighbor / ally, it is the duty of the Count as a nobleman to live within his station and all the codes (political and personal) that govern it.

The advice which Patronio illustrates with his second tale prescribes an alternate course of action similar to *exemplos* 16, 17, 31, 33 and 37, studied above. He explains to the Count that he should show no mercy whatsoever when dealing with the neighbor that is not his friend, and that he should do everything in his power to demonstrate his superior strength and determination: "mas al otro, con quien non avedes tales debdos, en ninguna guisa non le sufrades cosa del mundo, mas datle bien a entender que por quequier que vos faga, todo se aventurará sobrello" (227, "But in the case of the man with whom you do not have such ties, never take anything from him, but make him realize that whatever he does for you is for his own good" [160]). These two strategies can serve to represent the conflicting exemplary ethical strategies studied thus far that resist containment within the framework of the entire collection. Here these tensions are recreated in a single tale, and the very literary device designed to close off each narrative draws attention to the conflict it attempts to resolve: "Sienpre el Bien vençe con bien al Mal; / sofrir al omne malo poco val" (228, "Goodness always takes the prize, / To bear a bad man is unwise" [160]). Within the very device that attempts to synthesize a moral and exemplary behavior to follow, the tension between God and World cannot be satisfactorily harmonized.

I have intimated earlier that there are moments when Patronio's advice seems to conflict with the tale he tells, or at least depart from what would be the essential moral of his story. This conflict sets up another kind of friction in the collection that arises from the progression of narrative parts as they appear to lack a logical cohesion.

In *exemplo* 43 the same set of framing devices contain two tales that ethically collide with each other, drawing attention to a conflict that resonates throughout the collection. This tale is actually two stories within one narrative frame that strains to provide a summary of the lesson the reader should deduce; in fact, the concluding *viessos* express two contradictory exemplary behaviors. In the final analysis, it is the reader who must determine what kind of "neighbor" he or she is dealing with in order to put these *exempla* to use. There are many other cases of this type of friction caused by the equivocating advice Patronio gives to the Count before and after telling his exemplary tale. Among the many tales that in themselves dramatize these conflicts, *exemplo* 23, "De lo que facen las formigas para se mantener" ("How the Ants Provide for Themselves"), is a case in point. Here Patronio's advice and his reading of his own exemplary tale demonstrate how a story can be employed to legitimate more than one course of action, moving back and forth between two ethical positions.

In the frame story of this tale, the Count is in a familiar situation: his advisers tell him that now that he is wealthy he should rest at home and still be able to leave his children with good inheritances. Patronio's story is another tale that could be aligned with the moral expressed in *exemplo* 26, but his advice will provide an alternative course of action that does not flow directly from the central moral of his own exemplary tale.

The story that is intended to be a model of behavior for the Count tells of how the ants never stop gathering food, even when their nests are overflowing, and they have more than enough for the winter:

> Et aún fallaredes que, maguer que tengan cuanto pan les complía, que cada que buen tiempo faze, non fazen nin dexan de acarrear cualesquier erbizuelas que fallan. Et esto fazen reçelando que les non cumplirá aquello que tienen; et mientre an tiempo, non quieren estar de valde nin perder el tiempo que Dios les da, pues se pueden aprovechar dél (141-142, And you will also discover that although they have all the grain they need, every time there is good weather they do not fail to heap up all the

grains they can find. And they do this for fear that what they have will not be enough; and since they have it they do not wish to waste it nor lose the time God gives them, since they can profit by it [99]).

The moral is the same as many *exemplos* already studied here that suggest that one must take advantage of God's blessings, and that the pursuit of one's own good is also God's will. Patronio's first piece of advice will center on this general belief, but he will then offer a way around his own opinion, providing in the process an example of how to employ the *exemplo* to legitimate more than one interest and course of action.

According to Patronio's first reading of his story, the Count would do no less than the simple-minded ants; in fact, he is expected to do much better:

> Et vós, señor conde, pues la formiga, que es tan mesquina cosa, ha tal entendimiento et faze tanto por se mantener, bien devedes cuydar que non es buena razón para ningún omne, et mayormente para los que an de mantener grand estado et governar a muchos, en querer sienpre comer de lo ganado (142, And you, Sir Count, since the ant, which is such a small creature, has so much understanding and does so much to provide for herself, you should realize that it is not reasonable for a man, especially for one who has to maintain a large estate and govern a great many others, always to eat what is on hand [99]).

Patronio then immediately offers another interpretation, or at least another piece of advice, by suggesting that the Count does not have to follow the example of the ants exactly, demonstrating the interpretive possibilities available in his exemplary tale. He suggests that there is indeed a way for the Count to rest if he pleases, investing his estate wisely to promote his honor while always attending to his duties:

> Mas el mío consejo es este: que si queredes comer et folgar, que lo fagades sienpre manteniendo vuestro estado et guardando vuestra onra et catando et aviendo cuydado cómmo avredes de que lo cunplades, ca si mucho ovierdes et bueno quisieredes seer, assaz avredes logares en que lo despendades a vuestra onra (142, But my advise is that if you wish to eat and take your ease, do so

while always maintaining your estate, guarding your honor, and looking to and being careful of how you will have what you will require. For if you have a great deal and wish to do what is right, there are plenty of places where you can spend your wealth to your honor, and to the service of God, which is more important [99]).[21]

Patronio's personal opinion is that the Count does not have to obey the law of the ants to the letter if he does not want to; rather, there is a way that he can actually spend his treasure if he chooses to, so the ultimate decision is left to the Count and the readers who must apply the story to their own lives. Don Juan's final *viessos* attempt to strike a middle ground between these two options: "Non comas sienpre lo que as ganado / bive tal vida que mueras onrado" (142, "Eat not all you laid aside; / Live with honor, die with pride" [99]). These aphorisms are clearly not an adequate summary of Patronio's *exemplum*, since they do not capture the ants' philosophy of tireless pursuit of personal interests, nor the concept of taking advantage of the blessings (i.e., "good weather") bestowed by God for one's own benefit. On the contrary, Patronio's advice and Don Juan's maxims stymie the possibility of one univocal moral and exemplary behavior, leaving the burden of figuring out how to act on the shoulders of the readers. *Exemplos* 49 and 18 provide more evidence of this kind of interpretive latitude inscribed within the tales themselves that invites the reader to arrive at his or her own conclusions for each tale, and in the process learn Juan Manuel's rhetorical strategy of exemplification:

One of the underlying tensions of the entire collection surfaces in *exemplo* 18, "De lo que contesçió a don Pero Meléndez de Valdés cuando se le quebró la pierna" ("What Happened to Pero Meléndez de Valdés When He Broke His Leg"): how to respond to God's will. Should one accept it passively with faith in God's omniscience and mercy, or act upon it according to one's own interests?

---

[21] "[A]nd to the service of God, which is more important" does not appear in Blecua's edition of the *CL*, nor in Ayerbe-Chaux or Guillermo Serés' editions, but the license taken by Keller and Keating is interesting since it suggests an appreciation (perhaps even a preference?) of the "spirit" of Patronio's alternative advice in this tale and others where service to God is "more important" than "El Mundo." John England's translation of the same passage is a more literal rendition: "[F]or if you acquire great wealth and wish to do good, you will find plenty of opportunities to spend it honourably" (149).

By the end of this *exemplo* the Count must determine what kind of obstacle ("enbargo") he is faced with. This is a very serious decision, since a mistake could risk offending God's will. Patronio explains that there are two kinds of hardships: those that must be acted upon, and those that must be accepted faithfully. He suggests that the Count's illness is the latter kind, but that there are also problems that require action: "Et en los enbargos que se puede poner algún conseio deve fazer omne cuanto pudiere por lo poner y et non lo deve dexar por atender que por voluntad de Dios o por aventura se ende[re]çará, ca esto sería tentar a Dios" (122, "And in the case of obstacles about which one can take counsel a man should do his best to do so, and should not wait for the will of God or for matters to straighten themselves out by chance, for this would be tempting God" [86]). This is a very difficult matter to resolve, since the stakes are so high, but the idea of two kinds of problems that are both God's will opens up the decision-making process to the reader who can rhetorically rationalize two kinds of action for the same situation depending on which one of these categories he or she selects to define the *enbargo*.

In *exemplo* 49, "De lo que contesçió al que echaron en la ysla desnuyo quandol tomaron el señorío que tenié" ("What Happened to the Man Whom They Cast out Naked on an Island When They Took away from Him the Kingdom He Ruled"), Patronio explains the moral of the King-for-a-Day story (in this case King-for-a-Year), and argues that the Count should forsake worldly honors and riches in order to prepare his mansion in heaven, but the Count's advisers tell him that he should use his power to increase his treasure and honors on earth: "que faga cuanto pudiere por aver grand riqueza et grand poder et grand onra, et [que] esto es lo que me más cunple et más me pertenesçe" (254, "that I can do anything I please to acquire much money, great authority, and high honor; and that this is what is proper for me and what is most relevant" [178]).

Before telling his story and giving his opinion, Patronio qualifies his answer by arguing that any advice that has the Count's best interest at heart is good advice, and that he is taking a great risk by contradicting it–which is not exactly what he does. Patronio modifies his advice before he tells his story because the pursuit of fame, wealth and power is a noble endeavor for the Count, as seen in other *exemplos*. In this tale, the counselor is faced with reconciling the central ethical dilemma developed through the collection, and the task makes him noticeably tense:

> Señor conde –dixo Patronio–, este conseio que me vós demandades es grave de dar por dos razones: lo primero, que en este consejo que me vós demandades, avré a dezir contra vuestro talante; et lo otro, porque es muy grave de dezir contra el consejo que es dado a pro del señor. Et porque en este conseio ha estas dos cosas, esme muy grave de dezir contra él (254, 'Sir Count,' said Patronio, 'this counsel you require of me is a serious thing to give, and for two reasons: the first is that in this advice you ask of me I shall have to speak against your wishes; and the second is that it is awfully difficult to speak against the counsel given for one's master's advantage. And because there are these two things about this advice, it is hard for me to talk about it' [178]).

Patronio's final words of wisdom in this tale attempt to square his advice with that of the Count's other counselors by arguing that he should win salvation through good works performed with good intentions. After concluding that the honors of this world are "vanas et falleçederas" (256, "empty and perishable" [179]), Patronio claims that the Count should promote his honor on earth: "Pero seyendo estas cosas guardadas, todo lo que pudieredes fazer por levar vuestra onra et vuestro estado adelante tengo que lo devedes fazer et es bien que lo fagades" (256, "But with these works treasured up, I consider that you ought to do all that you can do to increase your honor and your estate, and it is well for you to do it" [179]). As Patronio explains before his *exemplo*, the Count's other advisers are partially correct: "vos digo que los que esto vos dizen que, en parte, vos conseian bien" (254, "And so I say to you that the men who advise you in part are counseling you well" [178-179]), but his final counsel brings the reader back to the central dilemma of the collection: how to attend to the path of God and the World at the same time. These tensions and paradoxes are exacerbated in a well-studied tale, *exemplo* 50, when the Count, appearing overwhelmed, asks Patronio for the best of all virtues, since there are so many dangers involved in deciding how to act properly.

Juan Manuel outlines in this tale the dichotomy put forward in the prologue, as well as many other *exemplos* in the collection; namely, how to do such works that will win both salvation and honors on earth. These two endeavors, paths or "carreras," Patronio will argue, must be acted upon equally. At the same time Patronio recognizes that this is an almost impossible task: "Et para las guardar amas, ha menester muy buenas obras et muy grant entendimiento, que tan grand cosa es de fazer esto commo meter la mano en l' fuego et non sentir la su calentura " (258, "And to keep to both [paths which are God's and the world's], great works as well as great understanding are needful, for it is as difficult to do as to thrust one's hand into fire and not feel its heat" [181]). Just as in the *Libro de los estados* and the *Libro infinido*, the only possible way out of this paradox is through faith in God's will and His miracles: "pero, ayudándole Dios, et ayudándosse el omne, todo se puede fazer; ca ya fueron muchos buenos reys et otros homnes sanctos; pues éstos buenos fueron a Dios et al mundo" (258, "but with God's help, and helping oneself, a man can do anything, for there have been many good kings and other saintly men, because they served God and the world" [181]).

Again Juan Manuel has linked the successful navigation of these two paths with sainthood, which, as observed in the *Libro de los estados*, was cause for some worry on the part of the pupil, but here Juan Manuel also adds the notion of man acting on his own behalf ("and helping oneself"), thereby reintroducing the dilemmas of understanding how to react to God's will, and the notion that the reader must apply "great understanding" to solve the paradox. These comments are certainly designed to encourage the Count, but there remain significant doubts and tension surrounding this paradox, and ultimately the reader is left to contemplate his own chances of success, and his own understanding of the context surrounding the paradox. Employing the same simile the author used to describe his perception of real conflict to his son in the *Libro infinido*, Juan Manuel's collection of tales recreates a homologous dynamic of tension and ambiguity that seriously challenges the framing argument of the entire collection.

In the political, ethical, and literary arenas, the reader, the Count, Patronio, and indeed Juan Manuel himself, are in a paradoxical situation, the solution to which cannot be found in the orthodoxy associated with the *exemplum*, nor in the conflicting ethical postures inscribed within and among the tales of the *CL*. The consequence of the paradox is that the reader must search for a solution to the matter of *Dios y el Mundo*, rather than relying exclusively on Patronio's authority. What is left is the reader's task to interpret the meaning of the book and apply it to his or her own life. In this tale, which may in fact have been the conclusion of a fifty-tale original version of Part I of the *CL*,[22] the search for a single moral, maxim, or "consejo" that can harmonize the paths of God and World is so seriously undermined that it must be abandoned.

But the author never did promise a solution in the first place, since the prologue merely states that it is the author's wish that his book aid his readers in their own deeds and decisions in order to win salvation and honors. Juan Manuel does not claim to have solved the paradox of God and World: "Este libro fizo don Iohan, fijo del muy noble infante don Manuel, deseando que los omnes *fiziessen en este mundo tales obras* que les fuessen aprovechosas [my emphasis]" (45, "This book was written by Don Juan Manuel, son of the noble Prince Don Manuel, with the wish that all men *should accomplish in this world such deeds* as would be advantageous" [39]). By following the array of homologous narrative parts, and comparing and contrasting the exemplary ethical behaviors recommended for identical questions, dilemmas and doubts, what may in fact be learned is Patronio's rhetorical method that appropriates the authority of the *exemplum* to legitimize ethical decisions. There may, in fact, be traces of a more pragmatic solution to the question of how to act properly in every occasion, such as in the second tale, but there are also others in which the author provides some explicit instructions on how to employ *enxiemplos* coercively, further calling attention to a rhetorical, as well as ethical, lesson in the *CL*.

---

[22] The authorship of the next tale, *exemplo* 51, which concludes Part I of the *CL* in manuscript S alone has been the subject of much debate, but most critics consider it to be the work of Juan Manuel. One of the most important voices on the subject is certainly John England, who defends Juan Manuel's authorship in "Exemplo 51 of *El Conde Lucanor*: The Problem of Authorship," as does David Flory, while others, most notably Alberto Blecua, have serious doubts. Like Flory, Ayerbe-Chaux proposes in his edition of the *CL* that it is an epilogue for Part I, since it has no title to separate it in manuscript S, although the editor does not mention that *exemplo* 49 does not have a title either in the same manuscript (14). The fact that Patronio makes concluding remarks in *exemplo* 50, referring to the fifty questions he has already answered suggests that at least one original version of the *CL* did indeed have an even number of stories, and that the fifty first was added at a later date. I will return to this tale, as well as England and Blecua's arguments on its authorship in chapter 4.

CHAPTER 2

JUAN MANUEL'S EXEMPLARY ART

IN the previous chapter I have argued that by following a medieval reading practice inscribed in the *CL*, Juan Manuel's method of writing itself–his rhetorical strategy of exemplification– can be the "meaning" of the book for those readers who can follow the progression of homologous narrative parts in each tale. The author's modal approach to writing, which ultimately is an expression of ethical reasoning and persuasion, can be learned to the benefit of those readers who must make decisions in their own lives about how to balance the seemingly contradictory paths of God and World. Don Juan's exemplary appropriation of the authority of the *exemplum*, employed as a kind of rhetorical armament to defend against criticism by authorizing an unknowable number of possible actions for any given situation, can aid the reader in his or her own ethical decision-making process, and sanction his or her final actions. I have also stated that Juan Manuel does not promise a single answer to the dilemma, at least not in his prologue where his intentions are most clearly announced.

In spite of this fact, many scholars have looked to the last three tales (*exemplos* 49, 50, and 51) in Part I of the *CL* as a solution to the conundrum, but these stories actually lead the reader away from the path of the world toward that of God, faith and humility, rather than actually balancing both *carreras*.[1] Juan Manuel's concluding

---

[1] In a lengthy note to *exemplo* 49, Guillermo Serés argues in his edition of the *CL* that the last three tales of Part I "están íntimamente relacionados" (201, "they are intimately related"). In addition to a thematic unity among the three tales (man must humble himself before God), they display a similarity of plot in the radical and miraculous reversal of identities that each protagonist undergoes in order to learn his lesson.

aphorisms sum up the gradual shift away from the tireless pursuit of wealth and honor, seen in other tales studied in chapter 1, towards the humility that endures God's divine will and order:

> Por este mundo falleçedero, / non pierdas el que es duradero (exemplo 49, Do not exchange God's endless day / For this brief one, however gay); La vergüença todos los males parte; / por vergüença faze omne bien sin arte (exemplo 50, Shame fights evil, as it should, / And makes it easy to do good); Los derechos omildosos Dios mucho los ensalça, / a los que son sobervios fiérelos peor que maça (exemplo 51, God uplifts the humble crowd, / And humbles soon the great and proud).[2]

Recently, important scholars have been paying greater attention to this same thematic progression through the entire five-part *CL* that concludes with pure faith in the articles and Sacraments of the Church in Part V, and there is no doubt that such a development exists, leading critics such as Laurence de Looze to conclude that the five-part *CL* "establishes [. . .] a clear hierarchy that places soul over body, the spiritual over the social, etc.–as it also enacts a movement from the one to the other" ("*El Conde Lucanor*, Part V" 150). At the same time, however, many of these same critics have discussed Juan Manuel's hermeneutic lessons and insights into the very contingency of language itself as an omnipresent theme.

As early as 1977, Peter Dunn uncovered the semantic possibilities in the *CL*, arguing that "the range of fictional situations [. . .] is such that they cannot be reduced to a dogmatic uniformity of meaning" ("Structures of Didacticism" 53). Following a similar line of inquiry, James Burke argues that the *CL* teaches the importance of being able to interpret signs, a theme he refers to as "the curse of mediacy" that is also present in the *Libro de buen amor* ("Counterfeit" 210), and John England acknowledges that Juan Manuel's book is designed to train its readers to be better able to make ethical decisions:

> The didacticism of *El Conde Lucanor* is, then, about making choices, choices which are difficult to get right because of the

---

[2] See the last note in chapter 1 on the polemical topic of the authenticity of this tale. I will return to a discussion of *exemplo* 51 as one of the idiosyncratic elements of manuscript S, and possibly one of the most significant examples of reading the *CL* ideologically "right" in the late Middle Ages.

dual nature of human beings and the complexity of the world in which they live. No single text can present the solution to every problem, but if the reader is receptive to the three different didactic forms which make up *El Conde Lucanor*–exemplary tale, maxim, discursive essay–, then he or she will be wiser and more sharp-witted in making correct decisions as and when the need arises, when there will be no time to consult advisers or reference-books. ("'Los que son muy cuerdos'" 364)

I would argue that an important lesson to learn from the *CL* in order to be "wiser" and "more sharp-witted" when making ethical decisions is that the *exemplum*, like any other sign, can only have meaning when mediated by a reader who defines and applies its ethical example. Derek Lomax reminds his readers that this is exactly how preachers employed the *exemplum* in their sermons for proofs and persuasion: "[A]ny preacher skilled in exegesis could extract what he needed from the stories and give them the most appropriate moral for his purpose" ("The Lateran Reforms" 309). Laurence de Looze sees this lesson clearly in *exemplo* 51, concluding that "there is no sign without an accompanying act of interpretation" ("Subversion of Meaning" 348).

Before moving on to an analysis of Juan Manuel's rhetorical use of *exempla* in two specific tales, I must clarify that by arguing that Juan Manuel's method of exemplification can legitimize a myriad of actions, by no means do I want to suggest that Juan Manuel was a moral relativist or subversive. Juan Manuel's faith in the teachings of the Catholic Church and acceptance of rigid medieval social hierarchies is unimpeachable; at least if we base our judgments on his words alone, as opposed to his actions. The *Libro de los estados* contains one of the best expressions of his orthodoxy: "creo et confiesso toda la sancta fe et todos sus artículos, así commo la sancta madre Eglesia de Roma lo tiene et lo cree" (297, "I believe in and confess to all of the Holy Faith and its articles as the Holy Mother Church of Rome states and believes"). In this same book, the author repeatedly expresses through the voice of Julio, the prince's counselor, his firm belief that every person within his or her own *estado* can be saved, as well as condemned:

> Señor infante, vós sabedes que yo, en la primera partida deste libro, vos dixi que en todos los estados en que biven los omnes en el mundo se pueden salvar, si quisieren. Et otrosí, non ay estado,

por bueno nin por sancto que sea, en que el omne non pueda perder el alma et aun el cuerpo muy bien, si quisiere (344, Sir prince, you know that I, in the first part of this book, told you that in every estate in which men live they can be saved, if they wish. Furthermore, there is no estate, no matter how good or holy, in which man cannot easily lose his soul and even his body, if he wishes).

But the author is also concerned in works such as the *Libro infinido* in passing on wisdom and advice on how to handle the very serious matter of balancing politics, ambition, and soteriology.

Juan Manuel's appropriation of a rhetorical strategy successfully employed by preachers, especially for persuading the under-educated–the *exemplum* was a far better persuasive tool for common audiences than the more erudite scholastic arguments used to elucidate and defend doctrine among the educated[3]–may well be one of the most useful lessons handed down to his readers. How to employ the rhetoric of exemplification to defend and authorize one's actions would have been a very useful lesson, especially for his aristocratic readers.

I must also clarify that I do not mean to suggest that Juan Manuel was a professional rhetorician. John England passionately argues against reading Juan Manuel as a "philosopher, logician, theologian, or linguist" ("'Los que son muy cuerdos'" 350), and it is patently obvious that he was none of those things. England goes on to defend Juan Manuel's famous pragmatism, claiming that "Juan Manuel writes [. . .] as a layman, seeking in works such as *El Conde Lucanor* to convey the fruits of his considerable experience of human behavior and society, in the form of exemplary tales in Part I, and maxims in Parts II-IV" (351); nevertheless, Juan Manuel had quite a lot to say about religion and even language itself.

In addition to Part V of the *CL* which takes on theological sub-

---

[3] James Murphy shows that as early as the parables of Christ, preaching to the masses with illustrative narratives was a preferred rhetorical device in preaching, witnessed in Christ's use of parables as "worldly reminders of superworldly things" (279). Larry Scanlon understands the Church's preference for the *exemplum* in preaching "not because it passively submitted to Christian doctrine, but, on the contrary, because the *exemplum*'s status as narrative gave it an ideological power doctrine often lacked [. . .]. The recurrent theme in ecclesiastical commentary on the *exemplum* from the fifth century onward was its persuasive power in contrast to reason or doctrine" (31).

jects of faith and the Sacraments, in the *Libro de los estados* Juan Manuel dedicates the entire second book to a discussion of Church hierarchies, and even the apparent self-contradictions in Holy Scripture. To begin with, the author acknowledges the dangers of writing on these matters, but with the divine seal bestowed upon him by the Holy Spirit, like all Christians who have received the Sacrament of Confirmation, he has faith that God will give him the correct words to speak on matters of the Church with authority:

> Et porque fablar en los estados de la clerezía es ý muy mayor mester el saber, entiendo que es aún mayor atrevimiento que el primero. Pero tanto es fuerte el tienpo en que agora estamos, que es de la Çinquaesma, en el qual tienpo et día envió nuestro señor Dios el Spíritu Sancto sobre los apóstoles, que les alunbró, así que sopieren todos los saberes et todos los lenguajes, tanbién los que nunca leyeron commo los que avían leído. Et otrosí, el poder de Dios es tan grande, que por la su virtud se alunbran los çiegos et andan los contrechos et fablan los mudos, et da poder a los que non an, quanto et quando Él quiere; por ende entiendo yo çiertamente que todo lo que Él quisiere se puede fazer (296-297, And because it is even more important that one have great knowledge to speak of the estates of the clergy, I know that [this second book] is even more audacious than the first. But the present time of Pentecost is very powerful, in which time and day our Lord God sent the Holy Spirit upon the apostles, illuminating them so that they could know all wisdom and all languages, allowing the illiterate to read as well as the literate. Furthermore, the power of God is so great that the blind have sight and the lame walk and the mute speak, and he gives power to those who have none, when and as much as He desires; therefore I am convinced that everything that He wants can be achieved).

With the power of the Holy Spirit behind him, Juan Manuel obviously believed that he did not have to be a theologian to write on matters of faith, Holy Scripture, or the Church itself.

In this same book Don Juan also acknowledges the fallen state of language, and its uselessness for conveying the mysterious truths of faith and Church doctrine. Referring specifically to apparent paradoxes in Holy Scripture (he cites for example that God's face has never been seen, and that God spoke to Moses face to face [*Libro de los estados* 308-309]), the author argues that one cannot use language to convince a non-believer that Scripture is true because of the very limitations of language: "Et en estas cosas, quien quisiere escatimar las palabras según las puede omne dezir, por fuerça fincará mal el que lo dixo, ca estas cosas alcánçalas el entendimiento, mas non se pueden dezir por palabra cómmo son" (309, "In these matters, if one chooses to debate another based on the words used to explain them, he who explains will inevitably fail, since these matters can be grasped by intelligence, but they cannot be expressed with words"). Here, as in the *CL*, "entendimiento" is a tricky word to translate into English. It can mean intelligence, understanding, reason, and, as in the quotation above, a natural ability to perceive truth behind apparent paradox; an ability akin to the Augustinian idea of a God-given inner-light that guides each individual toward the Truth that each person inherently already knows.

In the movements of an inward learning process, words are little more than reminders, as Augustine expresses in the last chapter of *Concerning the Teacher* (*De Magistro*): "man is only prompted by words in order that he may learn, and it is apparent that only a very small measure of what a speaker thinks is expressed in his words" (56). Juan Manuel seems to acknowledge this essential point of Augustinian sign theory, even though he avoids entering into a discussion of language itself; a wise decision since, as Augustine also remarks in *De Magistro*, an examination of the nature of language can be a very frustrating investigation: "For discussing words with words is as entangled as interlocking and rubbing the fingers with the fingers, in which case it may scarcely be distinguished, except by the one himself who does it, which fingers itch and which give aid to the itching" (20). It appears that Juan Manuel did not have to be a professional logician or linguist to understand the basic Augustinian concepts that each person is an individual learner, endowed with the power to decipher language and signs of all kinds, and that, as James Murphy paraphrases Augustine, a second person cannot debate, persuade or "*instruct* the hearer [. . .] by the force of the conventional signs he uses in communicating with him" (288). In Juan Manuel's words cited above, "he who explains will inevitably fail, since these matters can be grasped by intelligence, but they cannot be expressed with words."

Don Juan seems to approach the notion of the individual learner with his or her own private *entendimiento* as a measure of their essential virtue; to the degree that they are faithful believers, his readers will be able to not only understand Juan Manuel's meaning, but actually read his letters. In order to prevent his words on the delicate subject of Scripture and Church doctrine from being misunderstood, or even changed, Juan Manuel harnesses the ambiguity of language, inventing his own cryptography to test and limit his audience. The author was clearly aware that some readers would have the authority and intellect to correct his text, and he invites them to do so: "Et lo que ý fallaredes que es [dubdoso] de entender, emendadlo, et poned la culpa a mí, porque me atreví a fablar en tan altas maneras" (297, "And if what you find [in my book] is unclear or dubious, correct it and blame me because I dared to write on such high matters").[4] But there are other parts of his text that the author believes are infallible, and should only be read by true believers with proper *entendimiento*: "Et por ende, estas cosas en que los que lo non pudiese entender podrían tomar alguna dubda, por mengua de los sus entendimientos, estas tales cosas quiérolas yo poner por letras tan escuras que los que non fueren muy sotiles non las puedan *emendar*" (307, "And because those who cannot understand these things may have doubts because of their lack of intelligence, I want to write about them with letters so dark that those who are not clever enough will not be able to correct them").[5]

The author's secret code worked so well that it has left large blank spaces in the *Libro de los estados* as it appears in manuscript S. Apparently those who had to copy it did not have sufficient *entendimiento* to decipher Juan Manuel's code.[6] The use of a "dark" language is also found in the *CL*, in particular Parts II to IV where Patronio teaches through numerous maxims, many of which are ap-

---

[4] It is interesting to compare these comments with Juan Manuel's contemporary, Juan Ruiz, who also invites his more educated readers to alter his verses ("añadir e emendar si quisiere") in the often-cited *cuaderna* 1, 629 of the poem (*Libro de buen amor* 445).

[5] In Ian Macpherson and Robert Tate's edition of the *Libro de los estados*, cited here, the text reads, "que non fueren muy sotiles non las puedan *entender* [my emphasis]," but the text as it appears in manuscript S clearly reads "emendar" (Madrid, Biblioteca Nacional 6376, fol. 106ʳ). "Emendar" also makes perfect sense considering that in the first chapter of the second book which deals with the hierarchies of the clergy, as cited above, the author asks that if any of his writings are in error that they be corrected ("emendadlo, et poned la culpa a mí" [297]). Juan Manuel uses his *letras escuras* precisely to prevent readers from changing the parts of his text that he deems too serious to be tampered with.

[6] Barry Taylor has written an excellent study on these lacunae and Juan Manuel's cryptography in, "Juan Manuel's Cipher in the *Libro de los estados*."

parently paradoxical, even enigmatic. Part II is dedicated to Don Jaime, Señor de Xérica, a friend and ally who, according to the text, is not impressed with plain speech, preferring the more intellectually challenging "dark" manner of writing:

> [M]e dixo que querría que los mis libros fablassen más oscuro, et me rogó que si algund libro feziesse, que non fuessen tan declarado. Et so çierto que esto me dixo porque él es tan sotil et tan de buen entendimiento, et tiene por mengua de sabiduría fablar en las cosas muy llana et declaradamente (277, Don Jaime told me that he wanted my books be more esoteric, and he begged me that if I were to write a book that it not be so simple and direct. And I am certain that he told me this because he is so clever and has such great intelligence, and he believes that speaking clearly and directly shows a lack of wisdom).

Parts II and III contain many maxims that are not at all difficult to understand, while others, especially in Part IV, are more challenging to untangle. The first one in Part II is particularly troubling, especially when compared to Part I and the Count's plea for one good piece of advice: "En las cosas que ha muchas sentençias, non se puede dar regla general" (279, "In matters that have many sentences [i.e. judgments or expressions of wisdom], one cannot give a general rule"). Others are popular proverbs commonly used in modern Spanish: "Mejor sería andar solo que mal acompañado" (280, "Better to be alone than have bad company"), but as the reader progresses through the books of proverbs, the syntax of each becomes more difficult to parse, and, as in the first proverb of Part III, they may even be paradoxical: "Lo caro es caro, cuesta caro, guárdasse caro, acábalo caro; lo rehez es rehez, cuesta rehez, gánase rehez, acábalo rehez; lo caro es rehez, lo rehez es caro" (289, "That which is dear is dear, it costs dearly, it is dear to keep, it ends up being dear; that which is cheap is cheap, it costs little, it earns little, and ends up being cheap; that which is dear is cheap, that which is cheap is dear").

There are numerous other maxims and proverbs that take on topics such as governance, work, wisdom, common sense and good deeds, and some I would argue even display a playfulness found in tongue-twister type games. Some of these are so complicated that they test the limits of my modest translating abilities, or they simply do not "work" in English as they do in Spanish: "El rey rey reyna;

el rey non rey non reyna, mas es reynado" (284, "The king that is a king rules, and he who is not a king is ruled"). It would be challenging, and fun, to say this maxim in Spanish ten times as fast as you can.

Another one to try comes toward the end of Part II: "Si el fecho no faz grand fecho et buen fecho et bien fecho, non es grand fecho. El fecho es fecho cuando el fecho faze el fecho; es grand fecho et bien fecho si el non fecho faz grand fecho et bien fecho" (286), which is just about impossible for me to translate.[7] Still others are paradoxes that conceal a deeper truth:

> Todas las cosas paresçen bien et son buenas, et paresçen mal et son malas, et paresçen bien et son malas, et paresçen malas et son buenas (281, All things seem good and are good, and seem bad and are bad, and seem good and are bad, and seem bad and are good); Ay verdat buena, et ay verdat mala (283, There is good truth, and bad truth); El mejor pedaço que ha en l'omne es el coraçón, esse mismo es el peor (285, The best part of man is his heart, and it is also his worst); Del fablar biene mucho bien, del fablar biene mucho mal (285, From speaking comes great good, from speaking comes great evil); Del callar biene mucho bien, del callar biene mucho mal (285, From keeping quiet comes great good, from keeping quiet comes great evil).

The maxims of Parts II, III and IV have received comparatively less critical attention than Part I; in fact, some editions of the *CL* do not even include Parts II to V. Among those who have studied the entire five part *CL*, Laurence de Looze and James Burke have shed a great deal of light on the function of the proverbs in the whole book. Burke argues persuasively in *Desire Against the Law* that Juan Manuel included these enigmatic proverbs to test the intelligence of his readers, and to provide "explicit examples of how language can be twisted and convoluted" (239). Burke goes on to state that Juan Manuel's objective is to "teach [the reader] to untangle riddles posed to him and even to contrive enigmas himself" (239). Like Burke's analysis of Juan Manuel's proverbs, Laurence de

---

[7] I would like to thank the anonymous reviewer of this book who suggested the following translation: "If a deed is not a great and good deed, then it is not a deed; a deed is a (true) deed when it makes its own reputation; it is a great and well done deed, even when not done, if it has a positive outcome."

Looze also argues that the author attempts to expose for his audience the "obtuseness and obscurity of language itself" in order to teach how to become a better reader of signs ("The 'Nonsensical' Proverbs" 204).[8] De Looze sees these middle parts of the *CL* as steps in as series of lessons designed to force the reader to struggle with "difficult textuality," and to become a better hermeneutician ("The 'Nonsensical' Proverbs" 204):

> [I]t is the hermeneutic *process* of negotiating with the text that sharpens (*aguza*) the reader's capacity for understanding. The end point of resolving all obscurities and clarifying meanings matter little [. . .]. Instead, it is the process of the intellectual work involved in trying to understand a text that is of greatest importance, whether or not one 'solves', the obscurities in any definitive manner. ("The 'Nonsensical' Proverbs" 210)

De Looze and Burke concur that, for Juan Manuel, meditating on the nature of language itself is an important and useful exercise that can aid the reader in his or her own decision-making process. England does not entirely reject this argument, but he insists that the *CL* should not be reduced to a "text-book." Whether or not it was "outside his competence to compile a rigorously scientific textbook," as England argues ("'Los que son muy cuerdos'" 350), it is not out of the question, as I suggest in the previous chapter, that Juan Manuel's contacts and intense political experience taught him a great deal about the art of persuasion. The morals of each exemplary tale are not the only "fruits" Juan Manuel conveys; I believe that, as in Parts II to IV, the method of persuading with *exempla* itself can be at least one of the most important lessons in Part I.

England is correct in pointing out that Juan Manuel is not a "theologian," "philosopher," or "linguist," and he is also correct in stating that Juan Manuel writes from experience. Juan Manuel was a powerful, privileged knight and aristocratic governor. In his own

---

[8] In an excellent comparative essay that focuses on authors such as Juan Ruiz, Juan Manuel, Dante, and Boccaccio, Edmond Reiss demonstrates that the theme of ambiguous language preoccupies many of the most important authors of the fourteenth century: "by the fourteenth century, writers were less interested in restating moral or religious commonplaces than in investigating the possibilities and limitations of language [. . .]. [S]torytellers joined schoolmen in focusing not on truth itself but on such epistemological matters as the essential ambiguity of signs and the inherent complexity of language" (114).

writings (explicitly in the *Libro infinido*), he is a model prince, as he considered his son to be as well, equalled only by kings. He wrote from experience, political experience, the experience he would have gained at court and from listening to his Dominican friends and allies. He would have experienced first hand the power of the *exemplum* to persuade and coerce from clerics, theologians and philosophers. As a layman he had the best possible education available, which would have included at least a basic medieval training in grammar, rhetoric, and logic. Combining this basic education with a keen interest in learning, "hands-on" political experience, and an admiration for the Dominican Order whose hermeneutic example he was intelligent enough to grasp, Juan Manuel offers his readers a propaedeutic book that exposes and enacts the rhetorical strategies of the exemplarist for its reader to learn. England's point is on target, the *CL* is far too complex to be a mere "text-book."

The important work of the scholars mentioned above has contributed enormously to uncovering the interpretive potential of the *CL* that the author himself hints at in his prologue; some readers (the more simple-minded ones) will enjoy the pleasant tales for their own sake, and others (those with better *entendimiento*) will grasp the more "subtle meanings" of the book.[9] I will continue to suggest in this chapter that it is not exclusively the nature of language that Juan Manuel illuminates for his readers, but his rhetorical use of *exempla* to legitimize action, and even to coerce others to act according to another's will. In Part I, Juan Manuel offers his readers a series of demonstrations on how to employ the power and authority of the *exemplum* to one's own benefit. In order to put Patronio's rhetoric into practice, the reader must first learn that the *exemplum*, like language itself, is an ambivalent sign that can be charged with the meaning one desires. I believe that *exemplos* 2 and 21 provide some of the most patent evidence of Juan Manuel's exemplary art.

---

[9] Edmond Reiss recognizes that Juan Manuel, like Juan Ruiz and many other fourteenth-century authors, exploits the ambiguity of signs and asks his readers to work out their meaning: "The Archpriest's contemporary, Juan Manuel, offers much the same view [as in the *Libro de buen amor*] when, in the prologue to his collection of tales, *El Conde Lucanor*, he admonishes readers who, unable to understand well do not catch his subtle meanings" (116). Reiss' concluding remarks on the *CL* are particularly appropriate here: "*El Conde Lucanor* should not be taken as simply a series of obvious moral lessons" (121).

"De lo que contesçió a un omne bueno con su fijo"–*exemplo* 2– ("What Happened to a Good Man and His Son") is a simple tale on the surface, with some interesting thematic ties with *exemplo* 21, which contains the most explicit advice on how to employ *exempla*. *Exemplo* 2 begins, like all the others, with the Count's question for Patronio. The third-person narrator explains that "estava en grant coydado et en grand quexa *de un fecho que quería fazer* [my emphasis]" (61, "he was in great perplexity about *something that he wanted to do*" [47]).[10] An important detail of the Count's trouble in this tale is that, as in many other stories in Part I, the specifics of the Count's situation are completely–I would also argue deliberately–absent.

The Count's dilemma is entirely generic, allowing the reader's imagination to create a context and possibly even project his or her own experiences, questions, doubts and dilemmas into the story. The vague openness that frames Patronio's tale invites the reader to identify him or herself in the Count's enterprise, facilitating the recognition of one's own life in the text, as Juan Manuel promises his readers will be able to do in the prologue: "Et sería maravilla si de qualquier cosa que acaezca a qualquier omne, non fallare en este libro su semejança que acaesçió a otro" (45, "And it would be a wonder if in this book there will not be found something which has happened to someone else" [39]). The author is even more convinced in Part II that his books will relate to, and even mirror his readers' own personal experiences: "Et bien cuydo que el que leyere este libro et los otros que yo fiz, que pocas cosas puedan acaesçer para las vidas et las faziendas de los omnes, que non fallen algo en ellos" (278, "And I truly believe that whoever reads this book and the others I have written, that there are very few things that can happen in a man's life or business that they cannot find in them"). The one-size-fits-all frame narrative is the perfect device to ensure that every reader can identify with the Count. The invitation to imagine just what the Count wants to do allows the reader to tailor the story to his or her own imagination and private life.

The only piece of specific information about the Count's concern is that he knows that no matter what he does in this *fecho*, he

---

[10] This use of the third person narrator is not common in the *CL*, Part I. The only other tales that use this device to describe the Count's trouble / question are *exemplos* 36, 37, and 38.

will be castigated: "si por aventura lo fiziese, sabía que muchas gentes le travarían en ello; otrosí, si non lo fiziese, que él mismo entendíe quel prodrían travar en ello *con razón* [my emphasis]" (61, "If he went ahead, many people would criticize him for it, while if he refrained others would object" [47]).[11] The reader is not privy to exactly what he wants to do (the narrator simply states that he told Patronio "what he had in mind" [47]), but Patronio's *exemplum* is a very useful demonstration of how anyone can defend his or her own best interests in the face of dissenting opinions.

One of the first noticeable thematic parallels between *exemplo* 2 and 21 is that they both deal with how to teach, advise or *castigar* an intelligent youth on how to take charge of his responsibilities and business: his *fazienda*. But before Patronio gives his opinion, he reminds the Count that he has many other good counselors, and that he himself has been blessed with great intelligent: "et a vos dio Dios muy buen *entendimiento* [my emphasis]" (61, "and I know that the Lord has given you a good mind of your own" [47]). As seen in the Spanish text, the polysemic term "entendimiento" surfaces as the most important tool for deciphering hidden meanings, making ethical decisions and penetrating to the root of a problem or apparent paradox. This is an important introductory statement before Patronio's *exemplum* since the Count, like all private learners, must be the ultimate advocate and judge of his or her own actions.

Patronio's *exemplum* can be quickly summarized. A young man and his father have a farm, and because the son is so intelligent he can always show his father that whatever he wants to do on the farm may not work out according to plan. They live this way for some time, and the father is frustrated because he cannot do what he thinks is best for their business. In order to teach his precocious son a lesson, the father plans a trip to the market with a donkey to carry back their purchases.

---

[11] While Keller and Keating's translation certainly gets the main point across clearly, there is an important detail in the Spanish text that I believe is critical for understanding this *exemplum*. The Spanish reads "quel podrían travar en ello *con razón*" [my emphasis], emphasizing that those who would criticize the Count for his action (or inaction) would have good reason to do so. John England's translation of the same line is helpful here: "[I]f he did not do it, he could well understand why they would be right to criticize him" (45). This will be important when compared to what I call–somewhat playfully–the "donkey paradox," where all travelers who criticize the father and son are equally correct.

They set off walking with the donkey on the road to market where they encounter several travelers who give advice on how they should ride. One by one the passersby argue that the father and son are mistaken; first when they are both walking, then when the son rides and the father walks, then when the father rides and the son walks, and finally when father and son ride together. The two change the donkey's load with each traveler's advice because the son agrees that each is correct, and finally the father argues that it is impossible for them to continue their journey:

> Fijo, bien sabes que quando saliemos de nuestra casa, que amos veníamos de pie et traýamos la vestia sin carga ninguna, et tú dizías que te semejava que era bien. Et después, fallamos omnes en el camino que nos dixieron que non era bien, et mandé[te] yo sobir en la vestia et finqué de pie; et tú dixiste que era bien. Et después fallamos otros omnes que dixieron que aquello non era bien, et por ende desçendiste tú et subí yo en la vestia, et tú dixiste que era aquello lo mejor. Et porque los otros que fallamos dixieron que non era bien, mandéte subir en la vestia conmigo; et tú dixiste que era mejor que non fincar tú de pie et yr yo en la vestia. Et agora estos que fallamos dizen que fazemos yerro en yr entre amos en la vestia; et tú tienes que dizen verdat [. . .]. Pues en ninguna guisa non puede ser que alguna destas cosas non fagamos, et ya todas las fiziemos, et todos dizen que son yerro, et esto fiz yo porque tomasses exiemplo de las cosas que te acaesçiessen en tu fazienda (65-66, Son, you well know that when we left the house we were both walking and the donkey had no load at all. And you told me that you approved. Then we met people on the road who said this was wrong. I told you to get on and I walked, and you agreed to that. Afterwards we met other men who objected, so you got off and I got on. You said that was better. And because some other persons disagreed I told you to climb on with me. You agreed that it was better for you not to walk while I rode. Now people are saying it's wrong for both of us to ride and you agree with them [. . .]. Well, there is no way for us not to do one of these things, yet each one is said to be wrong. I did this to show you what happens on the farm [49]).

The *exiemplo* that the father teaches his son is actually a paradox. The "donkey paradox" is found in the oxymoronic notion that all manners of loading the beast are both correct and incorrect, an enigma similar to some found in the proverbs of Parts II to IV, such as "all things seem good and are good, and seem bad and are bad, and seem good and are bad, and seem bad and are good."

In many ways, this paradox defines the entire first part of the *CL* studied here in chapter 1. To the extent that the Count's troubles and questions are often identical, they are like the donkey itself. Patronio's advice for the Count is like that of the travelers, offering contradictory advice on how to handle ("load") the same situation ("donkey"). Following these comparisons, the Count is like the son, since he always accepts Patronio's advice which is always correct and good, as we are repeatedly told by Don Juan at the end of each tale. The final solution to the paradox is to load the donkey according to one's own needs, and this lesson can also be applied to the *exemplum* itself which can be loaded properly with the meaning necessary to defend one's ethical decisions. Each traveler interprets, or reads, the *exiemplo* of the father, son and donkey, and based on their own authority and good reason, each is correct in the load or meaning he assigns. The son, Count and reader must learn to do the same based on their own best judgment, private interests and *entendimiento*, as the father explains: "Et por ende, si tú quieres fazer mejor et más a tu pro, cata que fagas lo mejor et lo que entendieres que te cumple más, *et sol que non sea mal*, non dexes de lo fazer por reçelo de dicho de las gentes [my emphasis]" (66, "if you want to do what is best and most profitable for you, try to do what is right, or what will do you the most good. *So long as you are doing no harm*, do not stop because of what people say" [49]).

Even though the main point seems clear; that each must act according to what he or she believes is best, the seeds of doubt still remain in the father's final advice, since part of the paradox is precisely that there will always be someone who can argue that one's actions are harmful. Patronio's final suggestions return to this seemingly insurmountable obstacle:

> Et vós, conde Lucanor, señor, en esto que me dezides que queredes fazer et que reçelades que vos travarán las gentes en ello, et si non lo fazedes, que esso mismo farán, pues me mandades que vos conseje en ello, el mi consejo es éste: que ante que començedes el fecho, que cuydedes toda la pro o el dapño que se vos puede ende seguir, et que non vos fiedes en vuestro seso et que vos guardedes que vos non engañe la voluntad, et que vos consejedes con los que entendiéredes que son de buen entendimiento, et leales et de buena poridat. Et si tal consejero non falláredes,

guardat que vos non ar[r]ebatedes a lo que oviéredes a fazer, a lo menos fasta que passe un día et una noche, si fuere cosa que se non pierda por tiempo. Et de que estas cosas guardáredes en lo que oviéredes de fazer, et lo falláredes que es bien et vuestra pro, conséjovos yo que nunca lo dexedes de fazer por reçelo de lo que las gentes podrían dello dezir. (66-67, And you, Sir Count, as regards what you say you want to do, yet fear criticism, you must realize that you will be criticized even if you don't do it. You have asked for my advice. Here it is: before doing anything, look at all the possible advantages and disadvantages. Do not trust your own judgment, and avoid self-deception. Get advice from everyone whose opinions you respect and who is loyal and sensible. If you cannot find such a counselor do not rush into action but let a day and night go by; that is, if the matter will permit of the passing of time. When it comes to things you have decided to do for your own advantage, my advice is never fail to do them for fear of what people may say [49]).

By now the contradictions, or at least tensions, between Patronio's advice, the Count's problem, and the exemplary tale should be obvious. To name just a few troubling comments, the topic of having good counselors with good *entendimiento* (seen in the Spanish text), which many critics believe is a unifying theme of the entire collection, strains to make sense when compared with the travelers and the donkey. The fact that the Count's actions will inevitably generate contention and conflicting opinions is precisely the problem, and Patronio's *exemplum* demonstrates that advisers can give persuasive advice with good reasons, and contradict each other at the same time.

Another potential source of tension should be clarified, since the English translation actually creates a conflict where none really exists. An obvious didactic aspect of the moral of the story, and Patronio's advice, is that good judgment, intelligence, or "entendimiento" is a prerequisite for acting properly in any enterprise, but the English text translates "non vos fiedes en vuestro *seso* et que vos guardedes que vos non engañe la voluntad [my emphasis]" as "do not trust your *judgment* and avoid self-deception." The idea of "self-deception" seems a convenient way to handle "que non vos engañe la voluntad," but translating "seso" as "judgment," which is the same term used to translate "entendimiento" elsewhere, causes some confusion. Here "seso," which commonly means advice, has a meaning closer to an "idea" or "thought," "belief" or "desire." It should not be confused with the more important intellectual faculty, "entendimiento," which the Count himself has and must use to decide how to act.[12]

Finally, the implication that the Count should take care to do no harm exacerbates the paradox, because no matter what he does, someone will argue that it is harmful. Juan Manuel's *viessos* remind the reader of this tension: "Por dicho de las gentes / *sol que non sea mal*, / al pro tenet las mientes, / et non fagades al [my emphasis]" (67). Keller and Keating's translation of the maxim erases the problem in "sol que non sea mal" ("as long as it isn't bad"): "Unasked advice will seldom do, / Your own best choice is made by you" (50). Nevertheless, the English version highlights the most salient lesson of the tale.

Since the Count's business is so vague, as I argue above, it is inevitable that the reader speculate on the nature of his *fecho*, drawing on private experience. Since there is no specific problem for the *exemplo*'s lesson, as in other tales, this story is one of the most attractive for inserting one's own life experiences, and the moral is a very useful one, especially because of its generic nature. But there is another meta-rhetorical message in Patronio's *exemplum*, specifically in the "readings" applied to the donkey by each traveler. The son in this tale is persuaded by each adviser who interprets the *exiemplo* of the father and son on the road to market. In fact, the reader is told that the father staged the trip precisely to teach his son a lesson through an example, or *exiemplo*: "por castigar a su fijo et darle exiemplo cómmo fiziese en las cosas quel acaesçiesen adelante, tomó esta manera segund aquí oyredes" (63, "he decided to [teach him a lesson] and show him how to behave in the future. And this is what he decided to do" [48]), followed by the tale of the donkey and the travelers.[13]

How the travelers interpret the example of the father, son and

---

[12] John England translates this same passage as, "do not trust your own judgment; indeed, beware of being misled by your instincts" (49).

[13] I have chosen to slightly alter Keller and Keating's translation here from "punish," as it appears in their text, to "teach him a lesson." The original Spanish reads "castigar," which can indeed mean to punish, but it commonly means to advise, teach, correct, or instruct. John England translates "castigar" in this tale as "to advise" (44). King Sancho IV's book *Castigos e documentos para bien vivir*, for example, is not a collection of "punishments"; it is a book of teachings and advice.

donkey on the road to market is itself a lesson on the nature of the *exemplum* and how it can be charged with different meanings to support a decision or action; in this case, how to ride the donkey. According to the son, each traveler / adviser reads the *exemplum* of the donkey "right," in that they are all correct. With good *entendimiento*, the Count and the reader can learn to act according to their own best interests and defend their actions with their own authoritative interpretations of personal situations. *Exemplo* 21 takes the matter of interpreting signs and *exempla*, or *exempla* as signs, as its central theme, and teaches that not only can Patronio's rhetorical strategy be employed to legitimize one's actions, but can also be used to coerce others to act according to the interests of others.

In "De lo que contesçió a un rey moço con un muy grant philósopho a qui lo encomendara su padre" ("What Happened to a Young King and a Philosopher to Whom His Father Commended Him"), Count Lucanor comes to Patronio for advice on how to raise a young nobleman in his charge. The Count feels a debt to the young man's father that obliges him to raise the youth as his own son: "Et por el grand debdo et grand amor que avía a su padre, et otrosí por la grand ayuda que yo atiendo dél desque sea en tiempo para me la fazer, sabe Dios quel amo commo si fuesse mi fijo" (131, "And because of what I owed his father and my great affection for him, and also because of my expectation of what he will do for me when he is able, I have brought him up well, and God knows I love him as if he were my own son" [92]). The love that the Count feels for his ward is admirable, but it is clearly not a Christian kind of love (*caritas*); it is more a sense of duty and self-interested concern.[14] This will be an important detail to keep in mind for the conclusion of the tale.

Another interesting point of comparison with *exemplo* 2 is that part of the Count's concern stems from the inexperience of youth. Like the son in *exemplo* 2, the young man is very intelligent: "Et commo quier que el moço ha buen entendimiento et fío por Dios que sería muy buen omne, [pero] porque la moçedat engaña muchas veces a los moços et non les dexa fazer todo lo que

---

[14] Borrowing from Juan Manuel's thirteen definitions of "amor" in the last chapter of the *Libro infinido*, Ian Macpherson identifies the kind of relationship in this tale as "amor de debdo": a bond of friendship born of indebtedness ("Amor and Don Juan Manuel" 177).

les cumpl[ir]ía más, plazerme ýa si la moçedat non engañasse tanto a este moço" (131, "The boy is intelligent, and I trust to God that he will turn out to be a good man; but because appearances are often deceptive and boys do not achieve what they should, I shall be happy if youth and inexperience do not lead him astray" [92]).[15]

To help the Count be a better mentor, Patronio tells the story of a deceased king who entrusted his son to a philosopher. As Patronio's story goes, the young king became more stubborn, shirking his duties, and refusing to listen to good advice. The philosopher dutifully tries to persuade him to behave and take care of his kingdom: "ca ya muchas vezes provara de los castigar con ruego et con falago, et aun maltrayéndolo" (132, "admonishing him, urging him, and even punishing him" [93]). But no amount of urging or admonishing would suffice, so his teacher devised a plan to coerce the boy into behaving as a king should.

To trap the young king, the philosopher spreads a rumor in the court that he is a powerful soothsayer; more particularly, an expert reader of the signs of birds ("sabía catar agüeros" [132]). The youth, of course, wants to see him in action, accompanying him on an early morning excursion through the abandoned countryside of his kingdom to read the signs of the future. What follows is a "hidden" or "encoded" *exemplum*, deciphered by the philosopher after tricking the young king into believing that he eavesdropped on a conversation between two crows:

> Et desque passaron por muchas [aldeas yermas], vieron una corneja que estava dando vozes en un árbol. Et el rey mostróla al philósopho, et él fizo contenente que la entendía. El otra corneja començó a dar vozes en otro árbol, et amas las cornejas estudieron assí dando vozes, a vezes la una et a vezes la otra. Et desque el philósopho escuchó esto una pieça començó a llorar muy fieramente et ronpió sus paños, et fazía el mayor duelo del mundo (133, And when they had passed through a number [of deserted villages] they heard a crow cawing in a tree. And the king pointed him out to the philosopher who gave a sign that he had heard

---

[15] Note that the Spanish text does not exactly read "because appearances are often deceptive." A more literal translation might be: "because youth often deceives the young." John England translates this text as, "because young people often fall into error as a result of their immaturity" (135).

him.[16] And another crow began to caw in another tree, and the two crows kept it up, first one cawing and then the other. And when the philosopher had listened for a while he began to weep bitterly and tore his clothing and showed signs of overwhelming grief [93]).

After some convincing, the philosopher translates the birds' conversation, spinning a whole new tale within *exemplo* 21, which could be entitled "The Crows' Wedding Plans." According to the philosopher, the birds were celebrating what was bound to be a very successful marriage between their children since they both had inherited so much fallow lands that once were kept neat and productive by the deceased king, but now were quite neglected and full of delicious "culuebras et lagartos et sapos" (134, "snakes, lizards, and toads" [94]). After listening to the story, the king realizes the errors of his ways, accepts the good counsel of his teacher, and the kingdom is saved. But the story is never enough.

Patronio returns to advise the Count after his tale is ended, as he does in every story, and this time he gives explicit advice on how to use *exempla*: "Et vos, Señor conde, pues criastes este moço et querríades que se endereçasse su fazienda, catad alguna manera que *por exiemplos o por palabras maestradas et falagueras* le fagades entender su *fazienda* [my emphasis]" (134, "And you, Sir Count, since you are rearing this boy and you want him to straighten out his affairs, find some way either *by examples or by well-chosen words and flattery* to make him understand his *situation*" [94]).

Keller and Keating's translation is acceptable, with a few subtle, yet important clarifications. The words "por exiemplos o por palabras maestradas et falagueras" could also be translated as "by means of *exempla* or pleasing and deceitful words," rather than "by examples or by well-chosen words and flattery." John England translates this same text as "by example or by well-chosen and coaxing words" (139). Juan Manuel uses the adjective "maestrada" to mean cunning, deceitful, or evasive in another work, thus emphasizing the rhetorical and aggressively coercive deployment of *exempla* in this tale to control an impressionable king.[17] One last

---

[16] Note that the Spanish text reads, "fizo contenente que la entendía," which means "he made a gesture that he understood the crow [what the crow was saying]."

[17] Juan Manuel uses the adjective *maestrada* in the *Libro de los estados* to mean deceitful, and the author clearly associates it with lying. I will return to this important passage in *exemplo* 21 as it appears in manuscript P in chapter 4.

comment on Keller and Keating's translation is worth making here, since it ties this story with *exemplo* 2; the term "fazienda" is translated here as "situation," and in *exemplo* 2 it is often translated as "farm," both are suitable translations, but as seen in the prologue ("[el] infante don Manuel, deseando que los omnes fiziessen en este mundo tales obras que les fuessen aprovechosas de las onras et de las *faziendas* et de su estados [my emphasis]") and elsewhere in the *CL*, "fazienda" takes on a more global sense, meaning everything from "situation" to "business," "responsibilities," "estate," and "duty." Here in *exemplo* 21 the king's "fazienda" is the entire governance of his kingdom. Before commenting further on Juan Manuel's fascinating lesson on how and why one should learn to use *exempla*, "The Crows' Wedding Plans" deserves further attention.

The philosopher's story by itself tells us a great deal about how Juan Manuel handles the rhetorical power of the *exemplum*, since the reader is told that the youth refused to listen to sound teachings, and could only be lead to truth through the use of an illustrative tale manipulated by a clever rhetorician. What the story of the crows teaches is that an *exemplum* is a completely ambivalent sign that can be charged with any meaning necessary for the purposes of the speaker. In *exemplo* 21, the signs that construct the exemplary narrative are, in the finally analysis, the meaningless squawking of birds. The philosopher creates a narrative out of a cacophonous "conversation" so that the youth will believe that he has learned, by himself, what he must do. Nevertheless, from the very beginning the philosopher is in control of the entire learning experience. By exploiting the ambiguity of signs and the *exemplum* itself, the teacher traps his pupil and covertly guides him to the "correct" reading of "The Crows' Wedding Plans." In many ways, the cawing of the crows is similar to the sign language used in the famous debate between the Greeks and the Romans in the *Libro de buen amor*, but Juan Manuel goes beyond exposing the relativity of signs, and teaches a powerful rhetorical lesson on how to manipulate that same relativity for personal gain.

Michael Gerli describes this familiar theme in the *Libro de buen amor*, stating that "an underlying premise of the *Libro* seems to be that a sign itself possesses no meaning until interpreted' (510), which leads Gerli to uncover Augustinian ideas on the spiritual and intellectual processes of learning in Juan Ruiz's book. As Gerli demonstrates, the debate between the Greeks and the Romans exposes the "difficulty of transmitting intentions through signs" (502), since both the Greeks and the Romans interpret different meanings in the exact same hand gestures. Following these traces of Augustinian thought in the *Libro de buen amor*, Gerli convincingly argues that it is designed to induce the reader "to enter into himself so as to perceive the truths that are already there," offering the reader "food for moral thought" (503). On the surface, many of these same Augustinian notions appear to be at work in *exemplo* 21.

I would argue that there are at least three general Augustinian notions in play in *exemplo* 21; (1) the relativity of signs (the squawking of crows), (2) the impossibility of teaching with conventional signs (the philosopher has no success with direct instruction), and (3) that a person is only "reminded" by signs, and that one only learns by discovering within oneself what one knows to be true thanks to the divine Truth in every man and woman.

The contingency of a sign's meaning in *exemplo* 21 is not marked in the same way as in the debate between the Greeks and the Romans which concentrates on the relativity of signs by demonstrating how the same set of gestures can generate disparate interpretations. Since there is no "alternative" reading of the crows' cawing, the ambivalence of signs itself is not set up as the central theme in *exemplo* 21, instead it is left up to the reader to contemplate the nature of signs in this tale, and throughout the entire collection. Drawing on the analysis of chapter 1, the ambivalence of signs can be seen as another element of tension throughout the collection, witnessed in reoccurring homologous life situations that are interpreted differently by Patronio, concluding with self-contradicting "exemplary" behavior, or disjunctive ethical ambiguity. When Patronio gives his final specific instructions on how to use the power of narrative in *exemplo* 21, the reader must meditate on the nature of signs and how their meaning is always mediated by a "master" reader. Patronio's final advice invites the reader to meditate further on just what exactly the "exiemplos" and "palabras falagueras" are in this story.[18]

---

[18] Leonardo Funes has written an excellent study of this tale in which he concludes that Patronio's instructions represent "la síntesis de la concepción didáctica de don Juan Manuel; una combinación perfecta de narratividad, retórica e invención técnica puestas al servicio de una mayor eficacia didáctica de sus textos" ("Las palabras maestradas" 266-267, "the synthesis of Juan Manuel's concept of didacticism; a perfect combination of narrativity, rhetoric and technical invention at the service of greater didactic efficacy in his texts").

Other tales, however, expose more conspicuously the *exemplum* as a sign whose meaning is entirely contingent on its reader / reading. The best example may be *exemplo* 48. Here Patronio tells the familiar tale of "What Happened to a Man Who Tested His Friends," and extracts from it two different meanings and maxims. One piece of advice is practical and social: "Ca çierto seet que algunos son buenos amigos, mas muchos, et por aventura los más, son amigos de la ventura" (252, "for many friends, even most, are fair-weather friends"[176]). The second reading of the same *exemplum* is spiritual and theological, concluding that God is ultimately man's best friend: "Nunca omne podría tan buen amigo fallar / commo Dios, que lo quiso por su sangre comprar" (253, "Man could never find such a good friend / As God, who paid for him with his blood").[19] While this tale exposes the relativity of the *exemplum* as a narrative sign, the conclusion of tale 21 teaches that the interpretation of these signs can be a powerful rhetorical strategy.

Eloísa Palafox carefully unpacks the semiotics of the *exemplum* and concludes that it is much more than a literary form or genre, but a self-conscious discursive strategy (22), following Tubach's definition of the *exemplum* as a "paradigmatic sign" (523).[20] The salient feature of the *exemplum* in tale 21 is that in order for any sign to substantiate a belief, doctrine, or behavior, the otherwise relative relationship between narrative sign and signified behavior or belief must be mediated by the exemplarist in such a way that the listener or reader believes that he or she has fixed the paradigmatic meaning of the sign independently. Patronio's final instructions explain the importance of this mediation, since very often, and especially if the listener / learner is a haughty youth, a student may not always learn the desired behavior through conventional instruction:

> Mas por cosa del mundo non derrangedes con él castigándol nin maltrayéndol, cuydándol endereçar; ca la manera de los más de los moços es tal, que luego aborreçen al que los castiga, et mayormente si es omne de grand guisa, ca liéva[n]lo a manera de menospreçio, non entendiendo quánto lo yerra[n]; ca non an tan

---

[19] Keller and Keating's edition does not translate the Spanish *viessos*. John England translates the text as, "Man could never find such a good friend / as God, who deigned to redeem him with His own blood" (291).

[20] On the paradigmatic nature of Juan Manuel's narratives, see also María Jesús Lacarra (*Cuentística* 40).

buen amigo en el mundo commo el que castiga el moço porque non faga su daño, mas ellos non lo toman assí, sinon por la peor manera. Et por aventura caería tal desamor entre vós et él, que ternía daño a entramos para adelante (134-135, But by no means upset [the boy] with punishment or ill treatment, thinking thus to straighten him out, for it is the way of most boys to detest the one who [instructs] them, especially if he is a man of importance, for they regard it as a kind of scorn, not realizing how wrong they are, because no man is a greater friend than he who corrects a boy to keep him from harm. But boys do not take it thus, but in the worst possible way. And thus a disaffection might arise between the two of you, which would harm you both from now on [94]).[21]

In order to guarantee that the youth act according to the Count's definition of "proper" behavior, and to protect the personal gain that he hopes to reap from a good relationship with the youth, the Count must learn the art of "exiemplos" and "palabras maestradas et falagueras."

Once the relativity of the *exemplum* is exposed, the "real" reader can learn this same lesson to legitimize his or her own ethical choices and actions by following Patronio's rhetorical strategy.[22] Within the confines of the fictional world created in the *CL*, however, Patronio is the final mediator of all meaning, successfully convincing Juan Manuel, the inscribed reader of each story, that he has read his *exemplum* right. The literary persona of Juan Manuel is lead to believe that each action is correct as well, in spite of the potential contradictions within and among each tale studied in chapter 1: "Et porque don Iohan se pagó mucho deste exiemplo, fízolo poner en este libro, et fizo estos viessos que dizen assí: Non castigues moço maltrayéndo[l], / mas dilo commol vaya plaziéndo[l]" (135, "And because Don Juan was pleased with this story he had it placed in this book and wrote the following verses: Don't spank a boy for his misdeeds, / But show him rather how to please" [94]).

---

[21] Again, I believe that the verb "castigar" does not usually mean "to punish," even though here it is clear that Patronio is indeed referring to punishments as well as instructions. As in the story of the philosopher and the young king, the verb "castigar" means "to advise" or "to instruct."

[22] I use the term "real" here to simply mark the differences among the various types of readers present in the *CL*. As Gerald Prince points out, this "real or concrete reader" must "not be confused with the implied reader" (79), among others.

In the tale of the philosopher and the young king, the youth is tricked into believing and behaving as he should, and although on the surface it may appear that he discovered the truth within himself, the philosopher's plot combined with Juan Manuel's final remarks on how to employ the power of the *exemplum* teach that the Augustinian inner search for truth can be manipulated, and that the final discovery of truth on the part of the individual learner can be a mirage conjured up by a master exemplarist. How Patronio puts the *exemplum* to use for specific situations that preoccupy Juan Manuel in Part I, as well as a demonstration of the power of exemplification in Part V will help conclude the study of the author's appropriation of the *exemplum*. By remaining attentive to the method, rather than the "moral" or the "meaning" of each tale, Juan Manuel's audience can read the *CL* right if they learn to apply Patronio's rhetorical strategy to their own lives and private ethical decisions.

Chapter 3

THE *EXEMPLUM* IN ACTION

Of all the tales in the *CL* that express Juan Manuel's preoccupation with salvation and duty, *exemplos* 3 and 33 have often been singled out as the best examples, since they both address the theme of winning salvation with actions carried out according to the privileges and obligations of one's estate. Brian Tate identifies this topic in Juan Manuel's writings as a concern over the exercise of power and its potential to jeopardize man's salvation ("The Infante Don Juan de Aragón" 169-179). More specifically, Ian Macpherson does not believe that Juan Manuel was particularly worried about the plight of Man *per se* but with his own personal situation:

> [H]e concentrates on his own problems, which will be shared by those noblemen in Spain who are like him. How does a man, who finds himself by accident of birth a statesman and a soldier, constantly acting in the world to his own advantage, working for the advancement of his own power, honour, status, and business affairs, reconcile this pursuit of material success with a genuine concern for the salvation of his soul. ("*Dios y el mundo*" 30)

Exemplo 3 begins by exposing the dangers of "working for the advancement" of one's estate.

In this tale the Count confesses to Patronio that he has committed great sins against God. His actions are so wicked that by the end of the tale Patronio calls him a "cavallero del diablo" (74, "knight of the devil" [54]), and because his list of sins is so long, and old age has forced him to imagine his final judgment, he is not at all confident of escaping the flames of Hell. First among his crimes are constant wars against Christian kings and Moors alike, and although he claims to have never started a war himself, he could not avoid the fighting, and in the process caused great harm to the innocent: "Et quando lo ove con cristianos, commo quier que sienpre me guardé que nunca se levantase ninguna guerra a mi culpa, pero non se podía escusar de tomar muy grant daño muchos que lo non meresçieron" (68, "And when I struggled with Christians I always tried to avoid war, but when I fought many persons who did not deserve it were badly injured" [50]). This is only the beginning, and the Count confesses that he has committed many other offenses in the eyes of God ("otros yerros que yo fiz contra nuestro señor Dios" [68]) that the reader can only imagine.

The Count also recognizes that he will be saved or condemned according to his actions, and rather than seek out a priest to set his penance, he asks his adviser Patronio what he can do to redeem himself: "Et pues este bien et este mal tan grande non se cobra sinon por las obras, ruégovos que, segund el estado que yo tengo, que cuydedes et me conseiedes la manera mejor que entendiéredes porque pueda fazer emienda a Dios de los yerros que contra Él fiz, et pueda aver la su gracia" (69, "Now since my salvation or my damnation can be achieved only through deeds, I beg you according to my estate, to consider and advise me how best to make amends to God for the sins that I have committed against him, so that I may deserve his grace" [51]). Giving up his power and joining a religious order is out of the question since that would involve abandoning his duties, and Patronio even insinuates that the Count would not be able to endure the hardships of a monk's life. Be this as it may, Patronio is pleased with the Count's remorse and good intentions: "mas plázeme mucho porque dezides que querredes fazer emienda a Dios de los yerros que fiziestes, guardando vuestro estado et vuestra onra" (69, "But I am happy to learn that you wish to make amends before God for your faults, while keeping your position and your honor" [51]). To show him how to make amends, Patronio tells the story of King Richard's famous leap against the Moors.

Juan Manuel borrows the main *exemplum* from the *Gran conquista de Ultramar*, but it is the narrative frame and Patronio's advice that make this tale a *tour de force* of Juan Manuel's appropriation of the authority of the *exemplum*. This story, perhaps more than any other in the collection, demonstrates how, through the rhetorical deployment of narrative, in particular the narrative of a heroic figure from the past, the author can successfully co-opt specific belief systems, ideologemes, or what Larry Scanlon sees as "moral law" embodied in the narrative itself (33). In this case, Juan Manuel draws to himself the authority that conventionally flowed from the Church to the laity, also in the form of *exempla*; more particularly, the doctrines and beliefs surrounding the Sacrament of Reconciliation, and the viciously fanatical Holy-War ideology of the crusades, a belief system that still plagues us today.

As most readers will recall, the tale of King Richard's leap is a simple one: The King and his men, along with the King of France and Navarre, are faced with an overwhelming number of Moors protecting the port, preventing the Christians from landing. Rather than turn back, King Richard commends himself to God, spurs his horse and leaps from his ship into the sea. This act of faith earns God's divine intervention, the King and his horse do not drown, and the rest of the Christian troops follow the charge, vanquishing the Moors. While the outcome of the *exemplum* is predictable, Juan Manuel takes care to point out that the warrior king's behavior is in fact an act of penance, as well as a manifestation of faith in the doctrines of the Holy Crusade that teach that one act of violence against the infidel–preferably ending in one's own death–will undo a lifetime of sin and win eternal glory:

> [B]ien sabía que él avía fecho a Dios muchos enojos et muchos pesares en este mundo et que sienpre le pidiera merçed quel traxiese a tiempo quel fiziese emienda por el su cuerpo, et que loado a Dios, que veýa el día que él deseava mucho; ca si allí muriese, pues avía [fecho] la emienda que pudiera ante que de su tierra se partiesse, et estava en verdadera penitencia, que era çierto quel avría Dios merced al alma, et que si los moros fuessen vençidos, que tomaría Dios mucho serviçio, et serían todos muy de buena ventura (71, [King Richard] well knew he was a sinner in the sight of the Lord, that he had done many bad deeds and had always begged for a chance to mend his ways and that now, praise God, he saw the chance that he had so long desired; for if he died there and then, he would have made amends before leaving the earth, and he would die in a state of penitence and his soul would certainly enjoy God's grace. If the Moors were defeated, God would be well served, and all would be right [52]).

Not only can a suicidal act of aggression against the enemy win salvation, the reader has been informed earlier in the narrative frame of Patronio's *exemplum* that this single act of war is better in the eyes of God than an entire lifetime of prayer and good works.

Patronio's story begins with a pious hermit who is chagrined to learn from an angel of God that his companion in heaven will be the blood-thirsty sinner, King Richard the Lionheart: "Desta razón non plogo mucho el hermitaño, ca él conosçía muy bien al rey et sabía que era omne muy guerrero et que avía muertos et robados et deseredados muchas gentes, et sienpre le viera fazer vida muy contralla de la suya et aun, que paresçía muy alongado de la carrera de salvación" (70, "This news did not much please the hermit, for he knew the king well, knew that he was a very warlike man, and that he had killed, robbed and disinherited many people. He had always observed that he lived a life the very opposite of his own, and he still seemed a long way from salvation" [52]). The Lord sends his angel to the hermit a second time, this time to rebuke him, informing him that his life of pious acts is nothing in comparison with this great warrior: "He sent His angel to tell him not to complain nor to marvel at what he had been told, for certainly King Richard would do a greater service to God in a jump that he would take than the hermit had done with all his good works" (52). The Spanish text is even more devastating than Keller and Keating's translation, stating that the King is more deserving of salvation, and that the hermit will not be able to equal him in his entire lifetime: "[E]nviol dezir con el su ángel que non se quexase nin se marabillase de lo quel dixiera, ca çierto fuesse que más serviçio fiziera a Dios *et más meresçiera* el rey Richalte en un salto que saltara, que el hermitaño en *quantas buenas obras fiziera en su vida* [my emphasis]" (70). Patronio's final advice returns to the ideas of penance and duty, the latter being the source of the Count's troubles in the first place.

As the Count explains to Patronio, it is precisely because of his social standing, an "accident of birth"–borrowing again from Macpherson–, that he has sinned so terribly against the Lord. Furthermore, the Count makes it clear that these troubles are unavoidable, so when Patronio encourages him to make amends with those he has harmed, and leave his affairs in proper order before taking on the service of the Lord in holy war against the Moors, the Count is left to confront again the inherent dangers of carrying out the duties of his *estado*. Nevertheless, Patronio assures him that he can be saved:

Et vós, señor conde Lucanor, pues dezides que queredes servir a Dios et fazerle emienda de los enojos quel feziestes, non querades seguir esta carrera que es de ufana et llena de vanidat. Mas, pues Dios vos pobló en tierra quel podades servir contra los moros, tan bien por mar commo por tierra, fazet vuestro poder porque seades seguro de lo que dexades en vuestra tierra. Et esto fincado seguro, et aviendo fecho emienda a Dios de los yerros que fiziestes, porque estedes en verdadera penitençia, porque de los bienes que fezierdes ayades de todos meresçimiento, et faziendo esto podedes dexar todo lo al, et estar sienpre en serviçio de Dios et acabar así vuestra vida (73-74, And you say, Count Lucanor, that you wish to serve God and make amends for the evil that you have done, and that you do not wish to continue your present career, which is one of pride and vanity. But since God has placed you in a land where you can serve against the Moors, by sea and by land, do your utmost to see that what you leave behind is secure, and having done this, and having made amends to God for the sins you have committed, and being truly penitent, you may have credit for all the good deeds you have done, and in this way you may leave everything else and remain in God's service to the end of your life [53]).

Patronio promises that if the Count can do *all this* he will die a martyr, but the friction lies in the condition that the Count must take care of his business and duties at home before he can die in the service of God, and as seen in the Count's problem posed to Patronio, the Devil is in the details. The impossibility of guaranteeing that all these conditions can be successfully completed may explain why this tale–along with six others in the collection that deal with the question of salvation and good works–ends with a prayer, rather than the usual formulaic statement found in most every other story, surveyed in chapter 1.[1] The narrator's last words before Don Juan's appearance in the text to introduce his *viessos* describe the Count's prayer, enticing the reader to trust that he is sincere, and that he hopes to be able to fulfill his duties and save his soul: "Al conde Lucanor plogo mucho del consejo que Patronio le dio, et rogó a Dios quel guisase que lo pueda fazer commo él lo dezía y como el

---

[1] Of the fifty one tales included in Part I, seven end with a petition or prayer to God (*exemplo* 3, 33, 40, 42, 46, 49 and 51) which also have a formulaic syntax. Eight tales simply state that Patronio's advice was good, with no mention of the Count's action and profit (*exemplos* 9, 24, 25, 27, 29, 44, 48 and 50).

conde lo tenía en coraçón" (74, "And the Count was very pleased with Patronio's advice and he asked God to guide him so that he might follow it as he wished in his heart" [54]).[2]

The fact that the Count cannot put Patronio's advice into action successfully as he does repeatedly throughout the collection may remind the reader of the Count's original dilemma, but the prayer also works as the perfect narrative device to close off any further tension. There is no way to interrogate the Count's intentions, or any other person's for that matter, and the example of a famous warrior king authorizes the theoretical possibility for any prince in a similar situation to save himself. The *exemplum* even demonstrates how a life of sin can be pardoned, provided that the sinner is contrite, does penance, and always acts in the best interests of his estate, which brings him back to "square one," so to speak.

Beyond the apparent solution to the *Dios y el Mundo* paradox, which I would argue is a tautological solution at best, it is Juan Manuel's appropriation of discourses and doctrines that conventionally belong to the Church; namely, the doctrines of penance, reconciliation, and the discourse of the Holy Crusade, that makes *exemplo* 3 a fascinating demonstration of the *exemplum* in action. Juan Manuel is able to co-opt these discourses, and the authority associated with them, by successfully employing one of the most persuasive rhetorical vehicles–the *exemplum*–recruited by the Church to disseminate its doctrine to its under-educated lay audiences. As the author of the tales, and the inscribed author of the *viessos* that sanction each story, Juan Manuel draws the moral authority materialized in the *exemplum* toward himself, and becomes an authority (*auctor*) on Church doctrine as it pertains to princes.[3]

In *Narrative Authority and Power*, Larry Scanlon remarks that

---

[2] The other six stories that end with a similar petition also deal with the dicey situation of acting properly and performing good works that will win eternal life. The only exception is *exemplo* 46, which ends with a prayer to defend against the sin of hypocrisy, which is mentioned again in *exemplo* 51 as the most dangerous vice because it undermines good intentions, an indispensable prerequisite for all good works.

[3] Dayle Seidenspinner-Núñez describes Juan Manuel's audience as "the noblemen of 14th century Castile," but suggests further that his audience is divided into two groups within the aristocracy: the young and the old (260). For the young reader the *CL* is "a vehicle of indoctrination," while for the more experienced it "represents the confirmation of the traditional, conservative system of beliefs under siege in the 14th century" (261). On the audience of the *CL*, see also Barry Taylor, "Don Jaime de Jérica y el público de *El Conde Lucanor*."

the *exemplum* was the perfect vehicle for "the vernacular appropriation of clerical authority" (80), and in *exemplo* 3, Juan Manuel lays claim to Church doctrine and places it squarely at the heart of secular politics, circumventing the authority of the Church in the affairs of the ruling class. Together with other works such as the *Libro de los estados* and Part V of the *CL*, Juan Manuel sets himself up in *exemplo* 3 as an aristocratic lay authority on matters of faith, salvation, the Sacraments, and even Holy Scripture to help solve "his own problems," recalling Macpherson's comments cited earlier, which are also the problems of "those noblemen in Spain like him." *Exemplo* 33, "What Happened to Don Juan Manuel's Saker Falcon and an Eagle and a Heron" is linked to the third tale by Patronio's reference to it in his final words on the Count's question. The story duplicates the topic of war with Christians and Moors, and returns to the seemingly unavoidable pitfalls of acting according to one's best interests and duty.

To give the story a touch of realism, Juan Manuel places his own father, the *Infante* Don Manuel in Patronio's tale, an element of the text that has lead many critics to view *exemplo* 33 as an attempt to link the story with the author's own personal political affairs, particularly his rebellion against king Alfonso XI. Scholars such as Alexander Krappe and Daniel Devoto have read the story of the *Infante* Manuel's falcon fighting against an eagle that prevented it from capturing its prey as a symbolic representation, and justification, of Juan Manuel's political struggles and open war with Alfonso in the decade following the king's refusal to honor his marriage to Constanza, Juan Manuel's daughter, in 1327.[4] Aníbal Biglieri has written a detailed analysis of this tale, demonstrating that there is no reason to read any autobiographical elements into it, and that by no means does the story defend or promote rebellion. Biglieri warns against reading the entire collection as autobiographical (210), a critical trend that the scholar prudently corrects, and that in this particular tale, the *águila* does not represent Alfonso XI, nor does the falcon symbolize Juan Manuel (203; 208). In *Hacia una poética del relato didáctico*, Biglieri prefers to read this tale as anoth-

---

[4] Krappe's essay, "Le faucon de l'Infant dans *Le Conde Lucanor*," is one of the most cited studies that presents this reading of Patronio's *exemplum*. See also Daniel Devoto, "Cuatro notas sobre la materia tradicional en Don Juan Manuel," and *Introducción al estudio de don Juan Manuel* (422-423).

er allegorical and didactic expression of the larger socio-historical context that informs the *CL*, specifically the codes and virtues of the warrior class, based on strength of arms, that *exemplo* 33 celebrates and defends (206-207). I will return to Biglieri's important study of this tale further on, for now a brief rehearsal of the details of the text–the Count's trouble, Patronio's *exemplum*, and the counselor's advice–will show that, in spite of an attempt to ease the tensions of the Count's conundrum, this tale exposes the power of the *exemplum* to sanction a myriad of ethical decisions and actions, including war against Christian kings.

As mentioned above, the Count's concern deals with whether to rest or continue to aggressively pursue his ambitions; here this common theme is expressed in terms of war. As the Count explains his question to Patronio, he is often at war with "others" (persons who remain anonymous), and when his battles are over, his advisers present him with three different courses of action to choose from: (1) remain at peace, (2) make war with other people ("que tome otra contienda con otros" [191-192]), or (3) wage war against the Moors. Unlike other tales in which Patronio advises caution and warns against taking on new risky enterprises, the path of peace in this *exemplo* is immediately discarded.

The detail that troubles the closure of this story lies in the nebulous "other people," that linger on in Patronio's final judgment, and in the mind of the reader. If option 3 is war with the Moors, then war with *otros*–option 2–can only mean other Christian neighbors, as in *exemplo* 3, which Patronio cites as another tale for the Count to recall in this situation. In order to illustrate that the Count should strive to carry out war against the Moors, Patronio tells the story of the *Infante* Manuel's hunting expedition.

In Patronio's *exemplum*, the *infante*'s falcon is pursuing a heron when an eagle interferes with the hunt. Many critics argue that the eagle represents a superior power, and the text does state that the falcon was afraid of the regal bird, and was forced to abandon its prey: "El falcón con miedo del águila, dexó la garça et começó a foýr" (192, "And being afraid of the eagle, the falcon left the heron and began to fly away" [134]). But as the power struggle between falcon and eagle continues, they find themselves in a kind of stalemate. In spite of the falcon's attempts at chasing off his adversary, the eagle continues to interfere with the falcon's attacks on the heron, and in order to finally capture its prey, the falcon must strike a powerful blow against the eagle, breaking its wing.

While Biglieri makes a strong argument against making a direct association between the falcon and the author (208), Patronio does in fact make the connection between the falcon and its prey, and the Count and his duty:

> Et vós, señor conde Lucanor, pues sabedes que la vuestra caça et la vuestra onra et todo vuestro bien paral cuerpo et paral alma es que fagades serviçio a Dios, et sabedes que en cosa del mundo, segund el vuestro estado que vós tenedes, non le podedes tanto servir commo en aver guerra con los moros por ençalçar la sancta et verdadera fe católica, conséjovos yo que *luego que podades seer seguro de las otras partes*, que ayades guerra con los moros [my emphasis] (193, And you, Count Lucanor, since you know that your hunting and your heron and all your fortune in body and in soul is serving God, and you know that in your position there is nothing for you to do that is so profitable as to wage war on the Moors and thus enhance the true Catholic faith, I advise that *as soon as you are safe from other parties*, you should go to war against the Moors [135]).

As in *exemplo* 3, it is the unknown "other parties" and responsibilities to one's estate that undermine the Count's ability to engage in the cleansing war against the Moors.

Patronio cites *exemplo* 3 specifically on this matter, reminding the Count of his many sins against God, and promising a saint's death if he can manage to leave his kingdom secure and die in the service of God:

> Et si quier, parat mientes al enxiemplo terçero que vos dixe en este libro, del salto que fizo el rey Richalte de Inglaterra [. . .]; et pensat en vuestro coraçón que avedes a morir et que avedes fecho en vuestra vida muchos pesares a Dios, et que Dios es derechurero et de tan grand iustiçia que non podedes salir sin pena de los males que avedes fecho; pero ved si sodes de buena ventura en fallar carrera para que en un punto podades aver perdón de todos vuestros pecados, ca si en la guerra [de los moros] morides, estando en verdadera penitençia, sodes mártir et muy bienaventurado (193-194, And if you will kindly heed the third parable which I related to you in this book about the leap which King Richard of England made [. . .], then consider in your heart that you have to die and that during your life you have grieved God greatly, and that God is the lawgiver and of

such great justice that you cannot avoid paying the price of the sins you have committed. But if you are of goodwill, and find an act by which you may have pardon for all your sins, since in a war with the Moors you must die in a state of true penitence, you will be a martyr and blessed [135]).

In spite of the apparent lack of applicability between the Count's problem and Patronio's conclusion–here the Count does not specifically ask for advice on how to do penance or save his soul as in *exemplo* 3–Biglieri is certainly correct in pointing out that in this tale, like all the others, the author attempts to forge a kind of contract with the reader to limit the potential "play of meanings" ("'juego' de significantes") in the "field of possibilities" ("campo de posibilidades") uncovered in the text (198). Biglieri argues that the narrative frame, along with the reader's participation, is Juan Manuel's primary device for creating this closure (213).[5] Nevertheless, the "play" and "possibilities" remain in *exemplo* 33, and Patronio's illustrative tale and final advice seem to draw attention specifically to the possible obstacles the Count must face: all the possible symbolic meanings of the eagle.

Patronio never states that the eagle is a king, or a Christian enemy, or an unavoidable war, in fact, borrowing again from Biglieri, the eagle can be all of these things, and many other risks and challenges a nobleman must face in performing his duties and protecting his interests (203): the *otras partes* that must be dealt with first. *Exemplo* 33 picks up on a subtext in *exemplo* 3; namely, the notion of leaving one's estate secure before embarking on a war against the Moors, and exposes it as a dangerous situation that can lead a warrior to have to fight against his neighbors in order to stabilize his domestic affairs. By association with the Count's wars in the frame narrative of *exemplo* 33, and his confession to having battled against Christian kings in *exemplo* 3, the "other parties" that the Count must fight off could certainly include powerful monarchs. With the moral authority of this *exemplum* behind him, a noble warrior could potentially legitimize a wide range of behaviors while striving to act in the service of God. To the extent that the power of

---

[5] Marta Ana Diz proposes a similar reading of the function of the narrative voice in the *CL*, which, according to Diz, "comenta, juzga, guía incesantemente nuestra lectura" (86, "incessantly comments, judges and guides our reading").

the *exemplum* can do this, it does close off potential meanings in the narrative, once its interpretation has been set by the speaker.

At the heart of these two tales is not only the ambivalence of the *exemplum* as a narrative sign that can be loaded with the significance required to legitimize beliefs and behavior, but the ambivalence of ethical decisions and actions themselves, since what might appear to be a sinful act on the surface–war against Christians for example–may actually be a virtue, or at the very least an unavoidable consequence of political life that, if performed without malice of heart, may not be a completely evil act. Juan Manuel addresses the thorny subject of good and evil deeds, and actions that are not entirely good or entirely bad in the last book of the *CL*. To demonstrate his point on the apparent relativity of actions themselves, he draws again on the authority of the *exemplum*.

As the scholars surveyed in chapter 2 have demonstrated, the three often overlooked middle books of proverbs and maxims do appear to prepare the reader to interpret increasingly difficult linguistic signs. Critics such as James Burke, John England and Laurence de Looze have all demonstrated, from different angles, that these books bring textuality itself to the surface of the reading experience in order to hone the reader's hermeneutic skills. Reading through some of the more hermetic aphorisms, the exposition of the ambiguities of language itself is patent, but the proverbs also move the reader toward a deeper meditation on the very nature of man and his actions in the world. Patronio explains that even though his proverbs use fewer words than the fifty *exemplos* in Part I,[6] he tells the Count in the beginning of Part III that the more shrouded maxims should be studied carefully in order to learn their lessons: "sabet que non es menos el aprovechamiento et el entendimiento deste que del otro, ante es muy mayor para quien lo estudiare et lo entendiere" (288, "Know that this book is no less wise and beneficial than the other, instead it is even more so for he who can study and understand it"). One of the mysteries that Patronio asks the Count to consider in Part II, and again in Part V, is the paradox of man's fallen human condition.

---

[6] Juan Manuel mentions the fifty tales of Part I twice in the *CL*, both in the dialogue between Patronio and the Count in Parts III and IV. These references are often cited to trouble the authorship of *exemplo* 51, as Alberto Blecua does in *La transmisión textual de* El Conde Lucanor (114).

In Part II a first person narrator, or Patronio (it is not clear in the text), interrupts his proverbs with an apostrophe praising God's unknowable wisdom expressed in man himself. God's greatest creation is a mystery, since man is such a conflicted being; he cannot speak without erring, and he cannot remain quiet without showing his ignorance ("cuando fabla, yerra; quando calla, muestra su mengua" [279]), he cannot act correctly with reason, nor can he rest without losing his possessions ("si obra, non fará obra de recabdo; si está de vagar, pierde lo que ha" [279]). The list of failings amaze the speaker since God chose to create this pathetic being in his own image. Man is arrogant, stubborn, recalcitrant, tyrannical, ungrateful, short-tempered and selfish; in short, in all of his works man is a failure: "¿Qué diré más? En los fechos et en los dichos, en todo yerra" (280, "What more can I say? In both words and deeds, man errs in everything").

Many of the proverbs in Parts II to IV express this same mysterious imperfection in man, but Part V address the paradoxical nature of man head on, as God's most perfect and most imperfect creation: "Bien creed,"–Patronio explains to the Count–"señor conde, que entre todas las animalias que Dios crió en l' mundo, nin aun de las cosas corporales, non crió ninguna tan complida, nin tan menguada como el omne" (313-314, "Be certain, sir count, that of all the creatures God created, nor any other corporeal thing, he did not create any as perfect and as imperfect as man").

This statement is made toward the end of Part V, where Patronio addresses the nature of man, in particular his imperfections, and the three paths of the world: the contemplative, the active / materialist, and the path that balances the World with God. As in the *Libro infinido*, studied in chapter 1, Patronio alludes to kings and other great men who balanced their honor with service to God so well that they became saints ("sopieron obrar en guisa que salvaron las almas et aun fueron santos" [320]), but he also warns that those who choose the path of God *and* World can fail as easily as succeed: "los que passan en el mundo cobdiçiando fazer porque salven las almas, pero non se pueden partir de guardar sus onras et sus estados, estos tales pueden errar et pueden açertar en lo meior" (320, "those who live in this world desiring to do deeds that will save their souls, but cannot avoid protecting their honor and estates, these can err and succeed in the most important things"). Part of the difficulty, as in Part I, is knowing how to perform the good works that will ensure salvation.

Part V begins with a change of subject matter, away from *exemplos* and proverbs to another, "more profitable" topic ("fablar he un poco en otra cosa que es muy más provechosa" [300]). Since Patronio states that spiritual matters are the most important, he will explain how the Count can be saved. He lays out four apparently simple prerequisites; (1) faith in salvation itself, (2) adherence to all the articles of Church doctrine, (3) good works, and (4) avoidance of sinful deeds ("que se guarde de fazer malas obras" [301]). On the matter of faith, Patronio employs a brief *exemplum* of a simple elderly woman sowing in the sun as a metaphor for blind faith in the teachings of the Church, and if the Count needs proof that the Church's doctrine is indeed true, he refers him to the *Libro de los estados*, whose author, "don Iohán," is an authority on these matters.[7] After a detour through the Sacraments, Patronio returns to the subject of good and evil deeds.

When Patronio takes up the subject of good works again, he acknowledges right away that it is an extremely difficult and complicated matter to clarify, even though one could simply argue that in order for the Count to be saved he should do good and avoid evil, a tautological argument that Patronio exposes as useless:

> [Q]uien lo quisiesse dezir abreviadamente podría dezir que para esto non ha mester al sinon fazer bien et non fazer mal. Et esto sería verdat, mas porque esto sería, commo algunos dizen, grant verdat et poco seso, por ende, conviene que [. . .] declare más commo se pueden fazer estas dos cosas (308, to sum this matter up briefly, one could say that all that is necessary is to do good and not do evil deeds. And this would be true, but this would be, as some say, a great truth, but not very helpful advice, therefore, it is appropriate that [. . .] I explain in more detail how these two things can be done).

In his last book of the *CL*, I believe that Juan Manuel does finally solve, in an unexpected way, the ethical question of how to do such deeds that will win salvation while performing one's duty. He does so by exposing the relativity of actions themselves through the use of an exemplary story of a young knight who kills his father and

---

[7] As I demonstrate above in the case of *exemplo* 3, as well as in chapter 2, Juan Manuel had no qualms about writing on matters of Church doctrine.

lord at the same time; a double homicide that appears evil, but in the end is a virtue.

This *exemplum*, which could be titled "The Loyal Vassal," tells of a young knight who was forced to defend his lord against his own father in battle. When the paladin saw his *señor* in danger, he charged against the enemy, knowing it was his father and calling out to him to retreat. The father continues his attack and, with a miraculous blow, the son lances both his father and, by accident, his own lord. Overcome with grief, the knight turns himself over to a tribunal of kings and noblemen for judgment, and although the court admits that he had very bad luck, he did not commit a crime; on the contrary, he was rewarded for his loyalty: "lo preçiaron mucho et le fezieron much bien por la grand lealtad que fiziera en ferir a su padre por escapar a su señor. Et todo esto fue porque, commo quier que él fizo mala obra, non la fizo mal, nin por escogimiento de fazer mal" (312, "they praised him and rewarded him greatly for the loyal service rendered to his lord by injuring his father. And all of this because, even though he did an evil deed, he did not do it with bad intentions, or because he wanted to do an evil act").

An interesting detail in this *exemplum* is that it could easily be read as an example of loyalty, and as such it would corroborate Aníbal Biglieri's belief that the *CL* is a work that ratifies the social and political codes of conduct of the aristocracy, but here Patronio reads this tale as a example of the relativity of actions. Here Fratricide and Regicide are not the crimes they appear to be, but virtues. The important loophole that circumvents the law in this story, and in all actions that may appear evil, are the intentions that inform the knight's behavior.

Patronio defines good and evil deeds as actions that are chosen freely and performed with good or bad intentions, respectively.[8] One must choose freely to do a good work for its own sake and perform it with honest intentions. As an example, Patronio cites *exemplo* 40 from Part I which demonstrates that a hypocritical intention negates the virtue of a good deed. In *exemplo* 40 the seneschal

---

[8] Patronio explains in detail that a good work must "be done with good intentions, not for vanity or hypocritically, nor for any other intention than service to God," and furthermore, "he must choose it because it is good": "es mester que se faga bien, et esto es que se faga buena entençión, non por vanagloria, nin por ypocrisia, nin por otra entençión, sinon solamente por serviçio de Dios; otrosí, que lo faga por escogimiento [. . .], que escoja aquella porque es buena" (309).

of Carcassonne loses his soul because—as Patronio explains—"commo quier que él fizo buena obra, non la fizo bien, ca Dios non galardona solamente las buenas obras, mas galardona las que se fazen bien. Et este bien fazer es en la entençión, et porque la entención del senescal non fue buena [. . .], por ende non ovo della buen galardón" (212, "even though he did a good work, he did not do it well, because God does not reward good works alone, but only those works which are done properly. For good works lie in good intentions, and since the seneschal's intention was not good [. . .], he did not receive reward for it" [150]).

Without these prerequisites, a good deed is invalid, but more importantly for the story of the loyal vassal, an evil deed is not a sin at all if it is lacking in one of three conditions; (1) that it is an inherently evil act, (2) that it is chosen freely as an evil act, and (3) it is performed with malicious intentions: "lo primero, que non faga omne mala obra; lo segundo, que la non faga mal; lo terçero, que la non faga por escogimiento" (310). Rather than define what a sin *is*, Patronio shows what it is *not*, claiming that the Count can guard against sin if he can show that his actions lack one of the preconditions for malfeasance.

This negative method of defining an evil deed is noteworthy, since Patronio's point is that if only one of these three conditions is missing, the accused must be acquitted, like the loyal knight who killed two with one blow: "commo quier que fizo mala obra,"—following Patronio's summation—"porque la non fizo mal nin por escogimiento, non fizo mal nin meresçió aver por ello pena, nin la ovo" (310, "even though he did an evil deed, because he did not do it with malice, nor chose to do it freely, he did not commit the crime, and he did not deserve to be punished, nor was he"). My choice of language to describe this passage and translate Juan Manuel's text is obviously deliberate; it flows from the tale itself and the knight's trial, as well as what I perceive to be an almost lawyerly idiom to explain how, before the court of the Lord, a sin can be dismissed as evidence. As the Count's adviser Patronio clarifies the law at the end of his tale, a good or evil deed is ultimately contingent on the subject's intentions:

> Et assí, señor conde Lucanor, devedes entender por estos enxiemplos la razón porque las obras para que el omne vaya a Paraýso es mester que sean buenas, et bien fechas, et por es-

> cogimiento. Et por quel omne ha de yr al Infierno conviene que sean malas, et mal fechas, et por escogimiento; et esto que dize que sean bien fechas, o mal, et por escogimiento es en la entençión. (312-313, And in this way, sir Count Lucanor, you should understand from these *exempla* the reason why in order for a man to win Paradise his works must be good, performed with good intentions, and chosen freely for their own sake. And for a man to be condemned to Hell his deeds must be evil, performed with wicked intentions, and chosen freely for their own sake; and in order to say that a work is good or evil, or chosen freely or not, one must look to the intentions).

Part of the complexity of this tale, like others in the *CL*, is that in the text itself the exemplary action narrated in the *exemplum* has more than one explanation. The judges of the knight's behavior on the battlefield do not "read" his actions as an example of the three preconditions of an evil deed, but as an exemplary act of loyalty. Juan Manuel also clarifies in his narration of the knight's attack against his father that he was forced to do so because of his bonds of vassalage, exposing one of the many double-binds a nobleman may face in the performance of his duty. Finally, Patronio reads this same action, for all intents and purposes, as an example of the contingent nature of sin.

"The Loyal Vassal" is an extraordinary example of the semantic and rhetorical potential of the *exemplum* as an ambivalent sign that can be assigned more than one meaning in order to legitimize a range of beliefs. In this tale there are at least two lessons for the reader: (1) loyalty is an exemplary virtue of knighthood, and (2) sin is contingent upon intentions. The latter also implies another conclusion about exemplary behavior, since it exposes the very relativity of ethical decisions and actions.[9] Here the knight finds himself in

---

[9] While I have tried to frame my analysis of the *exemplum* in the *CL* within the field of ethics, Peter Dunn's view of the function of Juan Manuel's narratives goes beyond the realm of decisions and human behavior: "Whatever brilliance [the individual tales] may have is contributory to their function, which is to represent the variety and openness of the world, and to present this world to a mind which is capable of reflecting on it" ("The Structures of Didacticism" 53). María Rosa Menocal's comments on the moral of Patronio's stories is also worth citing here to demonstrate how other critics have interpreted this same sense of "openness" in the *CL*: "In the end, the only consistent 'moral' or 'lesson' to be drawn from the stories [is] that truth is highly contingent and relative, that absolutes are dangerous or evil, and that interpolation and judgment should avoid the temptations of closures and certainties" (482).

an ethical dilemma, and his choice to kill his father, which in a different situation would certainly be a sin, is sanctioned as the correct ethical decision.

The story of the loyal knight may be one of Juan Manuel's best aids to his readers, as he promises in the prologue, in their quest to "accomplish in this world such deeds as would be advantageous to their honor, their possessions, and their stations" (39), while saving their souls at the same time. Patronio's reading of the *exemplum* is itself very useful, since, as in *exemplo* 3 and 33 which end with a declaration of the Count's good intentions, the motivation behind one's actions is almost impossible to cross-examine. Intentions are ultimately subjective, even though the threat of hypocrisy lingers: "El mejor pedaço que ha en l' omne es el coraçón,"–according to one of Patronio's seemingly paradoxical proverbs cited in chapter 2–"esse mismo es el peor" (285, "The best part of man is his heart, and it is also his worst"). But Juan Manuel's rhetorical method of exemplification, employed to demonstrate this point, is just as profitable as Patronio's lesson itself. In this last *exemplo* of the *CL*,[10] the author exposes once again the ethical dangers of acting in the world according to one's *estado*, and demonstrates how a rhetorical strategy that appropriates the moral authority of the *exemplum*, like an expert witness in a trial, can circumvent any ethical conundrum.[11]

Before concluding this chapter, I must reiterate that by no means do I want to suggest that the author himself was a moral relativist. Furthermore, I am not entirely convinced that a return to an examination of authorial intentions is necessary to appreciate Juan Manuel's rhetorical use of *exempla*, or to defend my reading of the *CL*. Be this as it may, for those readers who have not completely given up on the relevance of authorial intentions, I would propose

---

[10] Juan Manuel actually uses four *exempla* in Part V; two are citations of tales in Part I (*exemplos* 40 and 45) which Patronio makes in order to prove a point, the others are the story of the old woman sowing in the sun as a metaphor of pure faith, and the *exemplum* of the loyal knight. This tale is the last new illustrative narrative of the *CL*, Patronio cites *exemplo* 45 at the end of Part V, but it is only a reference. Interestingly, Patronio refers the Count to *exemplo* 45 for proof of an entirely different argument than in Part I. The moral of *exemplo* 45 is to trust in God and never in the powers of the occult, while in the conclusion of Part V Patronio uses this same tale as evidence of the Devil's power to deceive man.

[11] As an interesting point of comparison, Sylvia Huot sees the same meta-rhetorical lesson in the fables of Marie de France: "Through such texts as these [fables], the lay reader is introduced to techniques of moralization and allegorization that he or she can then apply to other texts or even to real-life situations" (137).

the following compromise: Juan Manuel's appropriation of the rhetorical power of the *exemplum* in the *CL* is not at all intended to be subversive; instead, it is part of a pro-active strategy of self defense that works within the confines of late medieval notions of honor, duty, vassalage and salvation.[12]

In my reading of the *CL* thus far, I accept what appears to be an invitation to follow a medieval reading of the text, based primarily on an examination of *divisio* in Juan Manuel's narratives. By tracing these divisions in search of a univocal meaning in the array of homologous narrative parts, the reader is forced to contemplate a seemingly impenetrable paradox that exposes the relativity of the *exemplum* as a narrative sign. Like the donkey in *exemplo* 2, the ambivalence of the *exemplum* is a fundamental precept of the author's rhetorical strategy, since the narrative can be loaded according to the exemplarist's rhetorical needs. Juan Manuel puts the power of his exemplary art into action to solve a particularly thorny problem that would have been of interest to readers of his social and political standing, but more than merely providing a way out of the dilemma of acting in the world without getting burned in the next, Juan Manuel prepares his readers to contemplate his method of exemplification as yet another example of "how language can be twisted and convoluted," to borrow a phrase from James Burke cited in chapter 2. For the reader that has the proper *entendimiento* alluded to in the prologue, the *CL* can indeed be read as Laurence de Looze has suggested, as a "series of tutorials" ("The 'Nonsensical' Proverbs" 201), but the objective of the reader's intellectual exercise is not limited to developing a deeper appreciation of the ambiguity of signs, or even the ability to interpret them; instead, I would argue that at least one right reading of the *CL* involves learning how to appropriate the moral, ethical, even spiritual authority of the *exemplum* for the reader's benefit in his or her private journey on the paths of God and the World. The second part of this book attempts to show how Juan Manuel's earliest audience read

---

[12] Although Marta Ana Diz does not uncover a meta rhetorical lesson in the first part of the *CL*, she does, however, read Juan Manuel's tales as a kind of self defense. Paraphrasing Macpherson, Diz concludes that Part I is a text in which "Don Juan Manuel justifica ante otros y sobre todo ante sí mismo su propia existencia, como aristócrata poderoso y como cristiano preocupado por la salvación de su alma" (52, "Juan Manuel justifies to others, and above all to himself, his own existence as a powerful aristocrat and Christian worried about the salvation of his soul").

the *CL* "right" in at least two ways. First, by employing the rhetorical lesson of the *exemplum* exposed in the *CL*, which more than likely only reconfirmed a familiarity with the *exemplum* that the readers brought to the text; and second, by beginning a tradition of reading Juan Manuel's narratives as moral doctrine that essentially closed off the semantic potential of the *CL* for centuries.

PART II

FIXING THE MEANING OF *EL CONDE LUCANOR*

IN the introduction I describe my method of interrogating the manuscript evidence of reading the *CL* in the late Middle Ages by alluding to Siegfried Wenzel's materialist philology that reconsiders some of our modern, often unquestioned, assumptions about the medieval miscellany by taking seriously the possibility that a medieval compilation of various works may in fact have its own agenda and deliberate organization that can shed light on how each fascicle and the entire book were read and put to use by medieval audiences. Furthermore, as Ralph Hanna III reminds his readers, medieval anthologies, as opposed to printed books, are mediated by the needs of those who order their manufacture, producing "appropriations of works for the uses of particular persons in particular situations" (37). In the following chapters I will describe some of the organizing parameters that can shape a medieval anthology at work in two of the five manuscripts of the *CL*. An important idea to keep in mind is that very often the ties that bind individual works into a larger compilation must be searched for among what Sylvia Huot describes as "intermittent reminders" that require an associative reading attuned to thematic resonances in each collected work that together create a subtle overarching tone for the whole book (127, 138-139).

As I also state in the introduction, I am generally concerned with reading as the "primary literary activity" of the Middle Ages, as John Dagenais has argued (*The Ethics of Reading* 22), and in order to focus in on "lecturature," I will attempt to survey the overall manuscript landscape for evidence of reading the *CL*, rather than tracking each textual variant among the five manuscript witnesses, for example, or attempting to reconstruct the stemmatic relationships among them. Alberto Blecua's *La transmisión textual de* El Conde Lucanor is an exhaustive study of this type, and we can look forward to Laurence de Looze's forthcoming book on the variant meanings, and meaning of variance in the *CL* as it can be understood in the light of Paul Zumthor's notion of *mouvance*.[1] In keeping with my concentration on reading, and because every variant that can be described as a correction–as opposed to an error or difference stemming from the exemplar being copied–is also a reading of the text, I will restrict my study of this kind of variance, including scribal additions, to those changes which may reflect an ideological reading of the work which significantly affects its meaning beyond the level of vocabulary, grammar and syntax.

Nor do I indent to venture into the fascinating world of genetic criticism or the variance in medieval literature that Bernard Cerquiglini, among many others, have shown to be a rich field of research for more than a decade. Much of the evidence of reading that I will examine here, however, should be of interest to those scholars discovering the "joyous excess" of medieval literature, to borrow a now famous phrase from Cerquiglini (*In Praise of Variance* 33). More particularly, as Cerquiglini envisioned the creative exchange between reader and text in the Middle Ages, my study of the medieval reception of the *CL* often catches medieval readers in the act of rewriting and reshaping the *CL* in their own idiosyncratic performances of a work which they shamelessly appropriated as

---

[1] Zumthor defines the idea and aspects of *mouvance* in the second chapter of *Essai de poétique médiévale*, as well as in "Intertextualité et mouvance," arguing that it is a defining phenomenon of medieval culture ("Intertextualité" 9). According to Zumthor's almost poetic description of the medieval audience's interface with the ever-changing variance of literature, the medieval text is seen as fluid like the sea itself, and readers are also always potential writers who can contribute to the variance:

> Du point de vue des hommes du XIIe, du XIIIe, du XIVe siècle qui en furent l'origine, le moyen et la fin, auteurs, diffuseurs, consommateurs, l'ensemble de ces textes devait apparaître comme une vaste surface discursive, colorée, chatoyante, jetée par-dessus la brutalité de la vie et du monde, et mouvante comme une mer, avec ses courants, ses tourbillons, ses vagues toujours recommencées, don't aucune n'est tout à fait identifiable. ("Intertextualité" 13)

[2] In his ground-breaking book Cerquiglini celebrates the variance in medieval vernacular literature created by readers who took up a text as their own:

> In the Middle Ages the literary work was a variable. The effect of the vernacular joyful appropriation of the signifying nature suited to the written

their own.[2] Much of the manuscript study presented here will support these now familiar theories regarding the so-called "instability" of manuscript texts, or perhaps more specifically what Ramón Menéndez Pidal defined as "tradicionalidad escrita"; a concept akin to Pidal's theory of "tradicionalidad" as it applies to the transmission of oral poetry ("Poesía popular" 345).

Long before Zumthor or Cerquiglini rediscovered the "essential instability in medieval texts" (Zumthor, *Toward a Medieval Poetics* 45), Pidal compared manuscript textuality with the performative poetic tension found in traditional oral poetry (*Poesía juglaresca* 247). Pidal coined the term "tradicionalidad escrita" ("written traditionalism") to describe manuscript variance (*Poesía juglaresca* 247), and argued that the kind of variance caused by the spontaneous appropriation and improvisation that defines the oral Spanish ballad tradition ("Poesía popular" 341), is essentially the same as the more meditative variance found in manuscript texts (*Poesía juglaresca* 247). Many of the manuscripts that I will be studying in this second part of my book will support Pidal's prophetic theories, but as I have already suggested, I will go beyond providing more evidence of the unstable nature of manuscript textuality. Building on these theories, my argument here is that each act of rewriting, correcting and compiling–as physical and intellectual responses to the text–are simultaneously discrete acts of reading and interpreting the *CL*.

Since I am concerned primarily with the reception of the *CL* as it can be deduced from the entire manuscript environment of late medieval / early modern *CL* texts, I focus my attention on those manuscripts that contain the most evidence of reading. Two fifteenth-century manuscripts, in particular those known as P and M, have the most robust evidence of reading the *CL* primarily due to the fact that they are anthologies of various works, and as such contain a program of reading that can be followed from the very layout of the physical book to the more tell-tale traces of reading the *CL* in the manuscript texts themselves. The other three manuscripts (S, G and H) are also helpful in this enterprise and, studied together as a

---

word was the widespread abundant enjoyment of the privilege of writing. Occasionally, the fact that one hand was the first was probably less important than this continual rewriting of a work that belonged to whoever prepared it and gave it form once again. (33)

body of manuscript testimony, a clearer late-medieval horizon of expectations can be discerned surrounding Juan Manuel's work.[3] I will argue that all the manuscripts contain suggestive information, each demonstrating various degrees of use by their audiences, but it is not necessary to dedicate an entire chapter to each, since some can be surveyed briefly in order to draw out their place in the reception of the *CL* as supporting evidence for my general thesis. Chapters 4 and 5 will concentrate on the anthologies P and M, which span the fifteenth century,[4] while bringing in supporting evidence from the remaining three to provide a more complete picture of Juan Manuel's earliest traceable reception.

I will single out many significant physical characteristics of all the manuscript witnesses. Most editions of the *CL* provide the usual critical apparatuses including brief descriptions of the five manuscripts and of the first print edition known as A for its editor Argote de Molina.[5]

Manuscript S (Madrid, Biblioteca Nacional 6376) is the oldest and most complete copy of the *CL*, although it probably represents a later, five-part version of the *CL* that Juan Manuel revised for his complete-works volume.[6] Based on its rounded Gothic script, it is believed to be a late fourteenth-century codex. Manuscripts P

---

[3] Technically, manuscript S is also an anthology; it is a collected-works volume of Juan Manuel's writings, and as such it also displays an organizational plan that tells us a lot about how and who read this book. I will suggest further on that S was produced for a very limited audience, so much so that it is the least representative of how the *CL* was generally received in the late medieval and early modern era.

[4] Based on paleographic evidence, P is thought to be a late fourteenth, or more probably early fifteenth-century manuscript, while M falls in the later half of the fifteenth. Together they offer the most compelling evidence of how the *CL* was received in the late Middle Ages.

[5] One of the most complete description of the *CL* manuscripts can be found in Michael Hammer's doctoral dissertation, *Framing the Reader: Exemplarity and Ethics in the Manuscripts of the Conde Lucanor*. Eduardo Juliá's edition has often been cited for its description of the *CL* manuscripts, but Reinaldo Ayerbe-Chaux, José Blecua, and more recently Guillermo Serés, all provide satisfactory outlines in their critical editions. Most every modern editor, as well as Alberto Blecua in his study of the textual transmission of the work, include the first print edition in their reviews of the manuscript tradition of the *CL*, as Alan Deyermond's advises in "Editors, Critics and *El Conde Lucanor*" (620).

[6] Alberto Blecua concludes that Juan Manuel wrote the first part of the *CL* before the 1335 five-part version which was included in the complete-works volume prepared by Juan Manuel himself, creating the fascinating situation of two "original" *CL* texts with potentially independent histories of transmission (*La trasmisión textual* 124-125).

(Madrid, Real Academia Española 15) and M (Madrid, Biblioteca Nacional 4236) are both fifteenth-century works, as is manuscript H (Madrid, Real Academia de la Historia 9-5893). The manuscript that once belonged to Pascual Gayangos, known as G (Madrid, Biblioteca Nacional 18415) is a sixteenth-century humanist copy which also contains a version of the five-part *CL*. This last manuscript is of particular interest here for tracing the reading of the *CL* from the late medieval to the early modern era. I will discuss other important physical details of these manuscripts in the following chapters, but I must point out that I do not structure my study of the manuscripts chronologically, since I examine the entire body of evidence as the representation of a global, late-medieval response to the *CL*.

Chapter 4

THE IDEOLOGICAL READING OF *EL CONDE LUCANOR*[1]

THE ideological reading of the *CL* can be traced in many of its manuscript witnesses, but the codex housed in Madrid, Real Academia Española 15 (henceforth P) offers some of the most robust evidence of fixing the meaning of the *CL* in the late Middle Ages. It serves as an excellent foundation for an analysis of other, more inconspicuous traces of reading the *CL* "right" in the global manuscript environment of the work.

Since most scholars view manuscript S (Madrid, Biblioteca Nacional 6376), as the best text of the *CL*, most have limited their study of P to the text of Juan Manuel's narratives with little or no consideration of the other works bound together with it in the codex. Aside from its obvious value as one of the five manuscript witnesses of the *CL*, manuscript P, studied from cover to cover as a whole book is a fascinating expression of late-medieval manuscript culture. By drawing together examinations of scribal emendations and additions throughout the codex, its organization of materials, and comments on the other works included in the book, we can more fully appreciate how the codex itself and its version of the *CL* were read and put to use in late-medieval Spain. Among the other writings included in this compilation, two works in particular stand out; one is the only known copy of the *Libro de los engaños* which follows the *CL*, and the other is the *Lucidario*, an encyclopedic treatise on morals, religion and science.

---

[1] A version of my analysis of manuscript P in this chapter has also been published in *Hispanic Review*, "Reading and Writing Patronio's Doctrine in *Real Academia Española*, MS. 15."

In addition to these familiar works of didactic literature, the codex contains other, less familiar, writings such as San Pedro Pascual's gloss of the Lord's Prayer that unpacks the meaning of its seven petitions to God and prohibits Moors, bad Christians, and Jews from praying it. Following that, a copy of Alonso de Cuenca's will and testament preaches the joy of death as a second birth, allowing us to leave behind this valley of tears for the bliss of heaven wherein we eternally experience God's glory. This expression of a common medieval topos precedes a letter written by San Bernaldo advising Don Remón, knight of the castle of San Ambrosio, on how to live according to his station and save his soul. To sum up, the order of the works found in P is as follows: (1) *CL*, Part I (fol. 1^r-62^v), (2) *El libro de los engaños* (fol. 63^r-79^v), (3) San Pedro Pascual's *Glosa del Pater Noster* (fol. 80^r-85^r), (4) *El testamento del maestro Alfonso de Cuenca* (fol. 85^r-85^v), (5) a letter from San Bernaldo to Don Ramón (fol. 85^v-86^v), and (6) the *Lucidario* (fol. 87^r-159^v).

The physical condition of the codex is excellent, with the exception of the first folio which is illegible in parts. The Gothic cursive script is written in a clear, easy-to-read hand that appears to be the same throughout the codex, with the possible exception of the first column of folio 84 recto, where there appears to be a second scribe's hand, and finally a third hand has made many corrections and interlinear emendations that will be discussed further on. For these reasons, and especially because of the didactic nature of the other writings in the codex that make up its physical and literary context, manuscript P is an indispensable material witness to how Juan Manuel's *exempla* were read from the fifteenth to the early-sixteenth century.

The value of this manuscript has never been in question. Alberto Blecua, in his study of the manuscript transmission of the *CL*, appreciated its special evidence of the scribal reading process involved in manuscript production (71-72). Eugenio Krapf, its last private owner, went so far as to claim in his introduction to *El libro de Patronio* that this codex was "el más llano" and "primordial" of all those containing the *CL* (xxiv). More recently, Reinaldo Ayerbe-Chaux has suggested that this copy may in fact be more closely related, stemmatically, to a first writing of the book that Juan Manuel revised at a later date for his complete works represented by manuscript S (28).

As I intimate in the introduction to this second part of my study, I am not concerned here with reconstructing Juan Manuel's originally intended work; instead, I would ask the reader to place the notion of authorial intention aside, at least momentarily, in order to examine the physical evidence of this codex and arrive at a better understanding of how the *CL* was received and put to use by its late medieval and early modern readers. In this endeavor I wish to take advantage of Wenzel's notion of a "materialist philology," and for the sake of convenience I will remind the reader that this new philology "postulates the possibility that a given manuscript, having been organized along certain principles, may well present its text(s) according to its own agenda," and that "[f]ar from being a transparent or neutral vehicle, the codex can have a typological identity that affects the way we read and understand the texts it presents" (2).

More particularly, this chapter will examine how P displays a medieval reading process visible in the layout of the codex and its later emendations that resonates with a larger critical interpretation that set the ideological reading of the *CL*. An examination of this sort leads to an hypothesis that the traditional understanding of the *CL*'s doctrine and its didactic integrity is as much the result of the medieval interpretation and reception that P testifies to, as it is the product of Juan Manuel's design.

When holding this relatively small, portable codex which can be held and read easily in one hand, looking at the folios with enlarged decorative initials and running titles all in red ink, and meditating on the different works it contains, a simple question arises that is the starting point of this chapter. Does this book have a common theme and discernable purpose? Is there an agenda at work in this codex? An examination of the traces of the scholastic notion of *compilatio* that structures P provides a solid base of evidence to support the argument that it does indeed have its own "typological identity."

One can easily detect a compiler's hand behind the writings contained in this codex. Theo Stemmler outlines a number of parameters a medieval compiler could employ when designing the layout of a book, many of which are present in P. These "general organizing principles" include "author (one author / several authors), language (Latin / vernacular), form (prose / verse), genre (lyric / narrative / drama), [and] content (religious / secular)" (232). In P the most patent organizing principles are language (vernacular / Castilian) and form (prose), but beneath these integumental observations one can discern a coherency of content as well.

The first two works are collections of *exempla*, each considered to have useful didactic properties specifically for the instruction of proper behavior in worldly matters, as well as orthodox doctrines of salvation. The notion that these collections combine valuable secular and religious doctrine has been studied extensively; in the case of the *CL*, Ian Macpherson's classic essay on the two paths of God and World, cited earlier, comes to mind immediately. Other important scholars, many of whom have been mentioned already, such as María Jesús Lacarra, Derek Lomax, and María Rosa Lida de Malkiel have all concurred on a special characteristic of this kind of didactic short prose narrative: its perennial association with orthodoxy in both the religious and secular spheres, as well as its heavy imprint on the development of prose narrative in Spain. One of the most important scholars on the Spanish short prose narrative, Juan Paredes Núñez, has argued that throughout the Middle Ages there is no clear distinction between secular and religious *exempla* and that the Spanish term *exemplo* could be employed indiscriminately for any short prose narrative (20). This peculiar doubly-didactic valence of the *exemplum* cuts through P, since all the writings compiled in it deal with one or both of these fields of orthodoxy; it therefore forms one of the most important organizing apparatuses, under Stemmler's category of content, revealing a clearer picture of the "compiler's psychology"–to cite a phrase again from Stemmler–that planned this book (236).

A lengthy discussion of the notion of exemplarity in the *CL* and *El libro de los engaños* would be an unnecessary detour at this point, especially since it has been dealt with by many other critics who have edited these books and thoroughly investigated the history of the short prose narrative in Spain. One such scholar is John Keller, who argues in his introduction to *The Book of the Wiles of Women* that the *Libro de los engaños* is essentially a collection of entertaining stories with no serious didactic value: "Surely no one who reads the tales today can seriously consider them didactic, nor is it easy to believe that the Spaniard of the thirteenth century found them less amusing than we" (9). On the other hand, at the turn of the last century, José Amador de los Ríos opined that some of the tales included in *El libro de los engaños* were not offensive to good manners at all, and that others indeed contained valuable doctrine (3: 540). Unlike John Keller's reading, María Jesús Lacarra convincingly argues in "La mujer en la narrativa breve medieval" that the misogyny of this work, like that of *Disciplina Clericalis, Libro de los proverbios,* and *Poridat de las poridades,* was a commonplace in orthodox teachings presented in collections of aphorisms designed for religious instruction (104). Furthermore, *El libro de los engaños* as it appears in P testifies to the general assumption that the study of these tales, or listening to the stories of sages, will provide the necessary wisdom for salvation. One of the most important traces of reading manuscript P, in addition to its organization as an anthology, are the many deletions and interlinear corrections made by a late fifteenth-century reader that essentially create a double text.[2] I have marked the Spanish text with parenthesis and square brackets to indicate more precisely the scribal deletions and interlinear emendations, respectively:[3]

> oyendo las rrazones de los sabios, que quien bien faze nunca se le muere (el) [la fama] sab(er)[yendo] que ninguna cosa (non) (es) [ay mejor] para auer [de] ganar la vida perdurable si non (profeçía) [a el bien obrar y el saber]. [fol. 63ʳ]

I translate both versions into English, with the scribal correction translated with italics:

> By listening to the words of the wise, the wisdom of he who does good will never die, since there is nothing better than prophecy for winning salvation. *By listening to the words of the wise, the fame of he who does good will never die, knowing that there is nothing better for winning salvation than good works and wisdom.*

I will return to this interesting passage further on, but for now we should consider both the original and the amended text to be tools for winning salvation. Although it is helpful to note that these compilations of exemplary tales were received as an orthodox source of both religious and secular doctrine, there is further physi-

---

[2] For a description of the contents of manuscript P and the hand that edited the text, see the appendix of the beautiful facsimile edition, published by the Real Academia Española, which cites the entry on manuscript 15 from the *Catálogo de Manuscritos de la Real Academia Española*. According to this review of manuscript P, the corrections were made in the late fifteenth century.

[3] Quotations from the works compiled in this codex are transcribed from the facsimile edition published by the Real Academia Española. English translations and transcriptions of the manuscript text are my own.

cal evidence in P that sheds light on how these tales were read in this particular book.

The next group of works that appears after the *CL* and the *Libro de los engaños* deals more directly with matters of religious doctrine, as well as secular matters that go hand-in-hand with those of faith and salvation. Following the *Libro de los engaños* is a detailed explanation of the *Pater Noster*, copied without mention of its author. It is believed to be a gloss written by San Pedro Pascual while held captive by the Moors in Granada at the end of the thirteenth century for the instruction of the other prisoners there (Armengol Valenzuela, xxxii). In addition to its censure of Jews and Moors, it emphasizes the importance of understanding the meaning behind the words of this most important Christian prayer.

The place of this gloss in the anthology is also significant. It stands at the center of the codex as a kind of ideological anchor, and allows the reader to pause and meditate on a familiar prayer, even the act of prayer itself. In *El renacimiento espiritual*, a recent book that is bound to become an important contribution to the study of theological treatises on prayer and meditation in relation to literature, Armando Pego Puigbó recalls that the *Pater noster* is one of most basic and oldest subgenres of Christian doctrinal writings, taught by Christ himself (94). Together with explanations of the Ten Commandments, the Articles of Faith and the Sacraments, an explication of the Lord's Prayer, according to Pego Puigbó, forms a basic part of almost all catechisms: "[e]n casi todos los Catecismos, junto a la enseñanza del Decálogo, los Artículos de Fe y los Sacramentos, es básica la parte dedicada a la oración del *Pater noster*" (94). Its presence in P lends a voice of orthodoxy to the entire codex.

I will argue later that P is a kind of resource book of useful materials for a preacher, rather than a book to read or study from cover to cover, but the kind of "meditative reading" that Sylvia Huot identifies in this prayer as it appears in another medieval anthology (Bibliothèque Nationale fr. 24429) is helpful to consider here, since a concentrated reading on the themes of the Lord's Prayer train the reader to search for discrete thematic links among the other works in the anthology (129). In P, San Pedro Pascual's gloss helps to explain the presence of the other apparently miscellaneous writings in the codex that also deal with the subject of prayer and salvation. The gloss orients the reading of the other works as doctrinal texts.

Alonso de Cuenca's will, which follows this gloss, also exemplifies an orthodox doctrine, in particular a proper Christian attitude toward death and faith in a glorious afterlife. Among other lessons, it teaches against the fear of death and sorrow for those who have departed, and concludes with a short exemplary prayer for those close to death: "o rredentor mío, levanta mi alma e liévala a do aparesca ante la tu gloria que es perdurable sin fyn" (fol. 85^v, "oh, my redeemer, lift up my soul and bring it before your glory which is everlasting"). Following this prayer is the letter to Don Remón, which promises to teach how to live properly and save one's soul at the same time–a theme common to all of the works in this codex. Continuing the religious and secular didactic tone of the preceding texts, the matter of writing wills is taken up in the conclusion of this epistle, written in single column format across the bottom margin of the folio, followed by instructions on how and when to prepare a will, especially before one is too sick to do so: "pues, ordenar deves testamento ante de la enfermedat lo ordena. Muchas de vegadas algunos son siervos de la enfermedat [et] el sieruo non puede fazer testamento, pues que así eres libre faz testamento ante que seas siervo fecho de la enfermedat" (fol. 86^v, "therefore, you should arrange your will before your illness arranges it [for you]. Very often some are made slaves of their sickness, and a slave cannot make a will, so since you are free, write your will before your illness makes you a slave").

The thematic ties between Alonso de Cuenca's will and this letter are not immediately detected, but with a careful reading the points of contact become clearer; it may be more precise to describe the links as thematic "details and intermittent reminders," borrowing again from Sylvia Huot's description of a similar cohesion based on content that binds separate works into an anthology like those she studies in "A Book Made for a Queen" (138-139). But it is perhaps the last work of the codex, the *Lucidario*, that offers the most enlightening evidence of the compiler's criteria that can explain the production of P.

Scanning the folios that contain the *Lucidario*, one is immediately struck by its diverse subject-matter summarized in the running titles of each *capítulo* which restate the questions put to a teacher by his disciple on matters of theology and natural science, among other rather juvenile queries about human nature in general. The disciple's questions for his teacher range from some of the most hermetic and mysterious pillars of the Catholic faith, such as the Holy Trinity (in chapter 28 the pupil asks why the Trinity is made up of three persons), to other much more trivial questions dealing with religious and secular matters combined, for example: Why do the saints have different symbols? (chapter 16). Why does the Devil try to deceive only men instead of more simple-minded animals? (chapter 18). Why are there only four evangelists? (chapter 15). Why does the moon shine brighter when it is full? (chapter 14). How can God know what is in the hearts of all men all the time? (chapter 6). From which side did God take one of Adam's ribs? (chapter 56). The sophomoric nature of some of these questions is surprising, not to mention amusing, but they make more sense once the pedagogical nature and purpose of the *Lucidario* is understood.

In his edition of the *Lucidario* Richard Kinkade reproduces a prologue, not found in P, that explains its peculiar combination of theological and scientific queries. According to this prologue, Sancho IV ordered the production of the *Lucidario* in order to quell the disputes between doctors of theology and those of the "natural sciences": "veyendo la contienda que era entre los maestros de la thología e las de las naturas" (80). The prologue also suggests that the *Lucidario* was copied in order to provide authoritative answers to dangerous questions that should not be asked in the first place: "E estas preguntas tales, como quier que sean de grand sotileza, son a pedimento de tiempo de aquellos que las fazen e nasçe dellas mucho mal" (78, "And these questions, even though they are very intelligent, they are a waist of time to those who ask them, and from them much wickedness is born").

The prologue, however, is not copied in manuscript P, even though it is clear that the questions cited in the prologue are of the same tone, perhaps even flippancy, as the rest of the questions put forth in the *Lucidario*. Be this as it may, Kinkade explains that the *Lucidario* had a more general purpose as a trusted reference book for medieval professors, mostly clerics, who monopolized private instruction and the intermediate education of catechumens in cathedral and monastery schools (63).

Although the medieval church did control the majority of intermediate and higher education, individual instructors needed to compete for students in order to survive. In an amusing note that begs to be compared with our modern university system, Kinkade points out that these clerics had to keep things interesting for their students, even at the expense of a solid education, or risk losing their income (63). Whether it was used in the homes of students who could pay for private tutors, or clerics in cathedral schools, the *Lucidario* was considered to be a useful and officially sanctioned source of elementary orthodox instruction dealing with both secular and religious subjects: a useful tool of the teacher's trade (Kinkade 64).

Because of the subject-matter of the other works compiled in the codex, it is quite conceivable that the didactic pedagogical nature of the *Lucidario*, combining basic religious doctrine with secular topics, is a thematic parameter that the compiler had in mind for this anthology. It requires little imagination to see P as another kind of *lucidario* in Kinkade's most generic definition of the term as any compilation of useful materials for orthodox instruction (17). Nor does it seem unreasonable to suggest that this book was designed as an instructor's reference, or perhaps for a priest composing a sermon, and therefore compiled to address the needs of a more pragmatic reading practice.

Manuscript P was most probably not intended to be read from cover to cover; rather, the reader scanned the book for material to be incorporated into a lesson, disputation, or homily, all of which could use an exemplary tale to demonstrate a point or keep the audience interested and amused, following the classic rhetorical use of the *exemplum*. As the foregoing demonstrates, there is sufficient physical evidence in the layout of the codex itself to conclude that it was manufactured for these purposes and with a specific readership in mind.

This kind of scholastic reading practice required a new type of book that catered to academic needs in the form of a compilation that rearranged and packaged texts for reference purposes, making its material "easily accessible" (Parkes 127). P is an example of this type of medieval book. A new book also implies a new notion of authorship, bringing together works to create a compilation and, in so doing, superscribing upon them the compiler's reading of their content which is evidenced in the *ordinatio* of the new book produced (Evans 3-4). An inevitable consequence of reading and writing in this way is that whatever thematic unity, artistic creativity, or authorial intention the individual fascicles may have contained fade when they are brought into line with the compiler's vision of the new book. Looking at the *CL* as it appears in P provides further evidence of these medieval reading and writing customs.

One of the first examples of the scribe's rewriting of the *CL* that Alberto Blecua identifies in this manuscript are the concluding "viessos" of each tale (65). As Blecua demonstrates, these verses have been standardized according to the scribe's most familiar meters, in particular the "alejandrino" and "pie de romance" (65). What is significant about this systematic change is that it represents one level among many of a deliberate scribal reading and writing process that involves many degrees of interpretation and adaptation of the text to meet the compiler's overall design. It is an indisputable piece of physical evidence that testifies to the extra-textual ideological and aesthetic assumptions imposed on texts that were perceived as open and malleable by scribes who were also authors.[4]

This idea of an ideologically-bound reading practice physically present in the different classes of "scribal productivity" is borrowed from John Dagenais's outline of these often interwoven "registers" (*Ethics* 134). The ideological register that will be examined in P involves what Dagenais terms "not just a formal political, philosophical, or religious ideology that a scribe may impose upon the text," but also "vaguer systems of personal values held by the scribe" including aesthetics visible in changes of "rhythmic or metric patterns" (*Ethics* 143). I would propose an expansion of Dagenais's concept to encompass the notion of *compilatio* at work in P since it also registers the compiler's practical, aesthetic, and ideological thinking at the moment of production.

Furthermore, an examination of this scribal register in P can reactivate the rhetorical and interpretive potential that medieval compilers and scribes (or readers and writers) exploited in the *CL* precisely at the moment when they attempted to adapt and recast the meaning of Patronio's *exempla* by writing them into another book. Two general observations on P frame the following study of its version of the *CL*: (1) that there are traces of an overarching ideological reading that can be discussed in terms of *compilatio*, as well as evidenced in the accretions and emendations produced by the scribes of the codex, and (2) that the compiler and scribes exploited the "openness" of the text that invites such a reading.

One of the most surprising features of the *CL* as it appears in P

---

[4] For another excellent case-in-point of the collapse of the distinction between scribe and author in the Middle Ages, see Tim William Machan's essay "Scribal Role, Authorial Intention, and Chaucer's *Boece*."

are two apocryphal tales added at the end of the collection: *capítulo* 53, "De la emaginaçion que puede sacar a omne de entendimiento" ("How the Imagination Can Drive a Man Crazy"), and *capítulo* 54 "De commo la onrra deste mundo non es sino commo sueño que pasa" ("How the Honor of This World is Like a Passing Dream").[5] Aside from their literary significance–Krapf points to a possible relationship between *capítulo* 54 and Calderón de la Barca's *La vida es sueño* (206)–these tales are of particular interest here since they provide conspicuous evidence of the scribal reading and writing process that exploits the openness of the medieval book, and Juan Manuel's collection of tales as well.[6] As John Dagenais suggests in "That Bothersome Residue," there is an element of the performative in the medieval manuscript codex (255), and these tales are excellent examples of his point; they are unique story-telling performances that follow the didactic and literary example that precedes them since they are inscribed as two more tales of the *CL*. Furthermore, they are glaring examples of scribal participation as authors in the production of medieval literature.

But the scribal stories are very poor imitations of Juan Manuel's narrative technique. More than bad fakes, they suggest that no attempt at all was made to pass them off as authentic. They lack any kind of frame narrative; even Patronio, the Count, and Don Juan are missing. There are no *viessos* or aphorisms, and the plots of the stories are so superficially summarized that they cannot be seriously considered as attempts to decant their moral teachings; rather, they appear as mere running titles that serve to remind the reader that these stories are examples of how man's imagination can get the best of him, or that the honors of this world are fleeting:[7]

> Capítulo LIII, de la emaginaçion que puede sacar a omne de entendimiento e non se puede tornar de ligero sinon commo aquí dize. Contesçió esto a un omne: Un omne estaua doliente e començó a pensar en la muerte de guisa que pensó que era

---

[5] I have transcribed these tales in appendix I.

[6] María Rosa Menocal points to the fact that a fifty-first tale has "crept into" the *CL* in some instances, and she comments that it is an ironic case in point of the "fluidity and explicit openness of a genre Don Juan Manuel thought he could close" (488).

[7] See appendix I. The second of these two tales is incomplete, so it is impossible to say for sure if any attempt at interpreting its moral was made, but based on the structure of the preceding tale and the narrative similarities between the two, it does not seem likely that the second apocryphal story would offer much more than the first.

muerto (fol. 61ʳ-61ᵛ, Chapter LIII How the imagination can drive a man crazy, and how it is not easy for him to regain his sanity, except as in the following [example]. This happened to a man: A man was sick and he began to think about death in such a way that he believed he was dead).

The author does not frame or circumstantiate the narrative in any way except by simply stating that this happened to a man. Furthermore, the conclusion makes no attempt to interpret or apply the lesson of the story:

> E des que le contaron la manera, marauillóse ende mucho et así bivió toda su vida en su acuerdo commo ante. Por que se demuestra que la ymaginaçión saca a omne de entendimiento (fol. 62ʳ, And when they told him what happened, he was amazed and lived the rest of his life in sound mind as before. This shows how the imagination can drive a man crazy).

Clearly, no effort is made to follow the narrative model of the *CL*, yet these tales are included as two more *capítulos* in Patronio's book. As such, one can begin to extrapolate how the *CL* was read by one particular late-medieval audience.

These extra tales suggest that the reader / scribe viewed Juan Manuel's stories as little more than a random collection of tales with no thematic, artistic, or ideological coherency among them, so adding two more did not violate any notion of authorial intention. The physical presence of these scribal narratives tell us that for at least one group of medieval readers (those who worked on the production of P for a larger audience), the *exemplum* was a negatively charged narrative that could be infused with meaning according to various rhetorical needs. Juan Manuel's design disappears when these tales are added and his collection is copied into a new book with a new layout and organization. The extra *exempla* are witnesses to reading the *CL* within the larger framework of generic collections of didactic short stories intended to be used according to the needs of their readers, rather than read as the artistic expression and unique creation of an individual author.[8] These readers read

---

[8] Machan observes a similar scribal posture toward Chaucer's *Boece*, stating that "[t]he majority [of the scribes] evidently did not view the text they were copying as something sacrosanct: Chaucer's authorial intention was not their primary concern" (156).

the *CL* right because they recognized the rhetorical potential of Juan Manuel's *exempla* to be used, and even added to, for discrete purposes within a new literary and codicological context. My analysis of the *CL* in the previous chapters suggests that, by exposing the *exemplum* as an ambivalent sign, the work anticipates this kind of reading, at least by those readers with sufficient *entendimiento* to follow the textual and rhetorical clues.

Referring to the work of Malcolm Parkes and Murray Evans, I have stated above that the production of a compilation involved a new kind of authorship, and therefore the creation of a potentially new meaning for each fascicle bound together in the new book. In the case of the *CL*, I believe that the narrative thread created by the Count / Patronio discourse is cut–in P, *capítulos* 53 and 54 do not continue this device–thus erasing the author's original design, but while one manner of reading the collection is lost, another is taken up that aligns it with the entire anthology. The author's most basic didactic intention may have been followed by the scribe / author (i.e. the intention to write stories that can be used to teach a lesson), and the combination of secular and religious questions in the *CL* does resonate with the organizing principles behind the production of this codex, so one can imagine that reading the *CL* in P involved stabilizing the meaning of the collection by recognizing and exploiting certain attributes in the text while suppressing others. The compiler and scribe acknowledge the most superficial objective of Juan Manuel's stories, and actively participate, through writing and compiling, in drawing attention to that pedagogical goal. In so doing the scribe also registers for us the openness of Juan Manuel's work, as well as the appropriative ideological reading process involved in manufacturing a medieval book. Further evidence of this reading and writing process exists on folio 57 verso.

Exemplo 48, "De lo que contesçió a uno que provava sus amigos" ("What Happened to a Man Who Tested His Friends"), is incomplete in P, but the reading that the scribe wrote for it has not been lost. This tale is noteworthy because of Patronio's double exegesis, with one social and pragmatic reading, and a second "spiritual" interpretation of the exact same *exemplum*. It is also significant as an example of the relative nature of the *exemplum* that troubles the *CL*, since Patronio demonstrates how one tale can generate many lessons and interpretations according to the particular needs and circumstances of the reader. In manuscript P, the scribe obviously understood Patronio's lesson and applied his own hand at the exegetical project by providing another version of Patronio's allegorical reading, if not exactly a third original interpretation, which is worth citing in its entirety:

> En otra manera se dize este enxenplo, que todo omne que a tres amigos et al uno non sirve tanto nin lo tiene encargado, et el omne bive commo con el rrey que le toma cuenta de quanto a fecho et des que lo alcança por la cuenta tiene lo preso et quiere lo matar. E en aquella priesa va él a un amigo quel acorrerá et el amigo dizel quel dará algo de lo que tiene, mas non llegará con él [ante el rrey]. E lu[e]go va al otro et dízel que llegará con él fasta la casa del rrey et que luego se tornará a casa, et estos dos amigos son sus encargados. E el otro que non tiene tan encargado fue a él et dixo que llegase al rrey con él, et aquel le dixo; "nunca tanto me serviste commo a los otros, mas yo llegaré ante el rrey contigo, et rrogaré por ti." El primero amigo es el mundo a quien sirve omne mucho. De que muera para ir antel rrey que es Dios, va el omne al mundo que bivía con él et dale çinco varas de paño para una mortaja de quanto con él ganó et afanó. El segundo amigo es los parientes, et el omne va a ellos que le acorran et ellos le dizen que llegarán a la fuesa con él et se tornarán luego. El terçero amigo a quien non sirvió tanto es Dios que es amigo verdadero; este llega ante Dios et le rruega por él et lo salva el rrey (fol. 57ᵛ, One can explain this *exemplum* in another way. Every man that has three friends, one of whom he does not serve or help, lives as he who lives with a king who takes account of everything he does, and when he finds him he arrests him for what he owes, and wants to kill him. And in this plight the man turns to a friend who will help him, and the friend tells him that he will give him something of what he has to help, but he will not go with him [before the king]. And later the prisoner turns to another friend who says that he will accompany him as far as the king's house, then he will go back home, and these two friends are in debt to the man. And he went to the other friend who does not owe him any favors, and asked him to accompany him before the king, and this friend told him: "You never did as much for me as for the others, but I will go with you to the king, and I will beg him for your sake." The first friend is the World, whom man serves very much. And when he dies and goes before the king who is God, he turns to the World who gives him five yards of cloth for a burial gown for all of his work and effort. The second friend are family relatives, and the man turns to

them for help and they promise to follow him as far as the cemetery, before turning back. The third friend whom the man did not serve as much is God, who is a true friend; this friend goes before God and prays for the man, and the king saves him).

This accretion demonstrates that the scribe reads the *CL spiritualmente*, or ideologically. By comparison with Juan Manuel's allegorical reading of the tale, the scribe may have preferred to correct Patronio's version, since Juan Manuel cites the clergy as the second fair-weather friend (Keller and Keating edition 177). By writing in yet another religious allegorical reading, the scribe acknowledges and draws attention to the orthodoxy of Juan Manuel's work; through sheer repetition, imitation and correction, the reader / writer emphasizes the doctrine in Patronio's second reading, while indirectly suppressing the first, "political" reading which warns against trusting those who claim to be true friends. In this way the ideological reading of the *CL* cements the expectation that in this book one will find rhetorically useful, ideologically orthodox, conventional, and unproblematic lessons such as a medieval priest or teacher would expect to find in a *lucidario*. These expectations inform the overarching content parameter of the entire codex, and they rewrite the meaning of the *CL* automatically through association and conformation with the book that contains it.

As I mention in the introduction to this second part, I will argue that many of these ideological expectations endure to this day. For now, it is clear in P that this reading process includes writing into the *CL* the very doctrine that its late-medieval readers needed and expected to find. Completing the book necessitates writing the content of its components, and this is exactly what the scribe does in the accretions examined above. It also involves correcting the original text in order to bring it into alignment with its readers' ideological demands. Some of the most striking physical evidence of this is found on folio 22 verso which contains the conclusion of "What Happened to a Young King and a Philosopher to Whom His Father Commended Him," studied in detail in chapter 2; here in P it is "capítulo XXI De lo que conteçió a un rrey moço con un filósofo que dizié que sabié catar en agüeros."

As discussed in chapter 2, in this tale Patronio instructs the Count on the delicate art of teaching, made all the more precarious when one's pupil is a proud aristocrat. Above all, Patronio advises that the Count should never humiliate or scold his noble student; instead, he should tell him stories to make him feel as though he has deduced the moral and proper behavior by himself. I have argued in my analysis of this tale that the use of *exempla* is in fact a strategy to create an illusion of independent learning, with the final outcome predetermined by the master rhetorician. In P the passage reads as follows (again, I have translated the corrected version in English with italics, and marked the deletions and interlinear emendations of the Spanish text with parenthesis and square brackets):

> E vós conde señor pues criades este moço et querrades que se enderesçase su fazienda (catad) [buscad] alguna manera que por enxenplos o por palabras (maestradas) [de doctrina] et falagueras le faga(des)[ys] entender su fazienda, mas en (guisa) [manera] ninguna non derronpa(des)[ys] contra el, castigándolo nin mal trayéndolo cuydándolo enderesçar. Ca la manera de los más moços es aborresçer luego al que los castiga, mayor mente si (algo) [tienen algún poder] (que an en poder) (ca liévalo) [por que lo toma] a manera de menos preçio non entendiendo commo lo yerra, ca non ay tan bien amigo commo el que castiga el moço por que non faga su daño; mas ellos non lo toman así si non por la peor manera (fol. 22ᵛ, And you, sir count, since you are raising this boy and you want him to direct his affairs properly, find a way, either with *exempla* or with cunning and pleasing words, to make him understand his duties. *And you, sir count, since you are raising this boy and you want him to direct his affairs properly, find a way, either with* exempla *or with words of doctrine, to make him understand his duties.* But the way of boys is to hate the one who tries to instruct them, especially if they have some authority, and they find it humiliating, not knowing how mistaken they are. For there is no better friend than the one who tries to teach a boy how not to harm himself, but they do not see this, and they take it in the worst way).

Aside from Patronio's amusing sensitivity and understanding of the special challenges a proud youth can pose for any parent or teacher, it is the correction of "maestradas" that stands out among the other scribal alterations of the text seen in the Spanish transcription. Here a later second scribe has crossed out the word "maestradas" and written above them "de doctrina," so that the corrected version would read: "buscad alguna manera que por enxenplos o por palabras de doctrina et falagueras le fagays entender

MS P (Real Academia Española 15), folio 22 verso, showing scribal deletion of "maestradas" with interlinear emendation "de doctrina" on column B, line nine.

su fazienda." Obviously, "pleasing words of doctrine" does not convey the same message as "palabras maestradas y falagueras," nor does it follow the spirit of Patronio's advice, since to impose doctrine on the youth, which is what the philosopher in the story tries first, would certainly not make the boy feel as though he had discovered the lessons himself. On the contrary, the scribe's implied pedagogical method would certainly be received "por la peor manera" ("in the worst way").

Doctrina–this is what the reader expects to find in P, and since Patronio's advice does not exactly meet those expectations, the text is brought into line with them. Returning to the *Libro de los engaños* for a point of comparison, the scribe / corrector's religious attitude and doctrinal criteria can also be detected in the correction made in "there is nothing better than prophecy for winning salvation," changed to "there is nothing better than good works and wisdom." The alteration may seem insignificant if studied in isolation, but in comparison with the other corrections made throughout P, and particularly in *exemplo* 21, the scribal version is another patent example of reshaping and sharpening a vague, possibly problematic message into a more explicit teaching on the Christian virtue of charity. In a manner of speaking, doctrine is also what many modern readers have come to expect from the *CL*, as María Rosa Menocal acknowledges when she states that the conventional understanding of the *CL* has always been that it is "openly and positively and unambiguously didactic" (475). The folio cited above contains the evidence of this orthodox ideological reading in its earliest medieval manifestation.

No matter how one wishes to define "palabras de doctrina" on this folio, there can be no doubt that it represents a radical departure from "palabras maestradas," especially when Juan Manuel's other uses of this adjective are recalled. The *Libro de los estados* provides an excellent example when the young prince warns his trusted teacher, Turín, not to deceive him:

> Et bien cred que si me dizides otras palabras o razones encubiertas, que vos las entendré et avré de vos querella, ca si el amo [o el] servidor o el consegero del señor [es] entendido et dize palabras encubiertas o maestradas por encobrir la verdat, razón es que tarde o aína non se falle ende bien (82, And you can be sure that if you tell me any more tricky words or arguments, I will

catch you and I will have reason to quarrel with you, because if the master or the servant or the adviser of the lord is understood and uses cunning or deceitful words in order to cover up the truth, it is certain that sooner or later he will not be well).

"Palabras maestradas" is obviously associated with trickery and lying, and this could never be harmonized with the organizing parameters of the compilation that contain this tale, nor its ideological reading.[9] As part of the production of a compilation, such tensions and contradictions are not just glossed over, they are scratched out and corrected by professional readers and writers. An initial reading begins with the inscription of individual texts into a larger framework that imposes its own interpretation and agenda upon them, and a subsequent level of reading and writing takes place in the unique scribal practices witnessed throughout the book that register their response in accretions, deletions and interlinear emendations.

Having examined P from the general layout and the notion of *compilatio* at work behind it, moving from the outside in to the other works compiled within it, and finally to the idiosyncrasies of the *CL*, a number of conclusions can be deduced about how P was used by its late-medieval readers, about what kind of book it is, and how the *CL* was read and written into it. Some of these conclusions have been alluded to already, and still there are other general observations that should be noted.

Among these conclusions, one of José Amador de los Ríos's comments regarding the *CL* is worth recalling; the manuscript evidence in this codex, along with two other manuscript witnesses (H and M), suggests that in the late Middle Ages readers were most probably familiar with just the first part of the *CL* (3: 397).[10] This observation supports the hypothesis put forth here that Juan Manuel's late-medieval readers ignored any thematic, artistic, or ideological unity in the *CL* that many modern critics have painstakingly analyzed in the five-part book (for example, the triumph of

---

[9] As noted above here, as well as in chapter 1, Juan Manuel uses similar language, "palabras encubiertas o maestradas," in the *Libro de los estados* to mean lying and deceitful words. Likewise, in the prologue to the *Libro del caballero Zifar*, the narrator warns princes to be on guard against deceit in the form of "maestrías" and "sotilezas de engaño" (61).

[10] Only the manuscripts S and G contain all five parts of the *CL*.

the spiritual over the temporal, or any of the possible solutions to the entire God / World dichotomy). I believe, furthermore, that the medieval reading practices in P corroborate the notion that the *CL* is a text with more than one possible interpretation and use. By employing Juan Manuel's tales as *exempla*, these early readers either took the meta-rhetorical lesson on the relativity of narrative from the texts, or they found confirmation of their knowledge of the *exemplum* on display. Either way the medieval audience of the *CL* as it can be sketched from P, including those who manufactured it, read this lesson of the *exemplum* right, witnessed in their appropriation of Juan Manuel's tales for use in a new literary and ideological context that is P itself, not to mention all the virtual uses of the *exempla* in sermons, lessons and debates for which this anthology appears to have been prepared.

It is also clear that this book is not a mere miscellany. As Siegfried Wenzel reminds his readers, "miscellany" is often far too vague, even misleading, when classifying these kinds of medieval books that do indeed have their own agendas and organizing principles (3). Manuscript P is a book with a specific purpose as a reference tool for orthodox instruction dealing with both secular and religious subject-matter, with an emphasis on Church doctrine, faith, prayer, and obedience to dogmatic answers to potentially dangerous questions. P was most probably manufactured for a priest, teacher, or both, to refer to for uncomplicated solutions to common questions such as those found in the *Lucidario*, and as a bank of *exempla* to be employed rhetorically in a lesson or sermon.[11] These physical (i.e. the book) and virtual (sermons, lessons, etc.) contexts in which the *CL* was read betray the beginnings of a history of reception that consolidates one kind of reading, while suppressing others, essentially establishing the meaning of the text as "doctrine," void of complexity, contradiction, ambiguity or ambivalence.

Looking at the *CL* as it appears in this codex, one finds further evidence of this scholastic reading process, and the ideological assumptions made about the tales themselves. Disregard for authorial intention is patent in the apocryphal stories, and their presence cor-

---

[11] With the *CL* included as a bank of useful illustrative tales, P is a clear example of Fredrick Tubach's definition of one of the most common types of medieval collection of *exempla*, "serving as source material to the medieval preacher, but which are in fact independent tale collections separable from sermon use" (520).

roborates the idea that the *CL* was scanned by its readers for *exempla* that met their own rhetorical needs, rather than read as a univocal work of didactic literature with a central lesson or moral. While erasing Juan Manuel's exclusive authorship, these extra anecdotes, as well as the entire book that contains them, tell the modern reader that Patronio's stories were viewed as unambiguous, orthodox material sanctioned for pedagogical use. The additional allegorical interpretation of *exemplo* 48 also corroborates this argument, while aligning the *CL* with the other religious themes and exegetical practices that bind P together.

The last point brings to the surface one of the most challenging, perhaps even troubling, conclusions of this book regarding the reception of the *CL*. While it is certain that Juan Manuel's tales were considered ideologically correct, from a Christian / Catholic point of view, at times Juan Manuel's tales did not live up to those expectations and needed to be corrected, witnessed in the case of *capítulo* 21. The reader's assumptions seem to be that this collection of tales should not present any kind of ideological ambiguity or aporia, and it is not unreasonable to hypothesize that a continuum exists in the history of the reception of the *CL*, beginning with these medieval expectations and ending with the canonical understanding of Patronio's doctrine that has lasted at least until the twentieth century. What the physical evidence in P demonstrates is that this conventional reception of Juan Manuel's most famous work is as much the product of a reading and re-writing process, as it is the result of a masterfully written literary work of art. Manuscript P, I would conclude, presents the most robust evidence of reading the *CL* ideologically as "doctrine," and in the light of this evidence, some of the traces of reading in manuscripts H, G and S can be explained as part of this same interpretive tradition that fixed the meaning of the *CL*.

H was a well-used book, and before entering into a brief review of some of its most significant readings and rewritings of the *CL*, a simple perusal of this fifteenth-century manuscript shows that it was studied and mined for sentential wisdom and sound advice, witnessed in the many marginal keys and underlined text written by an early-modern reader. The margins were also used to practice calligraphy, and for doodling. One drawing sketched on several folios of a man with his tongue sticking out taunts the modern scholar, and tempts us to speculate about this particular reader's age and attitude toward the book. Was it a bored student's textbook? Or was the reader just a frustrated artist who made use of the source of paper at hand? It is impossible to know for certain, but together with the other marginal keys that appear to be of the same ink as the doodles, it appears that this book was studied more than consumed for its entertaining short stories to pass the time. The flyleaf also suggests that the *CL* as it appears in this book was viewed as an orthodox source of aphorisms and wisdom literature.

Written in the same hand with the same black and red ink as in the rest of the manuscript text, the flyleaf shows two more proverbs, authorized by an allusion to Scripture: "E por eso dize bien el proverbio que al auariento nunca le fallesçerá causa para negar" ("And therefore the proverb is true that says that a greedy man will always have a cause to deny"). This is followed by another scribal proverb written in red ink: "Aun non eres bien auenturado sy el pueblo non ha burlado de ty. Otro dize el evangelio" ("You are still not blessed if the people have not ridiculed you. Another according to Gospel"). The copy appears interrupted, but the general content is clear. The scribe has associated the text with additional sentential sayings, both popular and biblical, demonstrating an attitude toward the text that anticipated orthodox sources of practical and unambiguous doctrine, rather than entertaining short stories. These aphorisms suggest that manuscript H was read as a source of wisdom, and the association with other proverbs–a transtextual element that is found in other manuscripts of the *CL*–demonstrates that for this reader / writer, the material of the *CL* belongs to a family of doctrinal literary material created to be employed as such in different contexts.[12]

The intertextual link with additional proverbs may also tell us that the *CL* was viewed as a kind of wisdom book that invited the reader to create new lists of maxims, following Barry Taylor's argument in "Old Spanish Wisdom Texts," in which he states that "in practice the purpose [wisdom books] most commonly served was

---

[12] For the adjective "transtextual" I borrow from Gérard Genette's *Palimpsests*, in which "transtextuality" is described as a general concept of "all that sets the text in relationship, whether obvious or concealed, with other texts" (1). Here in M, the category of transtextuality that is most striking, as in manuscript P and the other manuscripts to be examined further on, is intertextuality, which, according to Genette, involves "the actual presence of one text within another," including quotation, plagiarism and the "less literal guise" of intertextuality, allusion (1-2).

to spawn other wisdom books" (78). Technically, Part I of the *CL* does not meet Taylor's definition of wisdom literature as collections of "brief sentences arranged paratactically" (71), but there is a strong connection made in H that links Juan Manuel's narratives with proverbial sayings in general, and it may be that the practice of freely associating Juan Manuel's maxims with others that came to the mind of his readers "spawned" new *sententiae*, some of which may have even made their way into one of Juan Manuel's stories.

Exemplo 13, "De lo que contesçió a un omne que tomava perdizes" ("What Happened to a Man Who Was Hunting Partridges"), as it appears in H and two other manuscripts–M and G–has another version of Juan Manuel's concluding couplet attributed to an unidentified "Suer Alfonso," of the Order of Santiago. Reinaldo Ayerbe-Chaux saw fit to include Suer Alfonso's verse in his edition of the *CL*, making *exemplo* 13 the only other tale, along with *exemplo* 1, to have two concluding maxims. Citing Ayerbe-Chaux's edition, Juan Manuel's *viessos* for this tale read, "Quien te mal faz mostrando grand pesar, / guisa cómmo te puedas dél guardar" (159, "From one who hurts you 'gainst his will, / Guard yourself with utmost skill" [76]), followed by the mysterious Suer Alfonso's *verso*: "Et sobre esta rrazón fizo otro verso Suer Alfonso, frayle de Sanctiago, que dize assí: Non pares mientes a ojos que lloran / mas a manos que laboran" (159-160, "And on this saying Suer Alfonso, friar of Santiago, wrote another verse as follows: Do not pay attention to eyes that cry, / rather, watch the hands at work").

Alberto Blecua is uncertain as to whether this *verso* is apocryphal or not (36), but regardless of its authorship, it is another indication that the tales and aphorisms in the *CL* lead its medieval and early modern readers (possibly even Juan Manuel himself) to gloss the texts at hand with allusions to other authorized sources of wisdom in the form of *refranes*, maxims, and proverbs.[13] In another early modern manuscript witness of the *CL* that I have studied elsewhere, the scribe chose to copy only the concluding *proverbios* in each tale, since, according to the scribe's own explanation, the proverbs were for all intents and purposes the condensed version of the entire tale and moral, so copying the narratives themselves was

---

[13] Of the most contemporary editions of the *CL* cited here, Ayerbe-Chaux is the only editor to include Suer Alfonso's maxim; Guillermo Serés, José Blecua, John Keller and L. Clark Keating do not.

not necessary. Furthermore, the scribe added a few more "modern" versions that came to mind while copying the *CL*.[14] All these glosses, allusions, and rewritings of the *CL* that associate the text with sentential sayings seem to suggest that the earliest reception of Juan Manuel's work overlooked its narrative entertainment value, and stabilized its meaning as terse and authoritative moral doctrine of the sort associated with wisdom literature. Some of the marginal notes indicate that not only were Juan Manuel's tales re-appropriated by an orthodox reader / scribe who aligned the text with wisdom literature and Scripture, but that Juan Manuel's method of exemplification was not lost either, perhaps confirming a reception that placed Patronio's tales within the larger tradition of the *exemplum*.

Much of the marginalia in H that highlights different passages with keys, underlined text, and pointing fingers mark exemplary characteristics of nobleman, possibly betraying the reader's aristocratic proclivities, typical of the fifteenth-century Castilian obsession with nobility that will be studied further in manuscript M. For instance, on folio 43 verso the reader has marked a passage in the story "What Happened to the King Who Wanted to Test His Three Sons," that describes the youngest prince's respect for and desire to serve his father. The highlighted manuscript text reads as follows:

> E non quiso que otro cauallero lo vistiese nin lo calçase sy non él et dando a entender que se tenía por de buenaventura que sy el rrey su padre tomase plazer o seruiçio de lo que pudiese fazer. E que pues su padre era que rrazón et guisado era de fazer quantos seruiçios et humildades pudiese (And he did not permit any chamberlain to dress him or help him or help with his shoes, for he expressed the idea that he would consider himself fortunate if the king his father should take pleasure in his efforts; and since he was his father, it was right and intelligent to do for him as much service and kindness as he could [102]).[15]

---

[14] The manuscript is Madrid, Biblioteca Nacional 19426, which I study in greater detail in "Reading to Pieces: *Divisio Textus* and the Structure of *El Conde Lucanor*."

[15] Transcriptions of the manuscript text are my own. As in the first part of this book, whenever possible English translations of the *CL* (Part I) will be taken from Keller and Keating's translation, while other Spanish quotations are from José Blecua's edition. Although there are slight differences in Keller and Keating's English edition when compared with manuscript H, their translation is accurate enough to grasp the content of the marked passage.

Pointing to another exemplary model of chivalry, on folio 46 verso, in the tale "What Happened to the Count of Provence and How He Was Freed from Prison by the Advice of Saladin," the reader underlined one of the concluding passages that celebrates the Count of Provence's son-in-law for his bravery, loyalty, and trustworthiness, as well as Saladin's notorious noble generosity. Another instance of marked interest in exemplary noblemen is found on folio 54 recto where the reader jotted a note summarizing a reference to "Don Alvar Fernandes," from the second *exemplum* in "What Happened to an Emperor and to Don Alvarfáñez Minaya and Their Wives." Here the reader marks the beginning of the second tale by underlining the text "Don Aluar Fernandes era *muy buen omne et muy onrado* et pobló a Yscar" ("Don Alvarfáñez was a fine man and an honorable man who settled down at Yxcar"). The marginal note simply reads "don alvar ferna[ndez] [po]bló yscar."[16]

Not all of the reader's notes point out cases of exemplary men, but most all do mark the advice and comments made by Patronio, even though there is a trace of the reader's sense of humor left behind in some of the keys that show an appreciation for Juan Manuel's better jokes. The reader did not miss Patronio's "serious" lesson in "What Happened to a Young Man Who Married a Strong and Ill-tempered Woman"; on folio 72 recto there is a key indexing the text that concludes Patronio's advice: "E aun conséjovos que con todos los omnes que ovierdes a fazer que sienpre les dedes a entender en qué manera han de pasar conbusco" ("And I advise you in all your dealings with others, always to let them know what you expect of them" [141]). At the same time, and on the same folio, the reader marked another key to highlight Juan Manuel's humor in the passage where the father-in-law attempts to make his wife behave, just as his son-in-law did with his stubborn daughter by killing one of his roosters, but to no avail since his wife knew him all too well: "E díxole su muger, 'A la fe don fulano, tarde vos acordastes que ya non vos valdrá nada aun que matasedes a [çi]ent gallos, que ya bien vos conóscemos'" ("But his wife said: 'Well now, Mr. So-and-So, you are a little late. It wouldn't matter to me now if you killed even a hundred [roosters, for now we know you]'" [140]).[17]

---

[16] Parts of the note have been trimmed from rebinding, but it is still clearly legible.

[17] I have slightly altered Keller and Keating's translation to better match the text as it reads in manuscript H.

THE IDEOLOGICAL READING OF *EL CONDE LUCANOR* 149

Folio 92 verso of MS H (Real Academia de la Historia 9-5893). This same doodle reappears on several manuscript pages.

One of the largest marginal keys and highlightings of text appears on folio 38 verso, which reproduces the conclusion to *exemplo* 21, "What Happened to a Young King and a Philosopher to Whom His Father Commended Him," studied in detail in chapter 2. There are, in fact, two marks and an underlined text on this folio; one mark is a rounded brace-like key, similar to most of the other keys throughout the book, but with a large loop added like a tail with a small circle inside it, forming the shape of an eye. The other mark is a smaller pointing finger which actually connects with the line that underscores the passage dealing with "the ways of boys." All together, the marginalia notes the passage on "palabras maestradas et falagueras" ("well-chosen words and flattery" [94]), but the reader seems to have been particularly interested in the nature of young aristocratic pupils. The following is a line-by-line transcription of the noted and underlined text, beginning on line four, just above the first key (the brace stands for the reader's key with eye-like flourish, and the arrow for the pointing finger that also underlines the text):

> que por enxienplos et por palabras maestradas et fa
> { lagueras le fagades entender su fazienda, mas por co
> { sas del mundo non derraguedes con él castigándolo ni
> { mal trayéndolo cuydándolo endereçar. [C]a[18] la mane
> { ra de los moços es tal que luego aborresçen al que los cas
> tiga. Et mayormente sy es omne de grant guisa, ca
> → *liéuanlo a manera de menospreçio non entendiendo*
> quanto lo yerran. (fol. 38ᵛ, either by examples or by well-chosen words and flattery to make him understand his situation. But by no means upset him with punishment or ill treatment, thinking thus to straighten him out, for it is the way of most boys to detest the one who punishes them, especially if he is a man of importance, for they regard it as a kind of scorn, not realizing how wrong they are [94]).

I find these notes particularly interesting in comparison with the other texts set off by the reader because they point to Juan

---

[18] Aside from adding accent marks, expanding abbreviations and adding minimum punctuation, I have not altered the manuscript text here, with one exception. The manuscript clearly reads, "*E*a la manera [my emphasis]" etc., not "Ca la manera," as I have transcribed it. I believe this is one of many scribal errors in H, and since "Ea" makes no sense, I have borrowed the "Ca" reading from Blecua's edition, as it also appears in Serés and Ayerbe-Chaux's editions.

Manuel's most explicit meta-rhetorical lesson concerning the *exemplum* in the *CL*. This marginalia indicates that the reader was especially interested in the use of "enxienplos" and "palabras maestradas" to instruct or coerce, which leads one to imagine that the reader was also acutely aware of the rhetorical potential of the book of *exempla* in hand. But the underlined text, as well as the passage set off by the marginal brace also offer a glimpse into the reader's reaction to, and perhaps even identification with, the student / teacher relationship. Was the reader identifying with the offended youth? Or was this a teacher's mark made to note a familiar experience, trick of the trade, or a universal pedagogical truth that all educators must learn? The last line pointed out with a finger and underlined, seems to emphasize the disapproval teachers (and parents?) have with young, haughty students who do not understand that their instructors always have their best interests at heart.

A survey of the reader's notes hints at both the social class and perhaps even profession of an audience that viewed the *CL* as primarily a bank of sentential wisdom and models of exemplary aristocratic behavior—it may even tell us that Juan Manuel's rhetorical strategy was recognized by his readers—but the notes do not determine the meaning of the text, at least not by physically rewriting the *CL*. Nevertheless, they do suggest that an audience, meaning, and use for the work had already been established.[19]

Most of the scribal corrections made in H have been documented by Alberto Blecua, who also comments on the decidedly antiwar attitude of the scribe who amended the text (95). Two of the most significant scribal readings and corrections made to the *CL* in H are found in *exemplos* 5 and 33, but overall Blecua concludes that all the corrections in H studied together demonstrate that the scribe altered the text according to moral and religious criteria (94). The ideological adjustment made to *exemplo* 33 that Blecua cites in its entirety is particularly important for my argument here because it is yet another case of shaping the ideology, even the religious significance of the *CL*, similar to the ideological reading and rewriting of Patronio's doctrine seen in manuscript P.

---

[19] My study of the audience in H here will contribute to my conclusions in the following chapter where I take up the subject again in manuscript M, but H also reveals the same kind of scribal authorship found in P that rewrote the *CL*, adjusting its meaning to fit the religious and moral expectations of the scribe.

MS H (Real Academia de la Historia 9-5893), folio 38 verso, with marginal key and pointing finger.

THE IDEOLOGICAL READING OF *EL CONDE LUCANOR* 153

Here the scribe of H eliminates Patronio's reference to *exemplo* 3 and King Richard's famous leap, along with the Holy War ideology of the *Reconquista* associated with *exemplo* 3, rewriting Patronio's final advice to focus on good works, the avoidance of sin, and faith in God's mercy for all men of every estate. The adjustment is cleverly worked into Juan Manuel's tale. The scribe did not change the entire conclusion of *exemplo* 33, and the beginning of Patronio's advice marked, as usual, with "And you, Count Lucanor," is present is H, along with the comments on service to God through war against the Moors: "non le podedes tanto seruir commo en aver guerra con los moros por ensalçar la santa fe católica et verdadera" (fol. 68r, "you cannot do [God] more service, enhancing the true Catholic faith, than by waging war against the Moors"). In an apparent effort to make a more seamless transition to a different moral, the scribe adjusts Patronio's last words to move the message away from war, aligning the lesson of the story with patient acceptance of one's *estado*, and faith in God's justice. The final advice does not exactly contradict Juan Manuel's message, but it does significantly blunt the crusader spirit of the original tale.

I have studied the conclusion to "What Happened to Don Juan Manuel's Saker Falcon and an Eagle and a Heron" in chapter 3, pointing out the place of the doctrine of martyrdom in the Christian crusade against the Moors; the following is the conclusion to *exemplo* 33 as it appears in H,[20] which radically reorients the ideological meaning of the tale:

> E pues a los señores es muy bueno et prouechoso, [here begins the scribal correction] a los otros omnes de buena guisa, cada uno en su estado, et non estar de vagar quanto pudiere et buscar en esto de que biua honestamente et a su honrra, guardándose de fazer et dezir cosas que non estén bien a Dios et al mundo, ca la pereza et grant folgura nunca fizo buen fecho. E aunque algunas cosas non vos sean asý como vós quisierdes, luego sed çierto que sy vós o otro que buscare otra baraja en este mundo, por bien beuir, guardando seruiçio et dios et bondad, que a la lengua Dios nuestro señor le dará gualardón et bueno (fols. 68r-68v, And since a cause is good and advantageous for noble lords, so too for men of good manners, each in their estate, not shirking their

---

[20] In H it is marked *Exemplo* XXX, but for the sake of clarity I will use the standardized numbering found in most every modern edition.

duty as much as possible, seeking to live honestly and with their honor, taking care not to do or say anything that is not good in the eyes of God and the world, because laziness and idle pleasures never did a good deed. And even though things may not turn out as you want, nevertheless be sure that if you or anyone else who searches for another hand in this life, by living properly, keeping safe one's service and God and goodness, by the word God our Lord will give him a good blessing).

The scribal version of Patronio's advice is striking for its ideological realignment, but it is also important to note that, although it is somewhat of an abrupt change in tone, an effort was made to weave in the new *consejo* without drawing attention to the scribe's authorship. The point in the text chosen for introducing the correction makes a good transition, since Patronio's comments deal with the topic of work, or a cause, or one's *mester*, and the scribe was able to use Juan Manuel's text to move further into the subject of work, then living according to one's estate and honor, and finally winning God's blessing through faith and righteousness, rather than martyrdom on the battlefield against the Moors. Aside for the scribe's artistry seen in this transition, the rewriting is also a convincing recasting of one of Juan Manuel's favorite themes; namely, that all men can win salvation within their own estate. Clearly, an effort was made to imitate Juan Manuel's style by picking out a familiar thematic thread in this tale, and aligning it with the more passively faithful approach to winning salvation and honor studied in chapter 1 in tales such as *exemplo* 26, "What Happened to the Tree of Lies."

Exemplo 5 is also noted by Alberto Blecua for its scribal addition (93-94). According to Blecua, when faced with a missing page, the scribe saw fit to finish an incomplete tale (93), but what is most interesting about the scribal addition is that it follows Juan Manuel's framing dialogue and formulaic divisions. Toward the end of "What Happened to a Fox and a Crow Who Had a Piece of Cheese in His Beak," the scribe did not forget to use Juan Manuel's transitional phrase to write Patronio's advice: "*E vos, señor conde,* sabed quel omne que tanto vos alaba sed çierto que vos quiere enganar e levar de vos alguna cosa [my emphasis]" (fol. 16ᵛ, "And you, Sir Count, know that the man who praises you so much wishes to deceive you and take something of yours").

Nor did the scribe leave off the Count's praise for Patronio's lesson and Juan Manuel's anticipated appearance, complete with *viessos*:

> E el conde touo este por buen consejo, et fízolo et guardóse ende bien. E quando don Iohan falló este enxenplo, fízolo poner en este libro, et puso estos versos que dizen asý: El que te alaba más de quanto en ti ouiere, sábete dél guardar ca enganar te quiere (fol. 16ᵛ, And the Count found this to be good advice, and he followed it and profited from it. And when Don Juan found this *exemplum*, he had it written it this book, and he wrote these following verses: From he who praises you for more than you have, know how to protect yourself for he wants to trick you).

Again, as in *exemplo* 33, the scribe demonstrates a great deal of narrative creativity, and an ability to disguise his work in Juan Manuel's style. This is an important observation, as Alberto Blecua also intimates, when studying other manuscript variants and even entire narratives that have conventionally been attributed to what Blecua calls "double compositions" of the author: "puede servir para ser muy cautos a la hora de hablar de dobles redacciones de autor" (94). Scribal authorship appears to have been a very common practice with the *CL* texts as they are found in H and P, and Blecua's warning seems to refer specifically to *exemplo* 51 of manuscript S, which I will look at briefly in the conclusion of this chapter, but a fascinating scribal addition found in manuscript G is worth noting here as yet another possible example of the ideological reading and rewriting of the *CL* from the late medieval to the early modern era.

The addition is found in the only other manuscript copy of Part V. Manuscript G reproduces a five-part, sixteenth century humanist copy of the *CL* that Alberto Blecua believes shared a common stemmatic sub-archetype with Argote de Molina's print edition (Blecua names this lost source β [78, 81]), but it is also a unique version of the five-part *CL*, distinct from the only other complete copy of it found in manuscript S. Few scholars have paid more than superficial critical attention to the meaning of another thirteenth-century Castilian didactic work, *Flores de filosofía*, as it is interpolated in G for the conclusion to Part V of the *CL*.[21]

---

[21] See appendix III for my transcription of this fragment of *Flores de filosofía*.

José Manuel Lucía Megías, Hugo Oscar Bizzarri, and Bary Taylor have all described the various manuscript witnesses of *Flores de Filosofía* in its two versions, generally referred to as the Longer and Shorter.[22] All together there are seven complete manuscript witnesses of *Flores*, and four fragments, one of which is found in manuscript G of the *CL*.[23] An important point to make about the fragment of *Flores* as it appears in G is that it was most certainly copied from a different source exemplar, or sources, than the one used for the *CL*, since the interpolated texts in G stem from sources represented by two different manuscript witnesses; namely Madrid, Biblioteca Nacional 9428 and Madrid, Biblioteca del Monasterio de El Escorial &-II-8 (Bizzarri, 48). Pascual Gayangos–from whom the manuscript derives its initial–also notes the fragment in his edition of the *CL* published for *Biblioteca de autores españoles*, transcribing it from what was at the time his private manuscript copy, although he did not acknowledge *Flores de filosofía* as its source (433-435).

Flores de filosofía is one of the oldest works of wisdom literature written in the Castilian language, as Hermann Knust pointed out in his 1878 edition (3), and Fernando Gómez Redondo speaks of it as the key piece of didactic literature that allows us to understand the thematic relationships among a number of medieval works which share much of their content with *Flores*, such as the *Bocados de oro*, *Libro de los cien capítulos*, *Libro de los treinta y cuatro sabios*, and the *Castigos del rey de Mentón* found in *El libro del caballero Zifar* (1: 260).[24] Hugo Bizzarri also defends *Flores* as an important work, not only for its survival in numerous manuscript witnesses, but also for its wide dissemination and adaptation in different didactic treatises (45), and as Gómez Redondo reminds his readers, in each of these different works, the text takes on a discrete meaning (1: 260). Yet few have taken an interest in the meaning of *Flores de filosofía* in the *CL*.

The fragments of *Flores* in G are made up of seven chapters, or *leyes* as they are found in Madrid, Escorial &-II-8, and one *capítulo*

---

[22] The Shorter has 35 chapters, or *leyes*, found in three manuscripts: (1) Madrid, Biblioteca del Monasterio de El Escorial h-III-1; (2) Madrid, Biblioteca Nacional 9428; and (3) New York, Hispanic Society of New York, HC371/217). The Longer version is found in two manuscripts from the Biblioteca del Monasterio de El Escorial: &-II-8 and X-II-12.

[23] See Lucía Megías for a concise list of these manuscript witnesses (151).

[24] See Barry Taylor's "Old Spanish Wisdom Texts: Some Relationships," for an excellent study of the connections among these works.

in Madrid, Biblioteca Nacional 9428. Comparing the *CL* as it appears in G with these other codices, the fragments begin with the second half of *ley* V, which deals with the subject of obedience to the king. The proceeding texts from *Flores* found in G (which correspond to *leyes* VI-XI following manuscript &-II-8), take up the following subject matter: the king as source and champion of justice (*ley* VI), advice for those who live with and counsel the king (*ley* VII), the king as leader and advocate of his people (*ley* VIII), the proper and efficient governance of the kingdom, which involves access to wise and loyal advisers (*ley* IX), the virtue of bravery and strength *versus* cowardice (*ley* X), and the mutability of history and the world, including the beautiful simile of life as a book (*ley* XI). The *CL* as it appears in G then concludes with a fragment also found in manuscript 9428 (*capítulo* 8), which deals with the benefits of education and catechism, especially for the young. As seen in appendix III, "quien castiga a su fijo quando es pequenio, fuelga con él quando es grande" ("he who teaches his son well when he is young, takes pleasure in his company when he is grown").

The fragments of *Flores* copied into G for the conclusion of its five-part version of the *CL* have patent thematic resonances with the Count's questions for Patronio in Part I. In addition to the obedience due to a virtuous prince, Part V in G concludes with the themes of good counsel, the cautious judgment of character, especially of those who would advise a prince, the honor gained through steadfast loyalty and strength, and the need of sound learning, advice and faith to perform works of charity. These texts appear to have been deliberately selected to conclude the *CL* along thematic and ideological lines, but it is impossible to determine if the exemplar used to copy the *CL* up to the interpolated texts contained a version of Part V like the one found in S, for example, or some other variant. It may be that the scribe's copy of the *CL* was incomplete, damaged, or illegible; nevertheless, the texts chosen to conclude the *CL* do not appear to have been selected at random, since they contain far too many "intermittent reminders" of the *CL*, Part I. There is another tell-tale trace of the scribe's introduction of new material into Juan Manuel's work that I believe demonstrates an ideological reading of the text, as well as an intention to rewrite the meaning of the *CL* in G.

Reinaldo Ayerbe-Chaux notes in his edition of the *CL* the precise point where the fragments of *Flores* were inserted into G, pointing out that no title or other paratexual information is provided to explain or mark the inserted texts (22); no further discussion of the variant is offered. The selected texts are added on seamlessly, as an authentic conclusion to this version of the *CL*, and in order to recast an original *CL* text, the scribe had to invent a transition to introduce the new material.

Part V of the *CL*, as most modern readers know it, based on manuscript S, ends in G on folio 122 verso. In editions based on S, Patronio concludes a discussion of the Sacraments by stating that, if he were pressed, he could prove that each is true and divinely ordained, just as the Sacrament of Baptism (a sacrament he defines and defends in greater detail than the other six):

> [B]ien vos diría tantas et tan buenas razones en cada uno dellos, que vós entendríades que eran assaz; mas déxolo por dos cosas: la una, por non alongar mucho el libro; et lo al, porque sé que vós et quien quier que esto oya, entendrá que tan con razón se prueva lo al commo esto (308, Indeed I could tell you as many arguments, and just as good, for each one of them, so that you would see that they were enough; but I will leave them for two reasons: one, so as to not drag on this book too long, and the other, because I know that you, and whoever hears this, will understand that the other [sacraments] are proved with the same reason as this one).

The scribe of manuscript G chose this point to move into a new set of texts, with a distinctly different ideological orientation:

> [V]ien vos dezía tantas e tan buenas razones en cada uno dellos que vos entenderedes que son asaz, mas déxolo por dos cosas: la una por no alongar mucho el libro, e lo al por que sé que vos e quien quier que esto oya *entre mala sospecha*, ca la obediencia es guarda de quien la quiere e castillo de quien la sygue [my emphasis] (fol. 123ʳ, Indeed I could tell you as many arguments, and just as good, for each one of them, so that you would see that they were enough; but I will leave them for two reasons: one, so as to not drag on this book too long, and the other, because I know that *an evil suspicion* may enter into you, or whoever hears this, therefore obedience is a guardian of whomever wants it and a castle for whomever follows it).

The *CL*, as it is known today from manuscript S, ends in G with "quien quier que esto oya" ("whoever hears this"). What follows is the scribes original, three-word transition–"entre mala sospecha" ("an evil suspicion may enter")–into the second half of *ley* V of *Flores*, which begins with "ca la obediencia es guarda de quien la quiere" ("obedience is a guardian of whomever wants it"). The shift is a radical departure from Juan Manuel's optimistic confidence in the faith of his listeners (perhaps it is an indication of a nervous, sixteenth-century Catholic attitude toward faith that was more acutely aware of dissent?). It is not impossible that the scribe was filling in a missing conclusion, but when one looks at the other cases of scribal authorship in the *CL* manuscripts, and the fact that the first interpolated text appears to have been selected from an entire "*ley*,"[25] it is not at all unimaginable that the presence of these texts from *Flores de filosofía* represent a scribal emendation; an ideological reading and reshaping of the *CL* that aligns the meaning of the work with the more practical political philosophy of the first part. If this is the case, then it may also be a suppression of the author's original text that is now missing in G.

The new material is copied into the text at a point of transition where the author moves into the potentially paradoxical subject matter of intentions and good works studied in chapter 3, and particularly in the *exemplum* of the loyal knight whose crimes of patricide and regicide are judged as virtues.[26] Given the catechetical, even theological tone of the rest of the subject matter in Part V as it appears in S, addressing topics such as God's creation of man as both a perfect and imperfect being, man's free will and reason, and a long list of natural imperfections found in God's greatest creation (i.e. man), it is all the more plausible that the *Flores* texts were selected and inserted to correct the meaning of the *CL*, inspired by a fear of heterodoxy, rather than an accidental contamination. The conclusion of the *CL* in G successfully cuts off access to Juan Manuel's meta-rhetorical lessons available to the reader of Part V in

---

[25] *Ley* V of *Flores*, "Cómmo los omnes deben ser leales e obedientes al rey" ("How man should be loyal and obedient to his king"), according to Knust's edition begins: "Sabed que obediencia es que [amades á vuestro] rey de coraçon e de voluntad" (22, "Know that obedience is that you should love your king with all your heart and mind"). There are no blank spaces in the manuscript text that would indicate a lacuna, or illegible text; rather, the scribe appears to have chosen a place in the *Flores* text, half way through the *ley*, that would make the best transition to a new subject, working off of Patronio's statement.

[26] It is also tempting to see a borrowing from the first suppressed word of the *CL* text represented in S: "entendrá" is changed to "entre."

MS G (Biblioteca Nacional 18415), folio 123 recto. Here the scribe introduces selections from *Flores de filosofía*, beginning on line three with "que esto oya". Also note the tachygraphic note for *est* to mark the beginning of a new section.

S, and by erasing the concluding paradoxical dilemma faced by those who would follow the paths of God and the World,[27] G establishes a more closed, orthodox and unequivocal meaning for the *CL* based on the unimpeachable doctrine and authority of a time-honored work of Castilian wisdom literature.

Thus far the evidence of reading in manuscripts P, H and G demonstrates that the reception of the *CL* in the late medieval and early modern era involved reshaping Juan Manuel's work, aligning it with ideological expectations and even pedagogical uses. The incorporation of the *CL* into anthologies of various works, as seen in P, is one of the most patent examples of reshaping the *CL*, and fixing its meaning through association with a discrete literary context invented in the mind of a compiler. Making these hand-made books also involved rewriting the tales themselves, and the various scribes of P, H and G display a surprising degree of creativity, invention, and a willingness to contribute to Patronio's stories by adding on extra tales, and even imitating Juan Manuel's style. More particularly, manuscripts H and G show a kind of scribal *usus scribendi* that took advantage of transitional points in the narratives to introduce new material. This last point is particularly important when reading one of the most idiosyncratic tales of the *CL* as it appears in all of its manuscript witnesses: *exemplo* 51 of manuscript S.

Unlike the other tales in manuscript S, *exemplo* 51 does not have a title, and it is only found in this one codex. Furthermore, it does not appear in the index in S, and it was not copied after *exemplo* 50 in the same manner as all the other tales. Laid out in double-column format on parchment, the stories of the *CL* are separated by blank spaces of approximately ten lines that appear to have been provided for an illumination, or *estoria*, introduced by the concluding statement of each tale: "Et la estoria deste enxiemplo es ésta que se sigue" ("And the story of this *exemplum* is as follows"). Manuscript S is clearly a carefully designed, deluxe, single-author

---

[27] As I have shown already in chapter 3, Patronio concludes in Part V as it appears in José Blecua's edition of S, by recalling that those who must live in the world and win salvation can succeed and fail in both endeavors: "los que passan en el mundo cobdiçiando fazer porque salven las almas, pero non se pueden partir de guardar sus onras et sus estados, estos tales pueden errar et pueden açertar en lo meior" (320, "those who live in this world desiring to do deeds that will save their souls, but cannot avoid protecting their honor and estates, these can err and succeed in the most important things").

complete-works volume, unfortunately left unfinished, but with all the traces of having a highly organized layout that makes the large lacuna on folio 178 recto all the more surprising.

In striking contrast with the layout of the first fifty tales, at the end of *exemplo* 50 approximately 22 lines of column A (the binding side) was left blank. *Exemplo* 51 begins at the top of column B, but many textual scholars, including Alberto Blecua, have been especially concerned with internal evidence in *exemplo* 50, and Parts III and IV, that suggests that there were only fifty tales in Part I. In *exemplo* 50, Patronio states that he has answered fifty questions, and Juan Manuel appears to conclude the collection of tales by alluding to the Count's fatigue, and his companions' impatience (José Blecua edition 266; Keller and Keating edition 187). In Parts III and IV, according to José Blecua's edition based on manuscript S, Patronio states that there are fifty tales in the first book: (Part III) "ca en l'otro ay cinquenta enxiemplos" (288, "since in the other book there are fifty *exempla*"); (Part IV) "en la primera parte deste libro en que ha çinquenta enxiemplos" (295, "in the first part of this book in which there are fifty *exempla*").

Alberto Blecua points to this textual evidence, and to the lacuna on folio 178 recto, among other codicological idiosyncrasies in S that lead him to believe that *exemplo* 51 is an apocryphal tale (*La transmisión textual* 113-16). Other critics, most noticeably John England, have written persuasive arguments in favor of Juan Manuel's authorship, while both scholars admit that it is impossible to be completely certain, leaving the question of authorship up to further debate.

Early in the twentieth century, one of Spain's most prolific and influential scholars, Marcelino Menéndez-Pelayo, commented on *exemplo* 51 in *Orígenes de la novela*, casting doubt on Juan Manuel's authorship (1: 153). Since then, the debate over *exemplo* 51 has become something of a quagmire that must be avoided, while most editors do include *exemplo* 51 as an authentic work.[28] But the internal textual evidence supporting a fifty-tale *CL*, Part I,

---

[28] Some textual scholars, particularly David Flory and Reinaldo Ayerbe-Chaux, argue that *exemplo* 51 is an epilogue that concludes Patronio's book of *exempla* (*CL*, Part I), originally composed as an independent work (Flory, "A Suggested Emendation" 88; Ayerbe-Chaux edition, *El libro del Conde Lucanor* 14). Alberto Blecua concludes that *exemplo* 51 had to have been added after the completion of the five-part *CL* (116).

MS S (Biblioteca Nacional 6376), folio 178 recto, with a large lacuna on column A before *ejemplo* 51.

has been dismissed in convincing fashion by critics such as David Flory and John England, who demonstrate that it was not uncommon for Juan Manuel to add on material to his works after completion (England, "*Exemplo* 51" 18), nor should it surprise us to find that Juan Manuel breaks with his own stated number of tales, since "[t]here is no section of the work, except the theological disquisition of the last part, whose numerical ordering corresponds exactly to the author's stated intention" (Flory 87). Finally, both of these critics defend Juan Manuel's authorship of *exemplo* 51 based on an appraisal of style and a measuring of the moral weight of the *CL*, Part I, as a whole. Both England and Flory are convinced that *exemplo* 51 is a fitting conclusion for the entire God / World theme of Patronio's *exempla*.

England defines his methodology as a study of "style, structure and moral" ("*Exemplo* 51" 19), concluding that Juan Manuel emended his original compilation of tales with *exemplo* 51, with its emphasis on humility, "to reduce the disparity between worldly and spiritual matters in the book as a whole" (26). Dismissing the notion of an apocryphal fifty-first tale, David Flory claims that *exemplo* 51 makes a tidy conclusion for "the dual path" of Part I: "Effectively, the strong admonition against pride and arrogance found in Ex. li provides both an answer and a fitting conclusion to a collection which addresses itself to this basic medieval problem [i.e. the dual path of God and World]" (88). John England goes even further, and suggests that Juan Manuel, after "re-reading" the *CL*, "became aware of the absence of one of the basic Christian virtues, humility, and so he added *Exemplo* 51" ("*Exemplo* 51" 26).

I am not entirely convinced that there really is such a "disparity" to begin with in Part I. In chapter 1 I demonstrate that there are clearly two ethical systems at work in the collection, often in conflict with each other, but a tally of "practical" and "spiritual" *exemplos* is unnecessary because these thematic threads are salient throughout Part I as a whole book. Humility *per se* may not turn up as a nominal virtue in other tales, but other virtues associated with it are common. The patient, obedient faith in God's will expressed in many of the tales studied in chapter 1 is a virtue easily associated with humility throughout the *CL*, Part I. Furthermore, as I also argue in chapter 1, the author makes no claim to solve a dilemma, or to balance the paths of God and World as so many critics take for granted; rather, the often-cited prologue text simply states that the author wrote his book with the heart-felt desire that his readers would know how to act properly. I believe it would be more precise to say that Juan Manuel aspired to aid his readers in the hard work of making ethical decisions that always involves the interpretation of signs or *enxiemplos*: "Este libro fizo don Iohan [. . .] deseando que los omnes fiziessen en este mundo tales obras que les fuessen aprovechosas de las onras et de las faziendas" (45, "This book was written by Don Juan Manuel [. . .] with the wish that all men should accomplish in this world such deeds as would be advantageous to their honor, their possessions, and their stations, and so that they would adhere to the career in which they could save their souls" [39]).

There may indeed be a "constrained" sense of "an inherent tension" in this statement, as Flory points out (88), which later becomes more patent in *exemplo* 50, for example, but there is no promise of a resolution in the prologue, which leads me to wonder if many modern critics have been searching of an answer to a question that the author does not ask directly, namely, how to follow both the path of the World and God at the same time? *Exemplo* 50, with the image of placing one's hand in a flame without getting burned, is, in my reading of the *CL*, a more appropriate conclusion for this paradoxically dual theme that the author never promises to unravel in the first place. But the essential trouble with studying this tale based on its style and moral is that style can be imitated, and as seen in the other manuscript witnesses, Juan Manuel's style was indeed copied, apparently with the intention of marking the moral content of his work. Furthermore, as Alberto Blecua demonstrates, there is ample stylistic evidence to support the apocryphal nature of *exemplo* 51 (*La transmisión textual* 117-21).

When placed within the entire manuscript landscape of the *CL*, what is most intriguing about *exemplo* 51 as it appears in S is not its moral, but the manner in which it is introduced in *exemplo* 50. Both John England and Alberto Blecua have observed the awkward transition made at the end of *exemplo* 50 that appears to contradict Juan Manuel's intention to conclude Patronio's tales. The entire passage is worth citing here in order to appreciate the consummative tone of *exemplo* 50:

> Agora, señor conde Lucanor, vos he respondido a esta pregunta que me feziestes et con esta repuesta vos he respondido a çin-

quenta preguntas que me avedes fecho. Et avedes estado en ello tanto tiempo, que só çierto que son ende enojados muchos de vuestras compañas, et señaladamente se enojan ende los que non an muy grand talante de oyr nin de aprender las cosas de que se pueden mucho aprovechar. Et contésceles commo a las vestias que van et non se aprovechan de la pro que ha en ello. Et ellos sienten el enojo de lo que oyen et non se aprovechan de las cosas buenas et aprovechosas que oyen. Et por ende, vos digo que lo uno por esto, et lo al por el trabajo que he tomado en las otras respuestas que vos di, que vos non quiero más responder a otras preguntas que vós fagades, que en este enxiemplo *et en otro que se sigue adelante deste* vos quiero fazer fin a este libro [my emphasis] (266-267, And now, Sir count, I have answered for you the question which you asked me, and with this reply I have answered all fifty of the questions that you have asked. And you have been so long here that I am sure your companions are annoyed by it, especially those who have no desire to hear or learn what can be of great profit to them. For it is with them as with pack animals loaded with gold, which feel the weight they carry on their backs, yet do not profit from its value. And they take umbrage at what they hear and do not take advantage of the profitable and good things they hear. Therefore, I tell you that for these reasons on the one hand, and on the other for the effort I have made in the other answers which I have given, I do not wish to answer any further questions which you may ask, for with this exemplary tale, *and with the one that is to follow*, I want to end this book [187-188]).

By returning to the notion of listening to and learning from exemplary tales, this ending resonates with the prologue in which Juan Manuel addresses the same theme, and successfully brings the collection to an end. The text I have noted above, "and with the one that is to follow," is only found in *exemplo* 50 as it appears in S, and has been the focus of much critical debate. As Alberto Blecua cites in his study of the manuscript transmission of the *CL*, the other versions of *exemplo* 50 make no mention of an additional tale. "Et por ende vos digo que lo uno por esto, et lo ál por el trabajo que he tomado en las otras respuestas que vos di, que vos non quiero más responder a otras preguntas que vós fagades que en este enxiemplo quiero fazer fin a este libro" (*La transmisión* 114, "I do not wish to answer any further questions which you may ask, for with this exemplary tale I want to end this book"). The variant in S, "and with the one that is to follow," does indeed contradict what appears to be a conclusion in *exemplo* 50, as it is in all the other manuscript witnesses, and it is interesting to note that this somewhat clumsy addition is placed in a conveniently transitional point in the text where Patronio mentions concluding his work with an *enxiemplo*.

Like the scribes of P, H and G, it appears that a reader / writer chose an opportune moment to add new material in S that would adjust the ideological meaning of the *CL*, adding weight to the moral component of the collection by emphasizing spiritual virtues, such as humility, over political acumen.[29] In P, as I have shown in this chapter, the scribe saw fit to add on a new version of Patronio's "spiritual" meaning of *exemplo* 48, not to mention two more stories at the end of the collection, and in H and G, a scribal custom of reading and writing can be observed taking advantage of transitional points in Juan Manuel's narratives to reshape them, and align the work with ethical, ideological, and perhaps even pedagogical expectations.

John England's defense of Juan Manuel's authorship of *exemplo* 51 is fascinating in comparison with my own analysis of scribal authorship in manuscripts P, H and G because England senses a similar attitude toward the text; more particularly, that the fifty-first tale is the result of a reception of the *CL* that engendered a desire to settle its ideological meaning through the act of writing. But England argues that it was Juan Manuel himself who was dissatisfied with the fifty-story version, as I have cited above in different occasions: "On re-reading the work (for the purpose of correcting the manuscript?), he probably became aware of the absence of one of the basic Christian virtues, humility, and so he added *Exemplo* 51 to reduce the disparity between worldly and spiritual matters in the book as a whole" ("*Exemplo* 51" 26).

This is exactly the sort of response to the *CL* that is found among Juan Manuel's earliest readers, who were also compilers and

---

[29] Even though there is no manuscript evidence to corroborate that these versions of *exemplos* 50 and 51 are not unique to manuscript S, it is not impossible that the scribe of S had access to another, now lost, copy of the fifty-one-story *CL*. Based on his assertion that *exemplo* 51 was added after the completion of the five-part version of the *CL*, Alberto Blecua doubts that there existed any other witness, since the only other five-part version of the *CL*, manuscript G, does not have the fifty-first tale either (113-114).

scribes, seen in manuscripts P, H and G, and although *exemplo* 51 is a much better imitation of Juan Manuel's style than the two apocryphal stories in P, the custom of reading and rewriting a work that England alludes to was equally common among scribes who were very creative in their imitations of Juan Manuel's style, as well as acutely aware of points in the author's texts that could be exploited for incorporating new material. Compared with the scribal *usus scribendi* found in P, H and G, that tended toward accretions and corrections based on ideological expectations, it is all the more likely that *exemplo* 51 is the work of another talented author / scribe, rather than the result of Juan Manuel's disappointment with his own work. Either way, *exemplo* 51 appears to be yet another example of how the reception of the *CL* implicated its readers and / or authors in reshaping the ideological content of the work, in an apparent effort to close its semantic potential, and secure a less complicated, transparent and orthodox meaning for the text. I will argue in the conclusion that this adjusted meaning of Juan Manuel's most important work was confirmed through the centuries, and still remains with us today as its most conventional understanding, but before moving on to a survey of some of the earliest editions of the *CL*, a study of the audience in manuscript M will serve as a conclusion for my study of the late medieval reception of Juan Manuel's *exempla*.

Chapter 5

THE LATE MEDIEVAL AND EARLY MODERN AUDIENCES OF *EL CONDE LUCANOR*[1]

I have already described some of the most informative and conspicuous traces of reading in manuscript M in the introduction to the first part of this book, and in this chapter I will take up where I left off in order to outline a profile of the audience of the *CL* in manuscript M, taking into consideration some of my conclusions from the previous chapter that also address the subject of Juan Manuel's earliest audience. As stated in my introduction, the scribal reading aid written in red ink in the margins throughout the *CL* as it appears in M is, without a doubt, one of the most telling indicators of how Juan Manuel's tales were read in fifteenth-century Spain, but the entire codex, as another anthology of various works like P (and together with P), outlines a profile of a particular audience that many critics have imagined for the *CL* based exclusively on internal textual evidence.

Reviewing some of the aspects of the reading aids that form part of the layout of the *CL* in M, it is worth recalling that the initial letters, internal paragraph marks, or *calderones*, original page numbers, and flourishes were systematically written into M in red ink. Juan Manuel's concluding *refranes* are also highlighted with red flourishes, and set apart from the body of the text by indentation.

In addition to the divisions of the page layout in manuscript M, I have described two types of marginal notes in each tale that stand out among the rest of the marginalia in this codex. One type marks the beginning of a new story, and the other points out where Patro-

---

[1] Portions of this chapter have been published in "Reading to Pieces: *Divisio Textus* and the Structure of *El Conde Lucanor*."

nio begins an exemplary tale to illustrate his point about the Count's particular query. The notes "c<apítul>o," followed by a roman numeral numbering each tale, and "enxenplo" appear in the margins in red ink, as mentioned earlier, and what is most interesting about the *enxenplo* notes is that they always appear across from the point in the text where Patronio makes a formulaic introductory comment like those I survey in the introduction to the first part of my study.[2]

John Dagenais makes several references to manuscript M of the *Conde Lucanor* in *The Ethics of Reading in Manuscript Culture*, and in particular the *enxenplo* notes. He concludes that this kind of marginalia are the traces of a medieval reading custom that divided and signaled changes in material within a text, a *divisio textus* that was "as basic and incontrovertible a tool of knowledge in the medieval period as the scientific method is in ours" (121). Dagenais's comments on the same type of marginal notes in manuscript G of the *Libro de buen amor* also apply in the case of manuscript M of the *Conde Lucanor*. These notes, Dagenais asserts, direct "future readers to material that is of potential use in preaching or writing, and also of benefit for personal moral instruction and entertainment" (160).

More than a means of noting different material on the page for future reference, Mary Carruthers has shown that, in general, marginalia of this kind facilitate the physiological workings of memory as they were understood in the Middle Ages, and that *divisio* in particular "serve[s] the function of textual heuristics, 'finding,' and mnemonic storage" (243). In this way the marginal notes written in manuscript M anticipate and aid the reader's desire to cut out and gather Patronio's stories from the context of the Count's questions, store them in memory, and reemploy them in another composition, in another context. I will return to these observations further on, but before a detailed study of the significance of this marginalia can take place, the more conspicuous evidence of medieval reading in M should be evaluated; in particular, the other works bound to-

---

[2] A convenient example of this marginalia appears on folio 27 verso of manuscript M which has all of the special features mentioned thus far: the indented *viessos* with red flourish, as well as the marginal notes "c<apitul>o" and "enxenplo." Nydia Gloeckner transcribes these notes in the margins of her edition of the *Conde Lucanor* as they appear in manuscript M.

gether with the *CL* that construct a discrete literary context for Patronio's stories, while adumbrating its intended audience.

Produced in the second half of the fifteenth century, Alberto Blecua describes M as one of the five manuscripts of the *CL* with the most innovative features (97), but he concludes that it is of limited use for editors (100). Blecua's appraisal of the manuscript seems to be corroborated by most of the critical editions of the *CL*, since almost all of them provide only a basic sketch of its physical makeup, overlooking one of its most interesting and obvious features; namely, that it is a late medieval Castilian anthology of various works. Surprisingly very few editors of the *CL* describe the contents of M in their introductions, or mention the other works bound in the codex by name.

Manuscript M is made up of 186 folios, the first 100 of which reproduce the *CL*, Part I. It is followed by the *Proposición contra los ingleses* (fols. 101^r-131^r), a translation of *Allegatio pro praecedentia regum Castellae prae regibus Angliae* composed by Alonso de Cartagena for the Council of Basel (July 19, 1434) in defense of the greater nobility of the Castilian crown and its privilege to speak first in the council. The next work in the manuscript is the *Cuestión sobre el acto de caballería* (fols. 132^r-148^r), consisting of a letter written by Íñigo López de Mendoza, Marqués de Santillana in 1444 to Alonso de Cartagena inquiring about the oath of knighthood, followed by Cartagena's reply, which according to Juan Marichal could be the first modern essay of the Castilian language (23).

After the *Cuestión* comes an anonymous work called the *Libro binario* (also *Binario de virtudes*, fols. 149^r-175^v) written in two parts; the first being a father's description of the seven virtues for his son, and the second part, also divided in two parts, being a discussion on the corporal and spiritual nature of man, followed by a series of questions put to the father about his treatise on the duality of human nature.[3] Folios 176 recto to 183 recto reproduce a Spanish translation of a selection from the *Vida de Jesucrist* (1397-1398) by Francesc Eiximenis on the symbolic meanings, especially for princes, of the three gifts of the Epiphany, as well as the punishments God sends to those princes who do not govern properly.

This last piece concludes what appears to be the original compilation, ending on folio 183 recto, with most of the recto side left

---

[3] To date, this work has not been edited.

blank, as well as the entire verso side. From folios 184 recto to 186 verso, and written in a different hand, are two additional pieces added at a later date. One is an incomplete description of Mérida that Michael Hammer has recently identified as a selection taken from chapter 156 of Pedro de Corral's *Crónica Sarracina* (54), the other text is an anonymous *exemplum*, the *Apólogo del filósofo que fue a una huerta a cortar verduras*.[4] These, then, are all the works included in M as we know it today, and at first glance there appears to be a general thematic uniformity among them; they are all works of interest for a ruling aristocracy fascinated with the world of chivalry, the true nature and virtues of nobility, and proper governance –all favorite themes of the Spanish nobility of this time as Jeremy Lawrence outlines in "On Fifteenth-Century Spanish Vernacular Humanism" (68-73).

Only by actually reading the other works as they appear in the manuscript can we appreciate the thematic resonances that bind all the works together in M; even the pieces added after the completion of the original anthology make sense within the framework of the codex. The *Descripción de Mérida* and the *Apólogo del filósofo que fue a una huerta a cortar verduras* are evidence of at least one reader's access to the manuscript, and they are indicative of the openness of medieval books for their readers, but the content of these extra tales also demonstrate a sensitive reading of the other fascicles bound in M. I will address just how the *CL*, and some of the anonymous works, fit into this compilation further on.

As in the case of manuscript P, I have used the terms "compilation" and "anthology" to describe this codex because it is clear that it was produced by that special breed of medieval author, the compiler, who created a new kind of book for secular, religious and academic audiences described by Malcolm Parkes in "The Influence of the Concepts of *Ordinatio* and *Compilatio* on the Development of the Book" (137-38), cited earlier in chapter 4. The act of creating a compilation is in fact a kind of medieval authorship that witnesses

---

[4] See appendix II for these two texts. The standard title for the *Apólogo* is cited as it appears in Carlos Alvar and José Manuel Lucía Megías's description of manuscript M in the *Diccionario filológico de literatura medieval española* (721), but it is interesting to note that the manuscript text itself, which does not give a title, reads that the "fylosofo" went to *buy* produce, rather than "cortar verduras": "un día el fylósofo fue a una guerta a conprar alguna verdura" (fol. 186^r). The transcriptions are my own from a microfilm copy of manuscript M.

not only the rewriting of various works and a discrete reading of each piece bound in the codex, but it also provides a profile of the implied reader, and possibly even intended uses of the new book.

Like manuscript P, "compilation" is also a better term to describe M, than "miscellany," for example, because a close examination of this codex uncovers a number of organizing parameters that bind the different fascicles of the codex into a cohesive book with its own agenda. Borrowing from Siegfried Wenzel's discussion of the various taxonomic descriptors used to catalogue medieval sermon collections, an even more precise term to describe manuscript M is "anthology," since it contains longer texts that are "in fact separate works," and have a noticeable "thematic unity" ("Sermon Collections" 19). The most superficial survey of the contents of M uncovers a unity of language (Castilian), and form (prose); upon closer examination, one finds a more inconspicuous consistency of subject matter, following Theo Stemmler's outline of the organizing principles that can be found in a medieval anthology (232).

At first glance, however, it may be difficult to catch the "intermittent reminders" that stitch all the works together in M, but even the pieces added on after the completion of the original anthology, the *Descripción de Mérida* and the *Apólogo del filósofo que fue a una huerta a cortar verduras*, make sense in the context of the compilation.

As seen in appendix II, the beginning of the *Descripción de Mérida* is missing in M. What appears on folio 184 recto is a description of the walls, towers, and other fortifications of the city at its greatest moment in history, which may have been of some interest for a fifteenth-century aristocratic reader interested in the patrician subject matter of the other pieces collected in the anthology. But it is the conclusion of this piece that clearly aligns with a theme that cuts across the entire codex: the rise and fall of great powers according to God's will, and the divine punishment placed on the prince that strays from virtue and faith. Here a direct link is established between the rise and fall of Mérida, and Spain herself:

> E agora podredes creer quel fecho de Mérida fue muy grande et de grand fama segund las cosas que oýdo avedes. E ora fagamos fyn en esta materia porque la su planeta et la de España me pareçe que an seydo de una guisa segund lo pasado et lo que agora es por que vos digo que nunca ninguno se deue tener por aquel que

> las gentes le dan la fama fasta que vea la su fyn sy está en egual del buen comienço. Et aun aý deue poner dubda ca todas las cosas han de aver fyn synon lo çelestial. Enpero durarán más unas que otras asý commo a Dios plaze (fol. 185ʳ, And now you can believe that the story of Mérida was grand and of great fame, as you have heard. And now we conclude this story of Mérida because its planet and Spain's seem to me to have followed the same path with respect to the past and what she is now; therefore I tell you that no one should ever believe that he is as great as his reputation until he sees that his ending is as great as his beginning. And even then he should have doubts, since everything must come to an end, except the heavens. Nevertheless, some things will last longer than others, according to God's will).

The idea that nations rise and fall according to God's will in this fragment added on to M appears to fit with a related subject in the excerpt from Eiximenis's *Vida de Jesucrist*; in particular, the notion that a kingdom's prosperity depends on virtuous and faithful leaders. The scribe introduces the "Maestre Françisco Ximenes" as an author who explains the symbolism of the three gifts presented at the Epiphany, especially for princes and kings: "dispone que es sygnificado a los prínçipes et rreyes de la tierra por los tres dones que aquellos santos rreyes ofreçieron al salvador" (fol. 176ʳ, "it defines the significance, for princes and kings of the earth, of the three gifts that those saintly kings offered to the Savior"). But the selected text goes on to explain the punishments wreaked on a kingdom ruled by sinful and disobedient lords.

Among the many sins mentioned are arrogance, vanity, laziness, a lack of good counsel, effeminate manners, and an over indulgence of the pleasures of the flesh, all of which are punished by God, as witnessed in the history of King Abdon of Syria. King Abdon is also an excellent example of the model prince who studies history as well as the art of war; learning from the mistakes of his predecessors, he turns away from sin and puts his faith in the Lord who rewards him by protecting his kingdom from potential aggressors:

> Et por otros muchos [pecados] Dios dio plaga a mis predeçesores et los fizo todos rreynar con muchas plagas dolores et afanes et penas et tribulaçiones. E yo sabiendo esto ayudándome la graçia de Dios dexé sus malos viçios et voluíme a las virtudes con-

> trarias et nuestro señor Dios a me manparado por su merçed et a todo mi rreyno fyrmado et comigo ligado et a mi et a él prosperado et asý me a confortado que non temo a ningunt rrey que sea enderredor. Ca confío que el señor que es Dios todo poderoso es mi amigo et comigo syenpre, pues que yo le syrvo de coraçón en el rregimiento que me a encomendado (fol. 181ᵛ, And because of many other sins, God sent a plague to my predecessors and made them all to rule with many pestilences, pains, trials, sufferings and tribulations. And I, knowing all this, and with the grace of God helping me, I gave up their evil vices and I turned back to the contrary virtues and our Lord God protected me by his mercy, and all of my kingdom he united and tied to me, and allowed me and my realm to prosper, and in this way he strengthened me so that I do not fear any other king that may be near by).

This passage calls attention to a salient theme of the anthology, taken up directly in the anonymous *Libro binario* which is organized around the medieval practice of reading in binary opposites, particularly applied to virtues and their opposite sins. In the *Libro binario*, a father instructs his son on how to ward off vices by opposing them (*contrastar*) with the Seven Virtues: "E es dicho aqueste libro binario por que fabla de dos cosas conuiene saber de syete virtudes et de omne, por tal que omne con las syete virtudes sepa ayudar a contrastar todos viçios" (fol. 150ʳ, "This book is called *Binario* because it speaks of two things; namely, of the Seven Virtues and Man, so that man can know, with the Seven Virtues, how to contrast all the vices"). Furthermore, this treatise on the Seven Virtues has a distinctly pragmatic purpose. It is designed to help a young lord govern prudently, combining secular wisdom with religious doctrine; a theme that clearly converges with the *CL*:

> Ca le veo enbuelto en los negoçios del mundo et puede syn sabiduría muy aýna peligrar. Por ende me oue a trabajar a le escriuir aqueste pequeñuelo libro en que lea, por tal que más conplidamente a Dios sepa seruir et onrrar et temer et amar. E sepa viçios que son pecados mortales fuyr et virtudes multiplicar et dellas usar (fol. 149ᵛ, Because I see my son engrossed in the business of the world, and without wisdom he may dangerously err. Therefore I felt obliged to write for him this little book that you read, so that he can more perfectly know how to serve, honor, fear and love God. And so that he know how to flee from vices, which are mortal sins, and multiply and employ virtues).

Here in the *Libro binario*, the reader encounters the familiar Manuelian theme of "Dios y el Mundo," and how to put secular wisdom and religious doctrine to use in a practical socio-political arena: "los negoçios del mundo." Considering the works in M studied thus far, with their attention to vices and virtues, it becomes more evident that manuscript M is a kind of instruction-book, similar in content and implied audience as those studied by Joseph Mosher in his now classic study, *The Exemplum in the Early Religious and Didactic Literature of England*. According to Mosher, toward the end of the Middle Ages a new class of *exempla* collections appear in anthologies "designed principally for the cultivation of persons of high rank" (134). In this new brand of instruction literature "which aimed to inculcate civic and moral rectitude," both secular and religious *exempla* were widely incorporated, as Mosher also explains (134-136), but with a tendency toward the more secular tale, like those found in the *CL*.

The other, more familiar works in M, such as the *Proposición contra los ingleses* and the *Cuestión sobre el acto de cavallería*, address the general audience of the entire collection, since they deal with the nature of true nobility and their most important virtues, embodied in the royal family of Castilla, the oath of knighthood, and the cultivation of arms and letters. While the royal house of Castilla stands out among the other noble families of Europe in the *Proposición* for its ancient royal lineage, natural resources, great cities, and its noble war against the Moors, Alonso de Cartagena applauds the Marqués de Santillana in the *Cuestión sobre el acto de cavallería* for his exemplary combination of intellectual activity with political responsibility and faithful service. The history and content of the oath taken by knights also addresses the common subject matter of the entire codex since it defines the most important virtue of the noble knight: fearless service to his country, its laws and its people, all embodied in the figure of the king.

All the works mentioned thus far–the *Proposición contra los ingleses, Cuestión sobre el acto de cavallería, Vida de Jesucrist, Libro binario,* and the *Descripción de Mérida*–appear to deal with the true nature and best virtues of the aristocracy, especially the seigniorial oligarchy charged with governance. Although M is not exactly a mirror of princes, it does appear to be an anthology with a distinctly pedagogical tone that could have been prepared for the instruction of young noblemen, or for the interest and edification of a fifteenth-century aristocratic audience enamored with its own history and identity.

As the *CL* can be informed by the context and content of M, it appears to follow a postulated theme and imagined audience for the entire anthology. The *CL* in M is not only a collection of *exempla*, common to instruction-books for princes, but it is also a series of realistic political and moral situations confronted by fictitious characters (i.e. the Count, Patronio, and *Don Iohan*) with whom an elite aristocratic audience could identify.

Typically, scholars have described the audience of the *CL* in terms of social class and education. Dayle Seidenspinner-Núñez suggests that the characters of the *CL* imply two "sectors" of Juan Manuel's audience, "the younger less experience nobility," and "the older, practiced nobility" (260), while Barry Taylor describes Juan Manuel's audience as an intelligent, although intellectually unrefined, class of noble knights (54). These critics attempt to sketch the author's implied contemporary readers, but manuscript M draws a much clearer picture of a well-educated and intellectually curious princely audience that turned to this codex for unambiguous wisdom for rulers, theological doctrine on virtue and the nature of man, as well as a definition and defense of their privileged standing in society.

Returning to the *CL*, these readers would certainly have taken serious note of the model relationship between a counselor and his lord, as well as the combination of religious and secular virtues necessary to achieve a balance between the political and spiritual spheres of influence. But what about the last *exemplum* added on to the anthology, and the marginal notes in the *CL* described earlier?

In the *Apólogo del filósofo que fue a una huerta a cortar verduras*, as seen in appendix II, a wise and educated man learns a lesson from his slave who unravels a riddle that his master could not. The question being, why do the crops cultivated by man require more work and time to grow than those plants that grow naturally? The philosopher cannot solve the riddle, and his answer is exposed as a ridiculous evasion of the question: "Et el fylósofo commo oyese esta quistión filosofal et non pudiese rresponder a ella, dize–estas semejantes cosas proceden de la providencia divinal, de lo qual el syeruo que el fylósofo llevaua con sygo se rrio muy de gana" (fol. 186^r, "And the philosopher, since he heard this philosophical question and could not answer it, says–these sorts of things come from Divine Providencia—which made the servant that the philosopher had with him laugh heartily"). The philosopher's slave, also a gardener (the text refers to him as the "ortolano"), laughs out loud at his master, who is enraged by his servant's insolence: "Et dízele su señor, –loco, rieste o escarrneçes –dixo el syervo– escarrnesco, non de ty, mas al fylósofo que te enseñó. Et que soluçión de fylósofo es, que por la divina providençia proçeden estas cosas tales. Eso tanbién lo saben los albarderos" (fol. 186ʳ, "And his lord says to him—Fool! Are you laughing or ridiculing me?–and the slave said–I am not making fun of you, but of the philosopher that taught you. And what a philosopher's answer it is, that these things come from Divine Providence. Even the saddle-makers know that").

The philosopher orders his servant to solve the riddle if he can, which he does, and wins all the vegetables he wants. Nature, the slave explains, is like a mother; she takes better care of her own children, in this case the plants that grow naturally, than her stepchildren, or the crops grown and harvested by man.

Aside from the symbolic role reversals common to this kind of didactic tale and the *CL* that James Burke has studied in "Frame and Structure in the *Conde Lucanor*" (270-71), the *Apólogo* raises the practice of solving riddles to the surface of the text, which establishes another connection with the *CL*, and eventually points to the theme of proper conduct for an aristocratic ruler that the entire anthology addresses.

In *Desire Against the Law*, James Burke considers Juan Manuel's primary audience to be the aristocratic "rulers" for whom he composed his *exempla* and proverbs in order to test their "mental agility" (229). Furthermore, Burke argues that the work of unraveling a riddle is, in the final analysis, an exercise designed to sharpen a person's ability to judge and act correctly in life: "[t]he solving of a riddle is then in essence an unmasking, and the person who learns to work with riddles also enhances his ability to uncover hidden intentions" (235). According to Burke, working out a riddle, parable or enigma, always translates into action in "the broader social sphere" (*Desire* 235), and this is where the marginal notes in the *CL* come into play again.

John Dagenais argues that the *enxenplo* notes in M indicate that for the medieval reader Patronio's tales, as opposed to the framing contexts or the concluding *viessos* were the "central focus" (75), and as such they offer further proof of the medieval reading subject's fragmented, "piecemeal" reading practices (213). I believe that this is a hasty conclusion.

The marginal notations do not mathematically tell us what was preferred by the compiler of manuscript M. They do let us know that the compiler / reader recognized that these narratives were made up of parts, as I have argued in the introduction to the first part of this book. Some critics may believe, along with Dagenais, that these markings prove that the manuscript demonstrates a preference for one part over another, when in fact they only show that the compiler is recognizing a division inscribed in the text itself. This is not an insignificant distinction. The marginal notes in M are more than simple markings on the page to indicate where one material stops and another begins, it means that the compiler was acutely aware of the structure of the *CL*. We should remember that each new story is indexed with a marginal note as well, *capítulo*, and the maxims are also marked with red flourishes. Clearly the scribe and / or compiler recognized that these tales were divisible, following their inscribed points of articulation. The traces of this structural reading also imply an awareness of a rhetorical strategy that the structure outlines. What the red marginal notes and flourishes point to is the *forma tractatus* of the *CL*; they tell us that these tales can be read in homologous pieces, that the parts are themselves autonomous, and that there exists a mode of thinking that structured the parts into a whole. I have attempted to follow this mode of writing in chapter 1.

At this point it will be helpful to recall again, and in greater detail, Judson Boyce Allen's discussion of *forma tractatus*, and especially *divisio* as expressions of a mode of thinking, or *forma tractandi* that informs and organizes much of the ethical writings of the later Middle Ages.[5] Allen demonstrates that medieval commentators read "backwards," working from a recognition of the divisions in a literary text as the "first step" of their critical analysis (90, 126).

---

[5] Although Allen's *The Ethical Poetic of the Later Middle Ages* is primarily concerned with poetry, the author acknowledges that he can "most directly account for the thinking that makes poetry by accounting for the late medieval logic of *exempla*, and for the implicit and explicit means whereby an *exemplum*, or a collection of *exempla*, may be significantly posited" (95). Aside from the obvious relevance for the study of the *exemplum* in the later Middle Ages, including the *CL*, many of Allen's conclusions are important for scholars interested in uncovering the ethical and rhetorical thinking of medieval authors in general.

An important consideration for my interpretation of the marginalia in M, also borrowed from Allen, is that the ultimate goal of reading backwards, beginning with *divisio*, is to uncover "some normative array of parts or some normative sequence, in terms of which the author's literal material has its full significance" (90).

Division, according to Allen, as a tool of medieval literary analysis "is the basis of any possible serious consideration of a text's wholeness, subject, or meaning" (126). While there is no doubt that the scribe of manuscript M points to the divisions inscribed in the *CL*, it is also possible that these marginal notes indicate the beginning of an analysis that seeks to find the "full significance" of each tale, or even the entire collection of Juan Manuel's short stories. What this scribe discovered by working backwards from *divisio* is impossible to determine, in fact the markings may serve the simple purpose of pointing out where to begin the analysis for future readers, as I have done in chapter 1. But there is another implicit conclusion about how, and by whom, the *CL* was read in M that can be deduced from the marginal notes.

As I have summarized above, Allen concludes that medieval commentators were ultimately concerned with a work's wholeness, but there is another aspect of *divisio* that is equally important for this study of manuscript M. Although the structural divisions of a text may lead a critic to understand an author's intentions, the parts themselves must be autonomous, and in the array of parts in any given work, they must be similar to each other. In order for division to be a successful rhetorical structuring device, it must create unity and diversity, similarity and difference. Allen clarifies this point in a passage from Raoul de Longchamp's thirteenth-century commentary on Alanus de Insulis's *Anticlaudianus*, found in a manuscript copy made in 1400:

> [W]hat is most important is that a fit division requires parts that are both like and different–'in aliquo conveniant et in aliquo different'. In the category which most nearly fits literary texts–that is, 'totius in partes,' what Raoul especially emphasizes is that the parts must be real and whole in themselves, they must be 'partes integrales,' they must make sense. (128-29)

Each part of an individual narrative in the *CL*–the Count's question / problem, Patronio's *exemplum*, Patronio's interpretation of his tale, and Don Juan's concluding *viessos*–can be read as discrete units or in their relation to the whole narrative. The scarlet "enxenplo" and "capítulo" notes, along with the red flourishes that highlight the concluding aphorisms, are marginal evidence of an educated reading process that recognized a rhetorically discursive structure in the text. Obviously, the scribe who marked the margins of manuscript M in red ink and indented the *viessos* was interested in indexing the material in each tale systematically, but there is no more evidence to suggest a preference. Nevertheless, the physical act of marking the page is enough to signal that the text had potential for more than one kind of reading.

As mentioned above, the framing narratives that surround Patronio's *exempla* resonate thematically with the other works of the anthology, so one can imagine that some late medieval readers would have read the entire collection of stories as they appear in M, driven by a fascination with exemplary aristocratic rulers, and their ideal relationships with good counselors. There is no reason to conclude, following Dagenais's profile of the "self-centered, greedy, disrespectful" medieval reader, that they were not interested in a more global message, or even Juan Manuel's "political or intellectual program" (213). It is quite possible that Juan Manuel's artistic and moral lessons were not lost on these readers; they did not have to scan and skip from *enxenplo* to *enxenplo*, but they could if they wanted to with the aid of the marginal notes. The notes could also have aided them in saving the various *exempla* and proverbs in their own storehouses of memory, and it is quite possible that they jumped from tale to tale for the pleasure of trying to "unmask" their meanings, trying their hand so to speak at the hermeneutic exercise Patronio and the philosopher's slave demonstrate, or to gather the various sentential *refranes* conveniently set apart from the body of the text, and highlighted with red flourishes.

The traces of *divisio* in M point to the places of convenient disarticulation. Through its divided and divisible structure, the CL as it appears in M anticipates multiple uses and interpretations. A reader can take the text apart in order to recontextualize the pieces according to his or her needs and interests, or, tracking the divisions "backwards," the reader can follow the layout as it is provided in the codex and potentially uncover the wholeness of the entire collection of tales, and even the thematic unity of the anthology that contains them. Either way, what these readings reveal is the dynamic processes of *divisio* and *compositio* which always go hand-in-hand according to Carruthers (189).

Manuscript M is a fascinating witness to the potential of the *CL* because it is an example of a new performance of the work according to a fifteenth-century aristocratic audience's expectations that the subject matter of the entire anthology denotes, and at the same time the anthology points future readers to the structural *loci* where the text can be taken apart again. In this way manuscript M both limits the reading of the *CL*, aligning its ideological significance with the other works that form this instruction-book for a distinct audience, "designed principally for the cultivation of persons of high rank," *and* it opens the collection, anticipating new contexts and used for the narratives by showing where to break them into pieces.

Following the omnipresent textual flags that structure the *CL*, a reader could separate, select, gather together, and even memorize the divisible parts of Juan Manuel's stories. Such a reader could easily locate an intriguing political, social, or moral problem to be contemplated, an amusing *exemplum* for practicing one's hermeneutic skills, an authoritative "unmasking" of the same problem and *exemplum*, or a useful *refrán* that could come in handy in any conversation, debate, or personal life situation. Whether or not such a reading actually happened is impossible to determine, but the potential was clearly mapped out in red for future readers. Be this as it may, the marginal notes written by at least one late-medieval reader of manuscript M appear to have traced the political doctrine found in the other works of the codex, more so than the religious doctrine, which suggests that the audience for whom this book was prepared followed a more guided reading of the *CL* than the thematic resonances studied in the entire anthology plot out for its readers.

Of all the works included in M, those of Alonso de Cartagena and Íñigo López de Mendoza, the *Proposición contra los ingleses* and the *Cuestión sobre el acto de cavallería* (fols. 104^r-148^r), have the most amount of marginal notes written by a reader whose markings suggest that he or she studied the codex for its political doctrine and history, rather than reading its collection of *exempla* for entertainment, or for meditating on the benefits and uses of the Seven Virtues. The most abundantly noted folios summarize and highlight content with catchwords, pointing fingers, brief summaries, or marginal keys in the shape of braces and crosses. A survey of these notes offers a glimpse into the reader's interests in manuscript M, and suggest that the *CL* was approached as a bank of useful secular *exempla* and sentential sayings for an audience of aristocrats, priests, or both.

The first hundred folios of M, those that contain the *CL*, are almost entirely devoid of any notes made by the reader of the *Proposición* and *Cuestión*. There is, however, one interesting piece of marginalia on folio 77 recto. Across the bottom margin of this folio, it is not clear whether the original scribe, or another reader, copied in a book hand the concluding aphorism of *exemplo* 42, "De lo que contesçió a una falsa veguina" ("What Happened to a Woman of Sham Piety"): the copy in the margin reads, "Para mientes a la obra e non a la semiança / si queres ser guardado," which is an incomplete version of the proverb as it appears in the body of the text of the same folio, indented and marked with a red *calderón*, as all the others in M: "Para mientes a la obra et non a la semejança / Si quieres ser guardado de aver mala andança" ("Look to deeds and not appearances / If you wish to be safe from bad fortune").[6]

The copy of the proverb here is reminiscent of the proverbs copied on the flyleaf of manuscript H, examined in the last chapter, and I believe that it is an indicator left behind by the scribe / reader of an interest in collecting the proverbial wisdom of the *CL*, not unlike the scribe of Madrid, Biblioteca Nacional 19426 that I have mentioned earlier. This manuscript contains a scribal explanation regarding the decision to anthologize Juan Manuel's aphorisms, ignoring the rest of the tales, offering to us an amazing view of an early-modern response to the *CL* that informs the traces of florilecture observed in M and H.

Manuscript 19426 is a sixteenth-century, humanist manuscript that suggests, together with manuscript H and M, that the late-medieval / early-modern audience of the *CL* placed a premium on its terse proverbial wisdom, over and above its narrative creativity, or Patronio's hermeneutic technique. It also suggests, like Argote de Molina's first print edition that will be discussed in the next chapter, that by the sixteenth century Juan Manuel's illustrious and noble lineage had become an indispensable component of the mean-

---

[6] Here the translation is my own. Keller and Keating provide another translation for the *refrán* of *exemplo* 42: "Not looks but deeds will surely test a friend; / Know this and foil what wicked men intend" (157).

ing of the *CL*. In manuscript 19426, the scribe explains exactly why he only copied the proverbs from the *CL*, while acknowledging the noble bloodline of the author at the same time:

> Este ynfante don Manuel, de que desuso se haze mençión, fue fijo del rey don Fernando de castilla tercero deste nonbre et de la reyna doña Beatriz; el qual dicho rey don Fernando es llamado El Santo, y el que ganó a seuilla. Este dicho ynfante don Manuel, fijo del dicho rey don Fernando et de la dicha reyna doña Beatriz casó con doña Costança fija del rey don Jayme de Aragón, et deste matrimonio obieron a este don Juan Manuel que es autor destos libros. Y en este de que agora se trata, que es el de los exemplos, quenta los casos como acaesçieron, y en fin de cada uno dellos pone un proueruio, o sentençia en breues palabras que se coge del caso et de lo que se vio por esperiençia para abisar a las gentes; et de aquí resalta la ynteligençia de lo que es proueruio que es una breue sentençia et abiso de lo que se vio por esperienç[i]a. Et por eso, aquí no porné los exenplos, sino solamente los proueruios de los dichos exemplos sacados de un señor que fablabaua con un su consejero; et dezían al señor conde Lucanor, y al consejero Patronio, casí comiençan los proueruios (fol. 35^r, This *Infante* Don Manuel, who is mentioned above, was the son of king Don Fernando of Castilla, the third of this name, and of queen Doña Beatriz; the above mentioned king Don Fernando is called The Saint, and is he who conquered Sevilla. This aforementioned *Infante* Don Manuel, son of said king Don Fernando and queen Doña Beatriz married Doña Constanza, daughter of Don Jaime, king of Aragon, and from this marriage they had said Don Juan Manuel, who is the author of these books. And this book which is being dealt with here, which is the book of *exemplos*, tells of cases and situations as they happened, and at the end of each case there is a proverb or sentence in a few words which are taken and understood from each case, and what was seen from experience in order to advise people; and this is what is meant by the word proverb, which is a brief sentence taken from something seen and experienced. And for this reason I will not write the *exemplos* here, rather only the proverbs taken from a lord who was speaking with his counselor; and the lord was called Count Lucanor, and the counselor Patronio, and thus begin the proverbs).

Returning to M, one can only speculate as to why the reader chose to copy the proverb on folio 77 recto–perhaps he was only practicing, or testing his instrument—but as one of the few indications of another reader's reaction to the text, it would seem to suggest a taste for the sentential sayings of the *CL* more so than a meditation on the paths of God and World, or Juan Manuel's rhetorical use of *exempla*.

Near the beginning of the *Proposición contra los ingleses*, on folio 102 verso, after a discussion of the nature of honor, and honorable kings, a pointing finger directs attention to a definition of tyrants, and a biblical reference on obedience to kings (1 Pet. 2.13-15). This is the beginning of an exhaustive reading, richly noted in the margins up to the end of the *Cuestión sobre el acto de cavallería* that displays a keen interest in Christian doctrine as it pertains to princes, political ethics, the nature of royalty and knighthood, and the honor of Castilla; all of which suggest that the reader identified with the class, nationality, and idealized codes of ethics associated with the aristocratic oligarchy of fifteenth-century Spain. The following is a line-by-line transcription of this first highlighted text, beginning on line 13, and marked with a pointing finger, represented here with an arrow:

> Et por esto se da honor et gloria et fama a los rreyes por
> que sean tenidos por esçelentes en virtud segunt que sant
> pedro dize: subjectos sed al rrey commo a omne muy
> → exçelente . j . pe. ii. Et los prínçipes que con esto non se
> contentan fázense tyranos segunt que aristótiles
> dize en el quarto de las héticas (fol. 102^v, And for these reasons one gives glory and fame to kings in order that they be received as excellent in virtue as St. Peter says: be subject to the king as an excellent man .1. pe. ii. And those princes who are not satisfied with this become tyrants according to Aristotle's fourth [book] of the *Ethics*).

Almost every folio, from 105 verso to 117 verso, of the *Proposición* is noted with a pointing finger, or more commonly with a catchword, or even a brief gloss of the content, which usually deals with the nature of honor, the order of knights, and the prestige of Castilla, especially in comparison with other nations, and particularly England. Various other marginal notes betray an interest in the place of Castilla in the history of the Roman Catholic Church.

A note made early on in the *Proposición* text marks the consistent attention paid to classes of nobility, and the nature of honor.

On folio 103 verso a key in the bottom left margin highlights the text that defines three kinds of nobility, and a brief note summarizes the content: "tres noblezas." The manuscript text defines "theological," "natural," and "civil" nobility: "Dize que se puede fazer que hay tres noblezas; la primera llaman thologal; la segunda natural; la tercera civil. La nobleza thologal es ser bien quisto de Dios" (fol. 103ᵛ-104ʳ, "It is said that one can distinguish three kinds of nobility; the first is called theological, the second natural, and the third civil. Theological nobility is being beloved by God").

Comparing this note with others that appear to index similar subject matter throughout the *Proposición*, it seems that the reader was equally interested in the theological content of M, which includes many biblical references, as the political observations on the royal house of Castilla. On both the verso and recto sides of folio 104 there are lengthy marginal notes paraphrasing the texts that take on the matter of "la nobleza civil," or the secular aristocracy, also named in the manuscript text as "fidalguía." On 104 recto there are three paraphrasing notes in the left and right margins, including a key to highlight the manuscript text that deals with "royal nobility" ("nobleça rreal"):

[. . . . .] La terçera nobleza se llama çiuil de que fablamos al presente, la qual comúnmente llamamos fydalguía et esta se difyne et declara por Bartolo asý: la nobleza çiuil es una calidad dada por el que tiene el prinçipado.⁷ Por la qual pareçe que el que la rreçibe es más quisto et amado del prínçipe que los onestos plebeyos que comúnmente llamamos pecheros (fol 104ʳ).	de la nobleça cevil que se llama fidalguía (on civil nobility which is called *fidalguía*)
[. . . . .] Et asý pues de los rreyes desçiende toda nobleza çiuil et fydalguía segunt que allí notó Bartolo. Et quanto más alguno se allega a la sangre rreal tanto más noble es. sýguese que los rreyes tienen la cunbre et soberana altura de la nobleza çiuil, pues que dellos commo de fuentes deçienden los arroyos de la nobleza çiuil et fidalguía, tanta que aun el hermano del rrey de padre et de madre non es tan fyjo dalgo commo el rrey (fol. 104ʳ,	que cosa es fidalguía et de donde viene (what is *fidalguía* and where it comes from)

nobleça rreal (royal nobility)

---

[7] This may be a reference to the fourteenth-century Italian jurist Bartolo da Sassoferrato (1313-1357).

> The third nobility is called civil, about which we will speak here, which is commonly called *fidalguía*, which is defined and explained by Bartolo in this way: civil nobility is a quality bestowed by he who has the principality. By which it appears that he who receives it is more favored and beloved by the prince than the honest commoners we commonly call *pecheros* [. . . .] And therefore all civil nobility and *fidalguía* descends from the kings as Bartolo noted. And the closer one gets to the royal bloodline the more noble one is. It follows then that the kings occupy the peak and sovereign height of civil nobility, since civil nobility and *fidalguía* flow from them like brooks from springs, so much so that even the brother of the king who has the same father and mother, is not as noble as the king).

There are numerous folios in M with this kind of marginal gloss. On the verso side of the folio cited above, another lengthy note summarizes Alonso de Cartagena's genealogy of King Enrique II, of the Trastamaran dynasty, who was a descendent of Saint Louis IX of France: "Et asý el rrey mi señor desçiende de sant luys rrey de françia" (fol. 104ᵛ). The reader also glossed passages in the *Proposición* that celebrate the most noble cities of Spain; specifically, Burgos, Leon and Toledo (folio 105ᵛ), but the majority of the reader's notes paraphrase texts that deal with the authority of kings, the responsibilities of the governing aristocracy, and the obedience due to princes, as seen on folio 142ᵛ where a red pointing hand directs attention to a passage from the *Cuestión* which defends the divine-right of kings to the loyalty of their subjects:

> [. . . . .] Jurauan los ca
> ualleros por Dios et por nuestro señor Jesús Cristo et por
> el espíritu santo, et por la magestad del prínçipe;
> la cual segunt Dios deue ser amada por el lina
> je humanal, que farán esforçadamente to
> → do lo que el príçipe les mandare. Ca aquel que tiene
> justo prinçipado deuésele auer fiel deuoçion et
> fazer diligente seruiçio commo a Dios sy fue
> se presente (fol. 142ᵛ, The knights swore an oath on our Lord Jesus Christ and the Holy Spirit, and on the majesty of the prince; which according to God should be loved because of its human lineage, that they would be bound to do whatever the prince commanded them to do. Since he who has the le-

gitimate principality should be given faithful devotion and diligent service as if God himself were present).

The reader's marginal notes throughout the *Cuestión sobre el acto de cavallería* display an equal attention to matters of chivalry, and the obligations of the nobility. In Alonso de Cartagena's reply to the Marqués de Santillana's question on the oath of knighthood,[8] the reader took note on folio 140 verso of a passage that is reminiscent of *exemplo* 3 in the *CL*, "How King Richard of England Leapt into the Sea against the Moors," which concludes with Juan Manuel's proverb for would-be knights: "Qui por cavallero se toviere, / más deve desear este salto, / que non si en la orden se metiere, / o se ençerrasse tras muro alto" (74, "If you are in truth a knight, / You'd rather take a leap in flight / Than live in within a convent's halls, / Or be a prisoner held by walls" [54]).

The noted passage from Cartagena's letter employs similar comparisons with monastic life to warn those who would take the oath of knighthood lightly:

> Ca no poco erraría quien cuydase que la cauallería da libertad para usar de deleytes et desordenados plazeres. Et commo que libra al que la toma de trabajar, por que quien bien acatare la rregla que tiene et con grant diligençia la quisyere obseruar, por ventura la fallará tan estrecha commo la de los encerrados cartuxos o de los menores descalços (fol 140^r-140^v, For he who may think that chivalry will give him leave from work and license to enjoy delights and unfettered pleasures is more than a little mistaken. And though it frees him from work, he who observes his rule of knighthood, and with great diligence wants to follow it, may find that it is as hard as the cloistered Carthusian monks or the Carmelites).

The reader's gloss on this passage concisely summarizes the main point of the text: "la estrechura de la cavallería" ("the austerity of chivalry"); while other passages are indexed only with a cross-like key made up of three points and a horizontal line forming the base

---

[8] It may be of interest to note here that the scribe of the *Cuestión sobre el acto de cavallería* in M wrote at the beginning of the letter that it was copied from an autograph of Íñigo López de Mendoza: "Copia de la letra del dicho señor marqués" (fol. 132^r).

of the cross, extending down the margin to draw attention to the important text.

Several cross markings and braces appear in the margins of folios 141 to 143, indicating a consistent interest in the figure of the king, and the duty of knights to give their lives for the honor of their sovereign lords and the laws of the land, as seen on folio 142 recto where a brace in the left-hand margin points out the following text:

> [. . . . .] Por ende el buen cauallero que su
> sacramento quiere guardar, deue tener en poco
> su vida, quando syntiere que a defensyón de la ley
> o a seruiçio et honor de su rrey, o aprouecho et
> bien de su tierra cunpliere morir, o poner en aven
> tura su vida. Et sy lo non faze, viene contra su
> profesyón, commo el frayle que quebranta su rre
> gla (fol. 142ʳ, Therefore the good knight who wishes to keep his sacrament should not place a high price on his life when he feels he should sacrifice himself, or place himself in harms way, in defense of the law or service and honor of his king, or for the benefit and good of his land).

Reviewing the marginal traces of an individual response to manuscript M surveyed above, the reader's attitude toward the book, and specifically its political ideology, comes into clear focus. The notes are so consistent in their selection of passages that define the nature and privileges of kings, and the responsibilities of his noble subjects, that it is more than likely that this reader identified with the class identity of an elite aristocracy for whom the entire anthology appears to have been prepared. Furthermore, the marginal notes point to a specific kind of *lectio* that scanned and studied the texts, rather than reading them for amusement. Manuscript M was studied for its sound political doctrine, and possibly even for its sentential wisdom, as witnessed on folio 136 verso where another pointing finger directs future readers to a proverb-like passage in the *Cuestión sobre el acto de cavallería*:

> → Ca nunca ay tanta priesa en que alguna
> ora vazía non falle el deseoso obrador, nin ay
> tiempo tan ancho en que achaque non quede al coraçón o
> çioso (fol. 136ᵛ, No matter how busy, the industrious worker will find a free hour, and no matter how unoccupied, the lazy heart will always find an indisposition).

The traces of a scholastic reading practice found in the *Proposición* and *Cuestión* texts may be clues to how the *CL* was read in the same codex. Assisted by the marginal reading aids that systematically point to the divisions in Juan Manuel's tales, a student / reader could pick out Juan Manuel's *viessos* and Patronio's advice as sound political and moral doctrine, while following the model of princely behavior caught in the very act of governing private and public affairs with the aid of a wise counselor. The red "enxenplo" and "capítulo" notes, along with the indented and decorated proverbs of the *CL*, when studied together with the organizing parameters of the entire codex that sketch a profile of a specific audience–an audience that also marked its response to the book in numerous marginal glosses–combine to shape the meaning of the *CL* as an authoritative expression of aristocratic political doctrine, supported by orthodox teachings on the proper behavior and virtues of the ideal prince. As a final note on the audience of the *CL* in the Middle Ages, manuscript S also presents a clear picture of a specific audience: Juan Manuel's own descendent family.

In a note published in *La corónica* (1987-88), Reinaldo Ayerbe-Chaux brought to light a rather obscure manuscript in which a scribe copied the concluding proverbs of the *CL* in Biblioteca Nacional 19426, which I have described above. In that same essay the distinguished philologist deciphered a hand-written note of the S scribe, found on the last folio of Biblioteca Nacional 6376. Written in the scribe's own "cursiva endiablada" ("diabolical cursive")–according to Ayerbe-Chaux–the note mentions the battle against the kingdom of Granada in 1483 that resulted in some 800 Spanish losses and 1,500 prisoners taken by commander Abdul Kasin's troops ("Manuscritos y documentos" 89).

Ayerbe-Chaux used this hermetic scribal note to further support his hypothesis that manuscript S was produced in Sevilla, and commissioned by one of Juan Manuel's descendents, fortunately, since it became the most complete manuscript witness of Juan Manuel's *opus* known today. The scribe, who appears to have signed his name in the bottom margin of folio 199 recto, "Juan Martínez," also practiced writing in the margins of other folios, possibly to start the flow of his quill, and very often by addressing a letter to a person I believe may have been the Manuel family patron: Doña María Manuel. On the top margin of folio 136 recto the scribe repeats the same salutation three times, in which the name "dona marya" ("Doña María") is clearly legible, especially in the third addressee: "a my señora doña marya manuel" ("to my lady Doña María Manuel").

In the later fifteenth century, there were two Doña Marías related to Juan Manuel that could have commissioned the manufacture of manuscript S; Doña María Manuel de Villena, the Third Lady of Montalegre y Meneses, great-grand-daughter of Juan Manuel, and her daughter, Doña María de Manuel Figueroa, daughter of Don Lorenzo Suárez de Figueroa, First Count of Feria.[9] The Lady of Montalegre y Meneses died in 1477, six years before the disastrous lose against Granada that the S scribe records (perhaps after the manuscript had been abandoned due to the death of its patron?). It is not impossible, however, that the work was commissioned by her daughter, who would marry Don Alvar Pérez de Guzmán, son of Juan de Guzmán, Duke of Medina Sidonia. Both women would have had the means to patronize a luxurious complete-works volume of one of the family's most famous patriarchs for display in their library.

Reinaldo Ayerbe-Chaux's hypothesis on the production of manuscript S, I believe, is corroborated by the marginal notes cited above, but what is certain is that manuscript S is a very different kind of book in comparison with the other four manuscript witnesses: S does not appear to have been designed for the same use and study as the rest, and although the intended audience was clearly an aristocratic one, as a deluxe, display volume, I would argue that of all the manuscript witnesses of the *CL*, S is the least indicative of how Juan Manuel's works were read in the later Middle Ages (as a large display piece, it may not have been intended for much reading at all). The significance of the *CL* in S is apparently referential to the Manuel family itself, and as a complete-works, single-author volume, it is the manuscript whose importance and meaning is most intimately linked to the person and idea of the author.

The place of the author as a mediating factor in the construction of meaning is patent in S, as it will be in Argote de Molina's first print edition of the *CL*, but in a distinct capacity. S derives its meaning for a limited audience as a symbol of wealth, wisdom, honor and power; all of which is alluded to in the figure of the leg-

---

[9] Doña María Manuel, Lady of Montalegre y Meneses married Lorenzo Suárez in 1435. She signed a will (Zafra, July 29, 1474), which I have examined in Real Academia de la Historia, Colección Salazar y Castro, M-5 (fols. 202-206).

MS S (Biblioteca Nacional 6376), folio 136 recto, with "doña marya manuel" written in the top margin above column B.

endary family author and prince, Don Juan Manuel, but the symbolic meaning is also materially present in the 216 parchment folios of the artifact itself. The meaning of S, and all the works within it was determined by those who commissioned and manufactured this extremely expensive book, but that meaning may not have been much more than a celebration and display of family prestige. As I have argued in these chapters, the manuscripts that present the most robust evidence of reading the *CL* are manuscripts M and P. S may be the best manuscript for editing the author's text, but the other manuscript witnesses, studied together with M and P fixed a meaning for the *CL* that lingers with us today.

Conclusions

THE MODERN CRITICAL RECEPTION
OF *EL CONDE LUCANOR*

THROUGHOUT this book I have alluded to a conventional interpretation of the *CL* which has its roots in the late medieval reception of Juan Manuel's exemplary tales, and as I demonstrate in the second part of my study, the late medieval and early modern response to the *CL* can be surveyed in the global manuscript landscape of the work. In particular, manuscripts P and M provide a great deal of evidence that suggests that the *CL* was understood "in comparison with works already read"–to borrow a phrase from Hans Robert Jauss cited in the introduction–namely, the *exemplum*.

The place of Juan Manuel's narrative in M and P displays an interest in their ideological content, and potential for pedagogical uses, more than an appreciation of their aesthetic value as creative and entertaining narratives. In manuscript P, for example, the *CL* is bound together with a work like the *Lucidario*, another catechetical and orthodox work with a specific didactic function. In P, the Count's questions and Patronio's lessons are rewritten into, and ideologically aligned with, the design and purpose of the entire codex. As a kind of resource book for an ecclesiastical and aristocratic audience, P reshapes the meaning of the *CL* by suppressing its semantic potential and meta-rhetorical message, while drawing out, even rewriting, its didactic signification as a collection of *exempla* with safe and sanctioned Christian doctrine for use in a lesson, sermon, or even for the edification of a private aristocratic reader interested in the moral, religious and political teachings bound together in P. Here Juan Manuel's tales were read as another bank of orthodox doctrine.

In M, a similar reading and writing practice capped the meaning of the *CL*, witnessed in the organizing parameters of the anthology, and the marginal traces of a late medieval response to the book as a whole. The implied audience of M, in comparison with P, appears to have been a more secular one, although the codex displays a similar combination of political, moral, and religious subject matter. The reader who studied M, and marked his points of interest in marginal glosses and highlighted text clearly responded to, perhaps even identified with, the portrait of the ideal king and aristocrat outlined in works such as the *Proposición contra los ingleses* and the *Cuestión de cavallería*. Returning to the *CL* in M, it is more than likely that the compiler who designed the book, and the readers who studied it, uncovered a doctrinal resonance with the ideological content of the entire book in the Count's questions, his relationship with Patronio, and Juan Manuel's sound ethico-political proverbial wisdom flagged in the very page layout of each story. Rather than studying the *CL* for its display of Juan Manuel's powerfully coercive rhetorical strategy, the *ordinatio* of the entire book suggests that the meaning of the *CL* in M was reduced to a collection of exemplary behaviors and values for an elite aristocratic audience.

What I deduce from the manuscript evidence of reading the *CL* in the later Middle Ages is that the didacticism of Juan Manuel's tales had been reshaped and aligned with the conservative, aristocratic, orthodox, and possibly even reactionary ideology of fifteenth-century Spain, long before the positivist tradition of textual criticism closed the meaning of the *CL* and situated it at the beginning of the Spanish prose canon, as María Rosa Menocal has argued (474-75). By the end of the Middle Ages, the *CL* had been read right, or "to the right," and its earliest reception was enriched over time, beginning with its first print edition, but I would like to hypothesize here in my conclusion that the early readings of the *CL* also channeled future critical responses, establishing a continuum among readers from generation to generation.

The first print edition of the *CL* in 1575 (A) offers an excellent example of how the medieval reading and meaning of the work persists, even while a humanist interest in the text enriched the significance of Juan Manuel's collection by constructing an image and function of the author that would last through the centuries. Argote de Molina's edition is extraordinary for various reasons, the first being its paratextual material; its ecclesiastic approbation, prologue, treatise on "ancient" Castilian poetry, glossary, and genealogy of the

Manuel family created by Molina himself who appears to have been motivated to publish the *CL* in order to ingratiate himself with an influential Manuel, Don Pedro Manuel, who was a member of the king's council. The title page celebrates the prestige of the Manuel family by recalling the author's–and Don Pedro's–royal lineage, followed by the Manuel family coat of arms prominently centered in the page:[1]

> El Conde Lucanor
> Compuesto por el excelentísimo príncipe
> don Juan Manuel, hijo del Infante don Manuel,
> y nieto del Sancto rey don Fernando.
> DIRIGIDO
> por Gonçalo de Argote y de Molina, al muy Illustre señor
> Don Pedro Manuel
> Gentil Hombre de la Cámara de su Magestad, y Consejo (A2ʳ, *El Conde Lucanor* composed by the very excellent prince, Don Juan Manuel, son of the *Infante* Manuel, and grand-son of the sainted king Fernando. Edited by Gonzalo de Argote y Molina, and dedicated to the illustrious lord Don Pedro Manuel, gentleman of His Majesty's chamber and adviser).

Argote de Molina dedicates his book to Don Pedro and the curious reader as an oddity from ancient Castilla, particularly interesting for humanists as an expression of the language and poetry of a pre-modern era, as well as a record of illustrious Castilians–the most important of them being Juan Manuel himself–who should not be forgotten. That Juan Manuel was viewed as a poet by the editor is fascinating,[2] but what is particularly important about Argote de Molina's introduction to the *CL* is that he distinguishes Juan Manuel's tales for their sound doctrine, as opposed to other fables and *novelas* of the sixteenth century:

---

[1] Juan Manuel himself describes his family heraldry in the *Libro de las armas*. The Manuel coat of arms, as it appears in Argote de Molina's edition, consists of a Renaissance shield with quarterly partitions, adorned with a crown. Diagonally from top to bottom, the partitions represent a lion rampant, and a winged hand holding a sword.

[2] Clearly, Argote de Molina did not share Ian Michael's view of Juan Manuel's *viessos*, which he describes as "atrocious" ("The Function of the Popular Tale" 180).

> [A]llende que en este libro no solamente se hallará lengua, mas justamente con esto doctrina de obras y de buenas costumbres y muy cuerdos consejos con que cada uno se puede gouernar según su estado [. . . .] Et si los libros de nouelas y fábulas tienen lugar y aceptación pública, los quales tienen un solo intento que es entretener con apazible, y algunas vezes dañoso gusto, mas justamente deue ser aceptado este libro, pues demás de ser gustoso tiene (como dicho tengo) tan buena parte de aprouechamiento (A4^v, Moreover, in this book one will find not only language, but together with it, doctrine of good works and manners and many sound pieces of advice with which everyone can govern their estates [. . .]. And if the books of novellas and fables have a public place and appreciation, which have only one purpose which is to entertain with pleasing, and at times harmful pleasures, this book should be all the more accepted, since in addition to being a pleasure to read, it contains, as I have mentioned already, such a great amount of profit for the reader).

The approbation provided by the king's chaplain, doctor Heredia of the Holy Inquisition (*Sancto Oficio*), gives permission to publish the *CL* for much the same reasons:

> Parece me obra cathólica, contiene algunas historias antiguas, exemplos y fábulas moralizadas, a manera todo de consejos prouechosos, el qual por la qualidad del autor y su lenguaje antiguo castellano [. . .] me paresce que no parara perjuyzio dar licencia para que se imprima (A3^r, It appears to me to be a Catholic work, having some ancient stories, *exempla* and moralizing fables, all in the manner of profitable advice, which, because of the caliber of the author and his ancient Castilian language [. . .], it seems to me that there will be no harm in giving permission to print it).

What I find especially important about these reviews is that the authority and orthodoxy of Juan Manuel's doctrine is at least partially derived from the august lineage of the author himself. The social and political rank of the author will remain an indispensable consideration for many critics who view the *CL* as a "limpid guide" for readers from Juan Manuel's same social class who may have had similar political and spiritual concerns, and for whom Patronio provides ideologically correct solutions ("all manner of profitable advice"), following a hegemonic, fourteenth-century aristocratic worldview. Finally, the editor's comparison of Juan Manuel's narratives with other books of *novelas* and *fábulas* continues a medieval reading of the *CL* as doctrine and not necessarily "literature," although Argote de Molina, like other modern critics, attempts to harmonize the two categories.

For a simple case in point of the modern reception of the *CL* that appears to follow the early-modern reading found in A, Pedro Barcia's *Análisis de El Conde Lucanor*, published in 1968, sets up the same distinction between literary narratives, and didactic literature that employs narrative as a vehicle for its lessons, not as an end in itself: "Con don Juan Manuel ya se sabe a qué atenerse: es literatura intencionalmente ejemplar, busca un efecto y se vale de lo narrativo como instrumento. Esta actitud medieval es extraña a nuestra sensibilidad actual frente a lo literario" (24, "With Don Juan Manuel one knows what to look for: it is intentionally exemplary literature, it seeks an effect and it takes advantage of narrative as its instrument. This medieval attitude is strange to our modern sensibility regarding what we consider to be literary"). It is also very tempting to note a continuation of the early-modern reception of the *CL* in Barcia's apparent apology for the didacticism of the *CL* when he states that in spite of its moralizing, it is still "a good read": "*El Conde Lucanor* está concebido como un manual de conducta que asocia relatos y preceptos, pero no por eso se privará de ser deleitosa enseñanza" (25, "*El Conde Lucanor* is conceived as a manual of conduct that relates stories and principles, but this does not mean that they cannot be pleasant lessons to learn").

A final observation on the 1575 edition of the *CL* is worth noting before moving on to other early modern, and modern commentaries on the meaning of Juan Manuel's *exempla*. As observed in several manuscript witnesses of the *CL* (M and G particularly), late medieval readers were clearly interested in scanning the text, searching its divisible parts for sentential wisdom, or perhaps for the "whole" meaning uncovered in the array of its homologous parts, or for the mere pleasure of meditating on the various conundrums faced by the Count and Patronio's repeated hermeneutic successes at reading the Count's questions and doubts correctly. Late medieval audiences could have read the *CL* in pieces, as seen in manuscript M for example, and Argote de Molina's edition appears to continue that same medieval reading practice.

Like manuscripts M and G, Argote de Molina chose to lay out

Juan Manuel's tales according to their structural points of articulation. In A all the proverbs that conclude each tale are indented and indexed with a decorated section mark (§), similar to manuscript M and G.[3] Throughout the book, printed in large type and centered in the middle of the page, the words "HISTORIA" or "EXEMPLO" appear where Patronio introduces his story, and in some instances "APLICACION" signals Patronio's interpretation and advice for the Count. Interestingly, this apocryphal format was corrected by Pascual Gayangos, who crossed these words out in his personal transcription of A (Biblioteca Nacional 17788) in an effort to put the pieces of Juan Manuel's masterpiece back together again for his edition of the *CL* in *Biblioteca de autores españoles*. The divisions in A and manuscript G, together with the maginal notes found in manuscript M, suggest a continuity of scanning and parsing Juan Manuel's stories from the later Middle Ages to the early modern era. Furthermore, I have observed many modern critical comments on the *CL* that view Patronio's *exempla* as divisible narrative units that can "stand on their own," so to speak.

In a very important textbook of Spanish literature, Bárbara Mujica chose to edit out part of "De lo que contesció a los dos caballos con el león" ("What Happened to Two Horses and a Lion" [Mujica 36]), specifically the concluding *viessos*, which leads me to question: Is this yet another instance of reading Patronio's tales to pieces? Regardless of the editor's rationale, it is a telling instance of reading Juan Manuel's narrative in a peculiarly medieval manner that tended to reduce the meaning of the tales to its divisible parts; in this case, Patronio's *exempla* and his interpretation of each one for the Count's specific question. Pedro Barcia, again, serves as an example of a conventional response to the *CL* that accepts a reading that parses each tale from the collection, and each part of each tale as discrete narrative units.

Barcia describes Patronio's *exempla* as the most "valuable" and "savory" part of Juan Manuel's tales–"la parte más sabrosa y valiosa" (27)–with an "independent life of their own" when cut out of the framing discourse between Patronio and the Count: "puede

---

[3] As I have described in chapter 4, Juan Manuel's *viessos* are indented and set off from the body of the text in G, but it also appears that the scribe marked each maxim, along with other divisions in Juan Manuel's narratives, with the tachygraphic sign for *est*: /~/ with a dot on top and bottom (Millares Carlo 121).

CONDE

& porque don Ioan entendio que este exemplo era muy
bueno fizolo escreuir eneste libro, é fizo estos versos que
dizen assi.

$ Del que tu enemigo suele ser
nunca quieras muncho del creer.

$ CAPIT V.XXXVI. Del consejo que Patronio dio
al conde Lucanor quando dixo que queria folgar &
tomar plazer, y el exemplo fue delo que contescio a
la Formiga.

Ablaua otra vez el conde Lucanor con
Patronio su consejero enesta manera.
Patronio loado Dios yo so assaz rico,&
algunos consejan me, que pues lo pue-
do fazer, que non tome otro cuydado
si non tomar plazer, & comer & beuer
è folgar, que assaz he para mi vida è aun
que dexe a mis fijos bien heredados,& por el buen enten
dimiento que vos auedes ruego vos que me digades lo q̃
vos paresce que deuo fazer enesto. Señor conde dixo Patronio, comoquier q̃ el folgar & tomar plazer es bueno,
para que vos enesto fagades lo que es mas aprouechoso,
plazerme ya que supiessedes lo que la Formiga faze para
mantenimiento de su vida. El conde le rogo le dixesse co
mo fuera aquello. Patronio le dixo.

HISTORIA.

SEñor conde Lucanor, ya vos vedes quan pequeña es
la Formiga, & segun razon, non deuia auer gran aper
cebimiento, pero fallaredes cada al tiempo que los omes
cogen el pan, salen ellas de sus formigueros, & van a las
heras è traen quanto pan pueden para su mantenimiēto
& me-

Argote de Molina's 1575 edition of the *CL*. This page (64v) shows how the editor divided Juan Manuel's work by setting off the maxims, and separating Patronio's story from the Count's question. In other tales, Argote de Molina points to where Patronio gives his final advice by inserting "APLICACION" in the center of the page.

cobrar vida independiente pues al arrancarla de su marco su factura queda impecablemente orgánica" (27). The medieval tradition of reading the *CL* in pieces inevitably closes the semantic potential of the collection as a whole; more particularly, any meta-rhetorical lesson, or hermeneutic example, is lost if the reader cannot follow the author's divisions and *forma tractatus*, which can only be uncovered by a comparison and contrast of homologous parts. I have attempted to follow this medieval reading of the *CL* in the first part of my study, which leads the reader to an appreciation of Juan Manuel's rhetorical use of *exempla*. But it appears that another tradition of reading inadvertently suppressed Patronio's method as the message of the *CL*. It may be that Juan Manuel's earliest readers simply recognized Patronio's rhetorical example and put it to use in new books, ultimately resulting in a reading of the *CL* that limited its meaning to practical advice for realistic, fourteenth-century aristocratic preoccupations with salvation and honor: a "right" reading that viewed the text as a "Catholic work," with "all manner of profitable advice."[4]

Ian Macpherson's classic essay condenses this conventional interpretation of the *CL* as practical political and ethical advice, and ultimately as a justification for real concerns and behaviors, particularly those of the author himself:

> There is also much in *El Conde Lucanor* to suggest that it is the work of one whole man, who is intelligent, preoccupied by this dichotomy [between the words in his writings and his deeds in life] in his make-up, concerned about the problems which it continually poses him, and driven by the desire not only to justify himself to others but also to justify himself to himself. The tales, with their introductions and their morals, illustrate different aspects of this central problem; no single one of them could be said to present the problem worked out as a coherent whole, but the whole body of them, when taken together, does offer a rounded answer, a coherent view of the meaning and purpose

---

[4] Although it may be due to a mere accident of history, the *CL*, as I have argued in chapter 1, was probably most familiar to readers of the later Middle Ages and early modern era only as a collection of exemplary tales between Patronio and the Count (i.e. Part I). Breaking up the entire five-part *CL* in this way may have also lead to the general lack of critical attention paid to the other four parts of Juan Manuel's book, as well as the common practice among many publishers to print only the tales from Part I for modern, non-academic audiences.

of the nobleman's mission as Juan Manuel saw it. ("*Dios y el mundo*" 29)

Macpherson's essay accepts *a priori* that there can be no meaning beyond answers and justifications that are ultimately referential to the author's own historical moment and personal life experiences. Furthermore, the statement above is indicative of a tendency to read each tale as an independent whole, since together they only provide a "rounded answer" that Macpherson qualifies as "unsatisfactory" for modern readers in the conclusion of his essay (38). I would argue that only if we read the *CL* as doctrine, informed by our modern views of authorship and fourteenth-century Spanish history, does the work fall short of a satisfactory answer. If the meaning of the *CL* is searched for in Juan Manuel's rhetorical strategy and appropriation of the *exemplum*, then the "meaning and purpose" of the collection can be a timeless lesson on how to employ the authority of narrative to coerce and legitimate action. Following the reception of the *CL* from the sixteenth century to modern scholars like Macpherson, the residue of the "right" medieval reading can be found guiding and framing appraisals of Juan Manuel's didacticism, glossing over the meta-rhetorical message of the work that scholars have been rediscovering over the past three decades.

In the seventeenth century, Baltasar Gracián wrote commentaries on the significance of the *CL* and Juan Manuel, as well as paraphrasing some of Patronio's *exempla*, but his remarks on the meaning of the *CL* betray the persistence of the medieval understanding of Juan Manuel as essentially a conservative moral and political apologist, whose collection of exemplary tales condenses ethics and moral philosophy in an anthology of didactic short prose narratives: "[R]eduxo la filosofía moral a gustosísimos cuentos" (158, "Juan Manuel reduced moral philosophy to very pleasant stories"). Above all, Gracián values Juan Manuel, and specifically the *CL*,[5] as a work of moral philosophy; for Gracián, the *CL* was ultimately concerned with ethics, although the author's pleasant style

---

[5] Gracián cites Argote de Molina's edition of the *CL*. It is more than likely that Gracián had access only to this particular edition. This is important since it would support the notion that during the Spanish Golden Age, most readers were only familiar with the tales from Part I of the *CL*.

did not go unnoticed: "Fue eminente en estas históricas ficciones el sabio, y prudente príncipe Don Manuel en su libro del *Conde Lucanor*, siempre agradable, aunque siete vezes se lea" (208, "Eminent in these historical fictions was the wise and prudent prince Don Manuel in his book of *Count Lucanor*, always enjoyable even after seven readings").

Apparently following the late medieval and early modern response to the *CL*, the historian, economist and politician, Antonio Capmany y Montpalau writes in the eighteenth century that Juan Manuel should be studied for his example of the best use of the Castilian language from the fourteenth century: "Esta obrita con el título del *Conde Lucanor* [. . .] es la que nos proponemos por muestra del lenguage más culto y puro de aquel tiempo (corriendo los años de 1327). Ciertamente no pueden dexar de aficionar á su lectura la propiedad y ancianidad de su locucion" (34, "This little work entitled *Count Lucanor* [. . .] is one which we propose as an example of the most educated and pure use of the language from that time (around the years of 1327). Indeed, one cannot help but appreciate in one's reading the propriety and antiquity of its locution").

In *Teatro histórico-crítico de la eloquencia española* Capmany y Montpalau expresses a similar interest in language found in Argote de Molina's edition, but the author's critique of the *CL* reduces Juan Manuel's stories to their proverbial wisdom and practical moral lessons by paraphrasing Patronio's advise and Juan Manuel's *viessos*. Again, the *CL* was not read as an achievement of Spanish prose narrative, nor as a book with a rhetorical message on how to employ and read *exempla*, but as a transparently didactic collection of narratives that effectively condensed pragmatic political attitudes in an organic fourteenth-century style and language.

By the middle of the nineteenth century, Juan Manuel's place in the history of Spanish prose appears to have been consolidated, so scholars such as Manuel Milá y Fontanals and Pascual Gayangos, two of the earliest modern editors of the *CL*, celebrate Juan Manuel's contribution to Spanish letters, but the medieval reading of the moral and doctrinal content of the work still informs these philologists' interpretation of the meaning of the *CL*.

In Milá y Fontanals' 1853 edition, after surveying Juan Manuel's turbulent life and summarizing his character as "indomitable" and "iron willed," the editor puts forth one of the earliest observations on the apparent contrast between the life of the author, who appears to have been obsessed with his personal honor and wealth, and the moral tone of his works:[6] "[N]o será tanta nuestra extrañeza, al observar que un hombre de tal condición presente en sus obras singular nobleza y rectitud de ideas, y que merezcan ellas de todo punto el dictado de obras morales; si bien se ve que la virtud predilecta de su autor era una mañosa prudencia" (vii, "Our surprise probably will not be too great, when we observe that a man of such a constitution presents in his works a singular nobility and rectitude of ideas, that truly deserve the honorable title of moral works, even though it is clear that the author's favorite virtue was a more wily kind of prudence"). Here we observe one of the earliest modern interpretations of the didacticism of the *CL*; it is a blend of noble and moral virtues ("singular nobleza y rectitud de ideas" and "obras morales"), a reading which I believe is far too similar to the medieval and early modern reception to be mere coincidence. Of course, most any attentive modern reader will be able to appreciate the advice, didactic tone, and perhaps even the aristocratic feudal worldview constructed in the *CL*. Be this as it may, I would also agree with several critics cited earlier such as Peter Dunn, Laurence de Looze, and Edmund Reiss that there is much more to Juan Manuel's tales than meets the eye, and that "*El Conde Lucanor* should not be taken as simply a series of obvious moral lessons" (Reiss 121).

Working at the turn of the century, Don Pascual de Gayangos, who had at his disposal all of the manuscript witnesses known today, summarized the aesthetic and didactic merits of the *CL* by blending the canonized image of the author, with his narrative style and moral tone to produce a reading of the *CL* that added to and continued the medieval response to Juan Manuel's work. Gayangos even hints at the medieval reception of Patronio's stories, insinuating that it was their doctrine and moral rectitude that attracted such a large medieval audience:

---

[6] Later in the twentieth century, Juan Manuel's biographer, Andrés Giménez Soler would recast this same observation (119), which would continue to inform the modern reception of Juan Manuel and his work, creating the so-called "dichotomy," referred to by Macpherson ("*Dios y el mundo*" 29), between the author's political actions, and his moral philosophy presented throughout his writings.

> Ya sea que lo ameno del asunto y lo agradable de la forma le hiciesen más popular y buscado, ya que las sublimes lecciones de moral cristiana y política en él contenidas fuesen más aceptables por estar dichas en estilo llano y familiar, aunque elegante y castizo, el hecho es que se reprodujo con más frecuencia, puesto que son ya cuatro las copias antiguas que hemos visto y disfrutado (231, Be it because of the pleasing subject matter and form, or the sublime lessons of Christian morals and politics contained in them, or because they were more widely accepted having been told in a plain and familiar style, although elegant and pure, the fact is that it was more frequently reproduced given that there are four ancient copies that we have seen and enjoyed).[7]

Comparing the *CL* with other didactic works, such as the *Castigos e documentos del rey don Sancho IV*, Gayangos points out Juan Manuel's lack of erudition, but nevertheless defends the *infante*'s exemplary tales for their profitable and sound teachings ("están llenas de aprovechamiento y enseñanza" [xix]). By the beginning of the twentieth century, this conventional reading had become ossified, and can still be found today in much of the scholarship on Juan Manuel and the *CL* that I have rehearsed throughout this book.

By far, the scholar who most authoritatively determined the meaning of the *CL* for the twentieth century was Marcelino Menéndez y Pelayo, whose *Orígenes de la novela* is often cited by scholars for its appraisal of Juan Manuel's style and ethics, in comparison with other fourteenth-century authors, particularly Boccaccio. As any reader familiar with this legendary Spanish philosopher, historian, and philologist knows, Menéndez y Pelayo is notorious for his celebration of the Catholic orthodoxy of Spanish literature, and Juan Manuel was no exception. Some of Menéndez y Pelayo's comparisons of the *CL* with the *Decameron* may appear to be, at first glance, minor criticisms, but given the author's strong Catholic prejudice, Juan Manuel's chaste style and sound Christian doctrine are precisely the elements of his work that deserve recognition and celebration.

In *Orígenes*, Menéndez y Pelayo categorizes the *CL* in the same family of Castilian didactic literature as the *Castigos e documentos*;

---

[7] Gayangos is referring to manuscripts S, M, P, and H, since he did not consider his own manuscript, G, to be a "copia antigua."

they are anthologies, or catechisms, on political and moral doctrine ("catecismo político moral" 121). When it comes to his study of the *CL* in comparison with Boccaccio, Menéndez y Pelayo's more subjective artistic tastes in literature shine through. According to the legendary philologist, Juan Manuel's style pales in comparison with the *Decameron*, which is "una perpetua fiesta para la imaginación y los sentidos" (150, "a perpetual feast for the imagination and senses"); but when it comes to morals and sound, timeless doctrine, Juan Manuel's *CL* by far outstrips Boccaccio's masterpiece, which in Menéndez y Pelayo's final analysis only panders to man's "worst animal instincts": "muchas veces adulando los peores instintos de la bestia humana" (151). Speaking of Juan Manuel and the *CL*, Menéndez y Pelayo appears to revel in Juan Manuel's orthodox didacticism:

> Criado a los pechos de la sabiduría oriental, que adoctrinaba en Castilla a príncipes y magnates, fue *un moralista filósofo* más bien que un moralista caballeresco. Sus lecciones alcanzan a todos los estados y situaciones de la vida, no a las clases privilegiadas únicamente. En este sentido hace obra de educación popular, que se levanta sobre instituciones locales y transitorias, y conserva un jugo perenne de buen sentido, de honradez nativa, de castidad robusta y varonil, de piedad sencilla y algo belicosa, de grave y profunda indulgencia y a veces de benévola y fina ironía [my emphasis] (151, Nurtured on the milk of Eastern wisdom, that which indoctrinated princes and magnates of Castilla, he was *a moral philosopher* more than an aristocratic moralist. His lessons reach all estates and stations in life, not only the privileged classes. In this sense, his is a work of popular education, that is above local and transitory institutions, and it preserves a perennial essence of common sense, native honor, robust and manly chastity, simple faith–at times a bit militant–of profound and serious indulgence, and at times a subtle and benevolent irony).

I would argue here in the conclusion of my work that the moral philosophy and doctrine has come down to us already mined from Patronio's stories, and this conventional "right" didactic meaning of the *CL* is as much the consequence of medieval readings and uses of Juan Manuel's exemplary tales, as it is the result of the author's original design. As I have argued primarily in the first part of this book, there is another lesson to be learned; it is a lesson on rhetoric and the rhetorical use of narrative, but it may also be a lesson on the very contingency of signs. Nevertheless, the orthodox reading of the *CL* as a work with "all manner of profitable advice" remains in many modern critical editions.

As early as 1920, F. J. Sánchez Cantón paraphrases the long tradition of reading the *CL* right by reducing the "important" part of Juan Manuel's collection to Patronio's stories (9), and by concluding that the *CL* is essentially a work of ethics and moral doctrine (16). Continuing the early modern focus on the relationship between the ideological content of the tales, and the author's own life, Eduardo Juliá insists that the meaning of the *CL* be understood in the light of the author's worldview expressed in his entire *opus* (xvi), and as recent as 1984, José Manuel Fradejas Rueda reduces Juan Manuel's entire work to its most superficial, terse and somber didacticism: "no pretende divertir, como ocurre en el *Libro de buen amor*, sino enseñar" (35, "Juan Manuel does not intend to entertain, as in the *Libro de buen amor*, rather his intention is to teach"). The examples abound, and a study of the modern reception of the *CL* would be a fascinating new investigation, beginning where this book ends, since it appears that the echoes of Juan Manuel's medieval readers are still audible in our most modern editions and critical debates over the meaning of the *CL*.

Appendix I

EXEMPLOS 53 AND 54 OF *EL CONDE LUCANOR* IN P[1]
[fols. 61ʳ-62ʳ][2]

Capítulo LIII. De la emaginaçión que puede sacar a omne de entendimiento et non se puede tornar de ligero sinon commo aquí dize; contesçió esto a un omne.

Un omne estaua doliente et començó a pensar en la muerte de guisa que pensó que era muerto. Et así fue que un día leuantóse su muger et díxole que si quería comer, et él díxole brauamente: ¡que veýa que estaua muerto et preguntáuale si quería comer! Et ella díxole que pues fablaua, que bivo estaua, et él porfiava que estaua muerto et diziéndole que fuese a llamar a sus parientes et que les fiziese saber commo era muerto et que le fiziesen onrra al su enterramiento. Et ella díxole que estaua loco et fuera de su entendimiento. E diziendo estas rrazones partióse dél, et guisó de comer et comió ella et él non quiso nada. Otro día des que ella se leuantó, fabló con él et díxole estas mesmas rrazones, et otro día eso mismo díxole que se leuantase. E él díxole: "¡Veres que loca muger esta! Vee que estó muerto et dize me que me leuante. Ve agora, llama mis parientes et diles commo so muerto et que me vengan a fazer onrra."

---

[1] I have included the following appendixes for interested readers who may want to follow up on some of the texts mentioned in this book which either have not been edited, or are found in out-of-print editions that are not readily available.

[2] Transcriptions are my own from the facsimile edition of manuscript P, published by the Real Academia Española. I have added accent marks and punctuation, and I have not altered the spelling of words. Eugenio Krapf edited the version of the *Conde Lucanor* as it appears in P (unfortunately he chose to edit only the *CL*, rather than all the works of P together), but it is a difficult book to find, so I have included these extra tales here for the sake of convenience. I have followed some of Krapf's sentence divisions and punctuation.

E ella veyendo que enflaqueçía et non quería comer dixo entre sí: este omne non muera por mal rrecabdo, quiero yr llamar sus parientes et pongan rrecabdo en él. E luego fue et llamó los diziendo que su marido estaua fuera de entendimeinto et dezía que los llamasen que le fuesen fazer onrra. E ellos ayuntáronse et fueron lo a ver et des que entraron por su casa dixiéronle: "Amigo, ¿cómmo estades?" Et él díxoles: "Veres en ora mala. ¡Veen que estó muerto et dizen me que cómmo estó! ¿Non vedes que estó muerto? Leuadme a la iglesia et fazedme mi onrra." E ellos de que esto oyeron començaron a rreyr diziéndol que estaua fuera del su entendimiento; et con esto fueron a llamar al físico que lo viese; et él vino luego, et era gran sabidor; et des que llegó a él, oyó aquellas palabras que dezía, díxol: "Mal fazen estos vuestros parientes en non vos querer fazer onrra et enterrar vos, ca muerto estades vos; et así, amigo, yo les diré agora que vos lieuen a la iglesia et vos entierren onrradamente." E díxole aquel omne: "A, señor, vos me entendedes bien ca estos otros non veen commo estó muerto et vós sí." E partióse de allý el físico; et su muger et sus parientes ayuntados todos díxoles: "Amigos, sabed que ese omne pensó tanto en la muerte que verdaderamente tiene que es muerto, et omne del mundo non lo podría así sacar de aquella ymaginaçión; pero vañaldo et leualdo a la iglesia a viesperas, et en la noche yo faré alguna cosa que torne a su entendimeinto," et ellos fizieron lo así.

E des que lo ouieron vañado et puesto en la cama díxoles que por que non trayán el clérigo, et dixiéronle que mejor era que le fiziesen su onrra en la iglesia que non en casa, et él díxoles que bien dezían. E así lo leuaron, et lo pusieron en la iglesia et fizieron así su onrra conplida, et sus candelas et todo su rrecabdo, et estudieron allý con él fasta que anocheçió; et en la noche dieron a entender que se yuan todos, et çerraua la iglesia. Et fincaron allý fasta seys o siete de sus parientes, et pusieron se nonbres de otros sus conosçientes et amigos que eran muertos, et vistiéronse sendas mortajas de lien[ç]o[3] et esudieron allí. Esto todo fue por mandado del físico. E luego el físico dioles una jarra de letuario confortatiuo de cosas que esforçasen el engenio et le tornasen a su memoria. Et fizieron lo que les mandó el físico en esta manera:

---

[3] The scribe actually writes "lienco," but it is obvious that the missing diacritic mark for /ç/ is an error. Eugenio Krapf's transcription shows "liençо," with no note on the scribal error (204).

Quando fue bien noche, vistiéronse aquellos omnes que fincaron en la iglesia sus mortajas, et andauan por la iglesia, et andando dauan del pie al ataúd en que estaua metido. E quando él los sintió, dixo: "¿Quién anda aý?" Et ellos dixiéronle: "Fulán et fluán, tus amigos, que bien sabes que somos muertos. Lieua, andarás aquí con nosotros." E des que los vido con sus mortajas, creyó los et andaua con ellos; et des que andudieron una pieça, dixo uno a otro calladamente: "Come más." Et el otro dixo al otro, et así todos fasta que lo oyó él, et díxoles: "¿Cómmo los muertos comen?" Et ellos dixiéronle: "Los muertos comen muy dulçes manjares que an en el paraýso terrenal, et dar te emos a comer dello." E luego fue uno et troxo la jarra del letuario, et comió cada uno un poco, et diéronle a él un pedaço bueno, et comió; et des que lo ouieron comido dixiéronle que se querían yr; et metiéronlo en su ataúd, et escondiéronse en la iglesia, [et] callando, echáronse a dormir. E des que fue de mañana, leuantáronse, et abrieron el iglesia, et él dormió tan bien después que comió el letuario fasta que le despertaron. E dende llamaron al clérigo et dieron a entender que lo leuauan a soterrar, et des que despertó dixo: "Amigos ¿Dó me leuáis, o quién me truxo aquí?" Et falló se en su acuerdo. E des que le contaron la manera marauillóse ende mucho, et así vivió toda su vida en su acuerdo commo ante. Por que se demuestra que la ymaginación saca a omne de entendimeinto.

Capítulo LIIII. De commo la onrra deste mundo non es sinon commo sueño que pasa.

Así fue que un rrey andando un día rribera de mar, vido estar un ferrero durmiendo que se auía echado bebdo en aquella rribera. Et era pobre et moraua en la çibdat do aquel rrey estaua, et violo el rrey et acatólo et dixo a los omnes que con él estauan: "Tomad este omne et leualdo al alcaçar a mi posada." Los omnes marauilláronse et tomáronlo durmiendo et lleuáronlo a su posada; et fue el rrey con ellos, et mandólo echar en su cama dormido. E mandó çerrar todas las lunbreras que auíe en todo el palaçio, et mandólo todo encortinar todo enderredor de la cama en manera que non veýa un omne a otro. Esto fecho, mandó a todos sus donzeles et escuderos et caualleros que ellos que fiziesen seruiçio et onrrasen aquel omne que auía mandado echar en su casa et en su cama, asý commo a él et más; ca él dixo que tenía en penitençia de estar un tiempo ençerrado en un palaçio, et non fablar a ninguno, et que querríe que aquel fincase en su lugar. Todos los suyos besaron le la mano, et dixieron que lo faría; et partido el rrey dellos, metió quanta vianda quiso en un palaçio, et metióse, et çerró contra sí. E esto fecho, el bebdo despertó et començó de esperezarse; et oyeron lo los seruidores del rrey que lo guardauan, et dixieron luego: "Señor, la vuestra merçed." Él, des que lo oyó, marauillóse, et en que lo vido todo escuro, tornóse a dormir, et durmió muy mucho en guisa que otra vez vino a despertar; et desque le dixieron, "Señor, ¿qué vos plaze?, marauillóse, et dixo que ¿quién lo auía allý echado? E ellos rrespondieron le: "Señor, vos os echastes, que vos sodes el rrey nuestro señor aquien nos somos tenudos de seruir." Et estando en esto, vistieron lo de los paños rreales del rrey et començaron le a dar agua a manos et peynallo et a allanar le los cabellos, et los paños quel vestían; et des que salyó fuera, fizieron le todo rreuerençia, et besaron le la mano diziendo: "Señor, mantenga os Dios." E él en esto marauilla[ua]se, et non sabíe que dixiese, sinon que dixo quel diesen de comer; et luego fueron puestas las mesas et posaron lo a comer et dieron le buenas viandas et a beuer con buenas traças, et siruieron lo rrealmente bien, así commo a rrey et a señor, taniendo juglares delante, faziendo le gran plazer. E el beyendo esto touo que así era de fecho et començó a fazer merçedes et a [...].[4]

---

[4] Here ends the tale as it appears in P.

APPENDIX II

DESCRIPCIÓN DE MÉRIDA AND *APÓLOGO DEL FILÓSOFO QUE FUE A UNA HUERTA A CORTAR VERDURAS* IN M.
Madrid, Biblioteca Nacional 4236

DESCRIPCIÓN DE MÉRIDA
[fols. 184ʳ-185ʳ]

[. . .] las veynte al sol leuante, e las otras veynte a sol poniente, e las otras veynte al medio día, e las otras veynte a setentrión. E abía çinco alcáçares, los quatro entre medias de los espaçios de las sobre dichas puertas. E cada alcáçar tenía una puerta e el otro alcáçar estaua en medio de la çibdad en una grand plaça. Este alcáçar avía veynte torres muy altas, que las más baxas dellas eran de veynte e çinco estados. Cada una de las sobredichas puertas avía dos calles una de una parte e otra de la otra. E todas venían a salir a la plaça grande e avía en las calles de ancho de una faz era a otra treynta codos. E de cada casa salía un caño por so tierra e entrauan todos estos caños en un caño grande que avía en cada calle por do corrían todas las aguas de la lluvia e eso mesmo toda la susiedad. E desta guisa non fallarían ninguna de las calles susia. E en el muro de la çibdad avía tres mill e seysçientas torres en que avía tan solamente a las puertas çiento e sesenta, que avían estas de altura quarenta estados. E cada torre de las otras del muro, avían cada treynta estados, e por cada puerta entraua un caño de agua que venía de muy lexos tierra. E por tal maestría era fecha que las yglesyas estauan sobre sý a mill pasadas del grand alcáçar, e todas en derredor que una non estaua más lexos ni otra más çerca. E en cada yglesia avía una grand torre, e de tal altura era que cada una avía un molino de viento que molía. E por que la çibdad fuese abastada de todo lo que nesçesario era, por tan buena ordenança era rregida que para la provisyón della avían rrepartido que los moradores de las villas e çibdades del su señorío fuesen tenudos de poner en cada un año a costa de la çibdad en cada alcáçar de los quatro veynte mill cargas de pan, las quinze mill de trigo, e las çinco mill de çebada e diez mill cántaras de vino colorado e çinco mill de blanco. E cada çinco mill carrneros, e quinientas vacas, e dos mill puercos. E todas las rrentas que esta çibdad avía del muro adentro eran para su provisyón, e lo que rrentauan las çibdades e villas del su señorío eran para conquistar villas e tierras que la obedeçiesen. E desde la primera v[illa] que fue puesto en esta çibdad la muchedunbre de [los] conplimientos que oýdo avedes quando ella se començó a poblar fasta que llegó al grand señorío que ovo, duraron trresientos años que nunca le faltó las cosas sobre dichas. E non ovo señor en España ni en Roma, que en ella non fiziese mucho. E non duró después la su grand prosperidad más de diez e syete años e ocho meses quando començó la su planea de abaxar. E algunos sabios dizen que quanto duró en sobir a la grande alteza e poderío que ovo que tanto durara en abaxar de grado en grado asý commo subió fasta que llegase a ser tal e de tan poco valor commo la menor villa que ella touo por sý. Enpero esto non sabe ninguno sy es verdad sy non sólo Dios. E agora podredes creer quel fecho de Mérida fue muy grande e de grand fama segund las cosas que oýdo avedes. E ora fagamos fyn en esta materia por que la su planea e la de España me pareçe que an seýdo de una guisa segund lo pasado e lo que agora es, porque vos digo que nunca ninguno se deue tener por aquel que las gentes le dan la fama fasta que vea la su fyn, sy está en egual del buen comienço. E aun aý deue poner dubda, ca todas las cosas han de aver fyn synon lo çelestial. Enpero durarán más unas que otras asý commo a Dios plaze.

APÓLOGO DEL FILÓSOFO QUE FUE A UNA HUERTA A CORTAR VERDURAS[1]
[fols. 186^r -186^v]

Un fylósofo avía un syervo esclavo et muy feo et deforme en su gesto et pareçer et commo quier que tal fuese era de muy agudo yngenio et muy sabio et acaesçió que un día el fylósofo fue a una güerta a conprar alguna verdura, et commo la conprase diola al

---

[1] Adolfo Bonilla y San Martín transcribed this tale in *Anales de la literatura española* (155).

syervo que yba con él et commo començase a se yr para su casa díxole el ortolano –"Ruégote, maestro, que me esperes un poco por que querría preguntarte una questión." Dize el filósofo –"Ya me plaze et te espero, fabla lo que te plazera." Et dize el ortolano –"maestro, las yeruas et ortalizas que diligentemente se syenbran et se labran con grand cura, ¿por qué vienen más tarde que las que nasçen por sý et non se labran?" Et el fylósofo commo oyese esta quistión filosofal et non pudiese rresponder a ella, dize –"Estas semejantes cosas proceden de la providencia divina, de lo qual el syeruo que el fylósofo llevaua con sygo se rrió muy de gana. Et dízele su señor –"¡Loco! ¿ríeste o escarrneçes?" Dixo el syervo –"Escarrnesco, non de ty, mas al fylósofo que te enseñó. Et que soluçión de fylósofo es, que por la divina providençia proçeden estas cosas tales. Eso tanbién lo saben los albarderos." Díxole el filósofo –"Pues, suelta tú la quistión." Responde el syervo –"Sy me lo mandas a mí, cosa ligera es de fazer." Entonçe el filósofo dixo, buelto al ortolano –"Non conbiene al filósofo que continuamente enseña en los estudios en las ju[n]tas rresponder et soltar las quistiones, mas este mi moço que en estas cosas es asás sabiente soltará la quistión, por tanto rruega a él." E dize el ortolano –"Ese non lynpio sabe letras, que mala ventura." Et dixo al syervo –"Tú, moço, ¿as conosçimiento destas cosas?" Al qual dixo el syervo, "pienso que sý, mas está atento; tú demandas ¿por qué las ortalizas que tú syenbras et labras creçen más tarde que las que de suyo nasçen, et non se labran? Abre las orejas et oye, asý commo la muger biuda que a fijos et casa con otro marido que tiene fijos, a los unos es madre et a los otros madrastra, et grand diferençia es entre los fijos et an[ten]ados.[2] Ca los fijos con grand afeçión et diligentemente son criados, et los antenados con negligençia et muchas vezes con aborreçimiento se tratan. Desta manera la tierra es madre a las yerbas que por sí nasçen, et a las otras que por mano de onbre se syenbran es madrastra." Et commo oye se el ortolano estas cosas díxole –"grand enojo me as quitado, de graçia te do las verduras, et quado las obieres menester vendrás et toma de graçia qualquier cosa de la güerta que querrás.
el inysio de los toneles del aseyte
el inysio de los mill florines perdidos

---

[2] The scribe seems to have mistakenly written, "andados." Given the context, and the appearance of "antenados" in the next line, I have chosen to make this small correction.

APPENDIX III

SELECTION OF *FLORES DE FILOSOFÍA* IN G[1]

Madrid, Biblioteca Nacional, 18415
[fols. 122ᵛ-127ʳ]

E quanto de los otros sacramentos son cinco, Penitencia, Confirmación, Casamiento, Orden postrimera,[2] vien vos dezía tantas e tam buenas razones en cada uno dellos que vos entenderedes que son asaz, mas déxolo por dos cosas: la una por no alongar mucho el libro, e lo al por que sé que vós e quien quier que esto oya[3] entre mala sospecha,[4] ca la obediencia es guarda de quien la quiere e castillo de quien la sygue, e lumbre de aquel en quien anduviere; e saved que quien ama a Dios ama a sus cosas, e quien ama a sus cosas ama la ley, e quien ama la ley deve amar al rey que la mantiene; e los que son obedientes a su rey son seguros de no aver vollicio en su reino e de no crecer cosa entre ellos porque se ayan a defazer su comunidad, e serán seguros de no salir de regla e de derecho. E non deve ninguno de los del reyno reprehender al Rey su señor por las

---

[1] Pascual Gayangos included this interpolated text in *Escritores en prosa anteriores al siglo XV*, published for the *Biblioteca de Autores Españoles* series.
[2] Here the scribe seems to have left out the word "unción." Given the many other errors in this copy, a skip is not unlikely, but it is not impossible that it did not exist, or was not legible, in the exemplar.
[3] "[Q]ue esto oya" are the last words of the *CL* (Part V) in G that are also in S.
[4] If indeed a different book was used for *Flores*, "entre mala sospecha" is the scribe's own writing to create a transition for the new conclusion to the *CL*. The rest of the text that follows are selections from *Flores de filosofía*, drawing on two manuscript witnesses. Hermann Knust identifies the selected texts in *Dos obras didácticas y dos leyendas*, and states that Gayangos's suspicion that a different book was used to interpolate the *leyes* from *Flores de filosofía* into the *CL* was correct (7).

cosas que pertenecieren e él fiziere endereçando su reino, ca todos los del su reino se deven guiar por él. E saved que con la obediencia se viedan las peleas e se salvan los caminos e haprovecen los vienes, e nunca fue hombre que pugnasse en desobedecer al rey que no le diesse Dios mal quebranto ante que muriesse.

Quando el rey fiziere justicia en su pueblo, abrá de Dios buen galardón e grado en su pueblo; ca el rey que non fiziere justicia no merece el reyno. E saved que el mejor de los tiempos del mundo es el tiempo del rey justiciero, ca mejor es el amo malo que viene en tiempo del rey justiciero,[5] que el buen amo que viene en tiempo del rey sin justicia. Ca el rey justiciero no consiente fuerça nin sovervia, e la más provechosa cossa del reyno es el rey, que es caveça dél, e la cosa porque más vale el rey es que sea justiciero e mercedero. E otrosí mejor es al rey no vivir so señorío del rey justiciero, que vevir sin él en guerra e en miedo; e quien faze lazdrar a sus vasallos por culpa de aquel, es rey sin ventura. E dixo Dios: "Quien se desviasse del vien, desviarse ýa el vien dél, e los que fazen justicia, esos son de luenga vida; e las que la non fazen, son de poca vida." E sabed que con la justicia aduran los vienes, e con el tuerto piérdense; pues el rey deve ser justiciero en sí mismo e en los de su casa; e en su pueblo o[be]decerlo han de coraçón e de voluntad, ca el rey justiciero ajúntansele los hombres a obedecerle, ca la justicia del rey allega los hombres que mejor, la sin justicia derrámalos. E el hombre que mejor lugar tiene ante Dios e ante los hombres, assí es el rey que faze justicia, e el rey es hombre que más deve temer a Dios, e que más deve amar a la verdad e fazer merced e mesura, porque Dios le faze merced e le dio el reyno que mantuviesse, e metió en su mano cuerpos e almas e averes de su pueblo.[6]

Sabed que quien enojare al rey, enozirle ha, e quien se le alongare no meterá mientes en él. E guardadvos de herrar al rey en algún hierro, ca él ha por manera de contar el más pequenio yerro por grande; e maguer le aya hombre fecho servicio luengo tiempo, todo lo olvida a la ora de la sania, e quien se le faze muy privado, el rey enójase dél, e quien se le tiene en caro, aluéngalo de sí [et] no lo ha muy gran menester; ca los reyess han por manera de enojarse de los

---

[5] Gayangos seems to have skipped over "ca mejor es el amo malo que viene en tiempo del rey justiciero," creating the following nonsensical passage: "es el tiempo del rey justiciero, que el buen amo que viene en tiempo del rey sin justicia" (434).

[6] Gayangos transcribes "cuerpo," but the manuscript text clearly reads "pueblo."

que se les fazen muy privados, e de querer mal a los que se tienen en caro; quanto más te llegare el rey a su companía e a su servicio, tanto le ave mayor miedo e mayor obediencia e le conocer mayor reverencia. E sabed que no ay peor sania que la del rey, ca en reyendo manda matar, e en reyendo manda destruir, e a las vezes faze escarmiento por pequenia culpa, e a las vezes perdona gran culpa por pequenia ruego, e a las vezes dexa muy grandes culpas sin ningún escarmiento; e por ende por todo eso non deve hombre ensaniar al rey, maguer lo maltraiga, e non se deva atrever a él maguer sea su privado. Ca en el rey ha braueza e ensániase como león, y el amor dél es penado, e de muy braua pena la mata horas ya con la primera lança que acaesce, viniéndole la sania, e después pone al vil en lugar del noble, e al flaco en lugar del esforçado, e págase de lo que faze sólo que sea su voluntad. E sabed que la gracia del rey es el mejor bien terrenal que hombre puede aver, pero dizen que el amor del rey no es eredad, e la semejança del rey es como la vid que trava con los árboles que falla más acerca de sí, e sobre ellos se e[x]tiende[7] qualesquier que sean, e non busca mejores, pues están aluenie della.

Saved que el rey e el reyno son dos personas, e como una cossa después que son partidos assí como el cuerpo e la ánima non son una cosa, e otrosí el rey e su pueblo no puede ninguno bien acavarse yendo desavenidos; e por ende la cosa que más deve pugnar el rey es de aver amor verdadero con su pueblo, e sabed que este mundo no ha mayor lazería que governar pueblo a quien lo quiere governar con lealtad e con verdad. E por esto dize un savio: El señor del pueblo más lazdrado es *que* el más lazdrado dellos.[8] E la mejor manera que el rey puede aver fortaleza con mesura e mansedad sin flaqueza, e no es bien al rey en ser quexoso, mas deve fazer sus cosas de vagar e con espacio, ca mejor podría fazer lo que non fizo que de fazer lo que ubiere fecho, todavía le deve venir en mente de fazer merced a los peccadores; ca el rey deve ser fuerte a los malos e muy derecho e merecedero a los buenos e deve ser verdadero en su palabra en lo que prometiere e deve aver por costumbre de amar los buenos e ellos que fallen en él verdad. E el rey deve

---

[7] The manuscript text reads "se entiende," but I believe Gayangos's correction–"se extiende" (434)–is appropriate for the context.

[8] Gayangos corrects the saying by deleting "que" as it appears in the manuscript text emphasized above. Gayangos's edition reads: "El señor del pueblo más lazdrado es el más lazdrado dellos" (434).

mucho atar tres cosas que él hubiere de dar.⁹ La segunda que no tarde el galardón aquel que lo hubiere fecho servycio por que lo merezca. La tercera es que cate muy bien las cosas ante que las faga. Otrosí deve guardar que sepa bien ante la verdad que juzgue, ca el juizio se deve dar en cierto e non por sospecha, pero sepa el rey que la justicia que él mandare del que mereciere muerte, aquella es vida ante Dios.

Sabed que el rey [que] se pospone¹⁰ las cosas, mucho lo nuze en su facienda; ca por eso dizen que quien pospone lo que oy ha de fazer para cras nunca aproveze su fecho. Quando el rey fiziere alguna cosa con consejo de sus hombres buenos maguer que non salga a bien lo que averná tarda, más vale que non se aventure a fazerlo sin su consejo, maguer salga a vien. E las peores maneras que puede aver el rey es de ser fuerte a los flacos, e flaco a los fuertes, e que sea escaso a quien no deve. E por ende dixeron que quatro cosas están mal a quatro personas; la primera ser el rey escaso a los que lo sirven, la segunda es ser el alcalde torticero, la tercera ser el físico doliente e no se saver dar consejo. E la 4ª es ser el rey atal que no osen los hombres que son sin culpa venir ante él, ca ma[s] de ligero se endereçarán las cosas grandes en el pueblo que la pequenia que es de endereçar en el rey; ca el pueblo quando es de mejorar, mejorarlo ha el señor, e si el señor es de mejorar no ay quien lo mejore sino Dios e por ende de aquel de quien atiende jusicia e derecho, no deve en el fablar sobervia nin braveza, ca quando se ensania es muy gran cuyta ca le semeja que le viene la muerte de allí donde espera la vida, e esto es atal como el hombre que ha sed e quiere vever del agua e afógase con ella, e no deven los reyes desdeniar a unas cosas que no conoçen de nuevo, ni tenerla en vil manera maguer sehan¹¹ pequenias. Ca las mayores cosas contecieron en los reynos pequenios, començaron e crecieron; e esto fue porque las daniaron de comienço e las tovieron en vil ca la pequenia pelea o el pequenio mal puede crescer tanto que fará muy gran danio, assí como el fuego

---

⁹ Here the text skips to the second attribute. According to Hermann Knust's edition in *Dos obras didácticas y dos leyendas*, in which manuscript G is cited for its fragments of *Flores de filosofía*, the first attribute is: "que dexe pasar la sanna ante que dé juysio sobre las cosas que lo ouier' á dar" (28).

¹⁰ Gayangos transcribes "si pospone." (434)

¹¹ I have chosen not to alter the spelling of the manuscript text as much as possible, but here Gayangos's correction–"sean"–makes perfect sense, and is worth noting (434).

que comiença de una centella en otra, e si luego no es amatado quema muy gran tierra.

Sabed que el esforçado esmedreçe sus enemigos e honrrase e defiéndese a sí mismo e a los que son con él; e el covarde desampara padre e hijo e hermanos e amigos, e ayuda a sus enemigos. E las peores dos maneras que hombre puede aver es ser escaso e covarde e no cuida el covarde de estorcer de muerte por su covardía si le huviere de venir, ca savida cosa es que los covardes caen siempre en ella e esfuércenla los esforçados, e mejor es recivir los golpes delante e morir como bueno que recevir los de otra guisa e morir como malo. E la primera cosa que gana el que es de buen esfuerço es que anda asegurado e non se espanta de sus enemigos; e saved que el desmayamiento naçe de la flaqueza del coraçón en el occasión de muerte en las vatallas. Ca savida cosa es que más son de los que mueren en las lides de los que fuyen, que no de los que tornan sobre sí. E sabed que el desmayamiento naçe de la flaqueza del coraçón en el occasión de muerte; e sabed que grande ayuda es la sufrencia, e el que es de gran coraçón lidia esforçadamente como si estuviesse en castillo. Ca con el esfuerço gana ho[m]bre honrra e es temido e recelado e defiéndese de fuerça e tuerto e de abaxamiento; e la franqueza e el esfureço fallaredes en los hombres de buena creencia, e el que fia en Dios es amparado dél en las vatallas.

Sabed que los tiempos buenos e malos han plaza e días contados en que han de durar, e pues si te viniere tiempo malo súfrelo hasta que se cumplan sus días e se cumplan sus días [sic] e se cumpla su plazo; e los mejores tiempos del mundo son los días en que viven los hombres a sombra del buen señor que ama justicia e mesura; ca la mayor partida de la mejoría del tiempo es en el rey. E sabed que el mundo es como el libro, e los hombres como son como [sic] las letras, e las planas escriptas son como los tiempos que quando se acava la una plana comiença la otra. E saved que según fuere la ventura del rey, atal será la ventura de los que viven so la su merced, e quando se acava el tiempo de los que ubieren vez, no les tiene pro la gran companía ni las muchas; e los que comiençan con la vez de la ventura, maguer sean pocos e flacos, siempre vencen e fazen a su guissa. E el mejor tiempo que los del reyno puede aver es que su rey sea bueno e merece ser amado de Dios, e aquellos son siempre bien andanates a quien él quiere ayudar.

Saved que el enseniamiento es como el guarnimiento de la espada, e sabed que el enseniamiento es manera del seso, e más vale enseniamiento a lugares que linage; ca el hombre bien enseniado conocerle han por su enseniamiento, e no le conocerán por su linage si no gelo mostraren e no gelo fazen saver; e el buen enseniamiento es como buen companiero a los que son fuera de su tierra,[12] e el buen companiero a la soledad. E saved que no puede hombre a su fijo mostrar mejor cosa que buen enseniamiento, e quien castiga a su fijo quando es pequenio, fuelga con él quando es grande. E todo hombre que ha en sí tres cosas, non habrá lazería nin abrá soledad; la una es que sea bien enseniado, e la otra que non faga mal a ninguno, e la tercera que non faga cosa que le esté mal. En el mundo no ha mejor heredad que enseniamiento bueno; e el que es más abondado de saver que de seso, es como el pastor que ha poco seso e guarda mucho ganado; e el que no es de buena creencia, quando más abondado es de saver que de seso, atanto es peor e más danioso. E el buen seso e el buen consejo, si es metido en obra que sea servicio de Dios, es bien, e si no, quando fuere más bueno aprovecharse ha de su seso e de su saver; si fuera su saver más complido que su seso, no se aprovechará de su seso nin del su saver; ca dizen que el saver es tal como el árbol sin fructo, e que quando es el hombre abondado del saver, es más menguado del seso, menos vale porque lo save.

---

[12] Gayangos seems to have skipped over "a los que son fuera de su tierra" (435).

BIBLIOGRAPHY

MANUSCRIPTS

Madrid, Biblioteca Nacional 6376 (Manuscript S of the *CL*)
Madrid, Biblioteca Nacional 4236 (Manuscript M of the *CL*)
Madrid, Biblioteca Nacional 18415 (Manuscript G of the *CL*)
Madrid, Biblioteca Nacional 19426
Madrid, Biblioteca Nacional 17788
Madrid, Real Academia de la Historia 9-5893 (Manuscript H of the *CL*)
Madrid, Real Academia de la Historia, Colección Salazar y Castro, M-5
Madrid, Real Academia Española 15 (Manuscript P of the *CL*)

EDITIONS OF *EL CONDE LUCANOR*

Argote de Molina, Gonzalo, ed. *El Conde Lucanor*. Sevilla: Hernando Díaz, 1575.
Ayerbe-Chaux, Reinaldo, ed. *Libro del Conde Lucanor*. Madrid: Alhambra, 1983.
Blecua, José Manuel, ed. *El Conde Lucanor*. Madrid: Castalia, 1982.
———, ed. *El Conde Lucanor*. Nota actualizadora de Fernando Gómez Redondo. Madrid: Castalia, 2002.
———, ed. *Obras completas*. 2 vols. Madrid: Gredos, 1982.
England, John, ed. *El Conde Lucanor: A Collection of Medieval Spanish Stories*. Warminster: Aris & Phillips, 1987.
Fradejas Rueda, José Manuel, ed. *El Conde Lucanor*. Barcelona: Plaza & Janés, 1984.
Gayangos, Don Pascual de, ed. *Escritores en prosa anteriores al siglo XV. Biblioteca de autores españoles (desde la formación del lenguaje hasta nuestros días)*. Vol. 51. Madrid: Sucesores de Hernando, 1905.
Gloeckner, Nydia R., ed. *El Conde Lucanor: An Edition of Manuscript 4.326 in the Biblioteca Nacional in Madrid*. Diss. The Pennsylvania State U, 1971.
England, John, ed. *El Conde Lucanor: A Collection of Mediaeval Spanish Stories*. Warminster [England]: Aris & Phillips Ltd., 1987.
Juliá, Eduardo, ed. *El Conde Lucanor*. Madrid: Librería General de Victoriano Suárez, 1933.
Krapf, Eugenio, ed. *El libro de Patronio ó El Conde Lucanor*. By Don Juan Manuel. 2nd ed. Vigo: Librería de Eugenio Krapf, 1902.

Keller, John E. and Clark Keating, eds. *The Book of Count Lucanor and Patronio: A Translation of Don Juan Manuel's* El Conde Lucanor. Lexington: U of Kentucky P, 1977.
Milá y Fontanals, M., ed. *El libro de Patronio ó El Conde Lucanor.* Barcelona: Juan de Oliveres, 1853.
Real Academia Española. *El Conde Lucanor y otros textos medievales: Códice de Puñonrostro.* Facsim. ed. Madrid: Real Academia Española, 1992.
Sáinz de Robles, Federico Carlos, ed. *El Conde Lucanor y Patronio: Libro de ejemplos.* 4a edición. Madrid: Aguilar, 1968.
Serés, Guillermo, ed. *El Conde Lucanor.* Barcelona: Crítica, 1994.

PRIMARY SOURCES

Augustine, Aurelius. *Concerning the Teacher (De Magistro) and On the Immortality of the Soul.* Trans. George G. Leckie. New York: Appleton-Century-Crofts, 1938.
Bennett, William J, ed. *The Book of Virtues: A Treasury of Great Moral Stories.* New York: Simon & Schuster, 1993.
Cervantes, Miguel de. *Novelas ejemplares.* Ed. Harry Sieber. 2 vols. Madrid: Cátedra, 1990.
[Cicero], *Rhetorica ad Herennium.* Trans. Harry Caplan. Cambridge and London: Harvard UP, 1999.
García de Castrojeriz, Juan. *Glosa castellana al 'Regimiento de príncipes' de Egidio Romano.* Ed. Juan Beneyto Pérez. 3 vols. Madrid: Instituto de Estudios Políticos, 1947.
Gracián y Morales, Baltasar. *Obras de Lorenzo Gracian.* Vol. 2. Barcelona: P. Escuder and P. Nadal, 1748.
Gran Crónica de Alfonso XI. Ed. Diego Catalán. 2 vols. Fuentes Cronísticas de la Historia de España 4. Madrid: Gredos, 1977.
Latini, Brunetto. *The Book of the Treasure (Di Livres dou Tresor).* Trans. Paul Barrette and Spurgeon Baldwin. Garland Library of Medieval Literature, Series B, Vol. 90. New York and London: Garland, 1993.
Libro del caballero Zifar. Ed. J. González Muela. Madrid. Castalia, 1982.
Manuel, Don Juan. *El libro de los estados.* Ian R. Macpherson and Robert Brian Tate, eds. Madrid: Castalia, 1991.
——. *Libro infinido y tractado de la asunçión.* Ed. José Manuel Blecua. Colección Filológica 2. Granada [Spain]: U of Granada, 1952.
Ruiz, Juan, "Arcipreste de Hita." *El libro de buen amor.* Ed. G. B. Gybbon-Monypenny. Madrid: Castalia, 1988.
Sancho IV, "El Bravo." *Castigos e documentos para bien vivir ordenados por el Rey Don Sancho IV.* Ed. Agapito Rey. Humanities Series 24. Bloomington: Indiana University Publications, 1952.
Sancto Victore, Hugonis de. *Didascalicon de Studio Legendi.* Ed. Brother Charles Henry Buttimer. Diss. The Catholic U of America. Washington D. C.: The Catholic UP, 1939.

SECONDARY SOURCES

Allen, Judson Boyce. *The Ethical Poetic of the Later Middle Ages: A Decorum of Convenient Distinction.* Toronto: U of Toronto P, 1982.
Althusser, Louis. "Ideology and Ideological State Apparatusses." *Lenin and Philosophy and Other Essays.* Trans. Ben Brewster. New York: Monthly Review Press, 1971. 127-86.

Alvar, Carlos. "Contribución al estudio de la parte V de *El Conde Lucanor.*" *La corónica* 13 (1985): 190-195.
Alvar, Carlos, and José Manuel Lucía Megías. *Diccionario filológico de literatura medieval española: Textos y transmisión.* Nueva Biblioteca de Erudición y Crítica. Madrid: Castalia, 2002.
Alvar, Manuel. "Alfonso X contemplado por Don Juan Manuel." *Actas del congreso internacional 'La literatura en la época de Sancho IV'*. Alcalá de Henares [Spain]: Universidad de Alcalá de Henares, 1996. 91-106.
Amador de los Ríos, José. *Historia crítica de la literatura española.* 7 vols. Biblioteca Románica Hispana 9, Facsímiles. Madrid: Gredos, 1969.
Armengol Valenzuela, P. Fr. Pedro, ed. *Obras de San Pedro Pascual, Mártir.* Vol. 3. Rome: Salustiana, 1907.
Ayerbe-Chaux, Reinaldo. "Critical Editions and Literary History: The Case of Don Juan Manuel." *The Politics of Editing.* Ed. Nicholas Spadaccini and Jenaro Talens. Minneapolis: U of Minneapolis P, 1992. 22-38
———. El Conde Lucanor*: Materia tradicional y originalidad creadora.* Madrid: José Porrúa Turanzas, 1975.
———. "Manuscritos y documentos de Don Juan Manuel." *La corónica* 16.1 (1987-88): 88-93.
Baquero Goyanes, Mariano. "Perspectivismo en *El Conde Lucanor.*" *Don Juan Manuel: VII Centenario.* Murcia: U de Murcia, 1982. 27-50.
Barcia, Pedro L. *Análisis de* El Conde Lucanor. Enciclopedia Literaria 27. España e Hispanoamérica. Buenos Aires: Centro Editor de América Latina, 1968.
Battaglia, Salvatore. "L'esempio medievale." *Filologia Romanza* 6 (1959): 45-82.
Biglieri, Aníbal A. *Hacia una poética del relato didáctico: Ocho estudios sobre* El Conde Lucanor. North Carolina Studies in Romance Languages and Literatures 233. Chapel Hill: U.N.C Department of Romance Languages, 1989.
Bizzarri, Hugo Oscar. "Deslindes histórico-literarios en torno a *Flores de filosofía* y *Libro de los cien capítulos.*" *Incipit* 15 (1995): 45-63.
Blecua, Alberto. *La transmisión textual de* El Conde Lucanor. Barcelona: Universidad Autónoma de Barcelona, 1982.
Bonilla y San Martín, Adolfo. *Anales de la literatura española.* Madrid: Viuda e Hijos de Tello, 1904.
Bremond, Claude, Jacques Le Goff, Jean-Claude Schmitt. *L' "exemplum".* Typologie de Sources du Moyen Âge Occidental 40. Turnhout-Belgium: Brepols, 1982.
Buceta, Erasmo. "La admiración de Gracián por el infante don Juan Manuel." *Revista de filología española* 11 (1924): 63-66.
Burgoyne, Jonathan. "Ideology in Action: The Consequences of Paradox in *El Conde Lucanor*, Part I." *La corónica* 30 (2001): 37-65.
———. "Reading and Writing Patronio's Doctrine in Real Academia Española MS 15." *Hispanic Review* 71 (2003): 473-492.
———. "Reading to Pieces: *Divisio Textus* and the Structure of *El Conde Lucanor.*" *La corónica* 32 (Fall 2003): 231-55.
Burke, James. "Counterfeit and the Curse of Mediacy in the *Libro de buen amor* and the *Conde Lucanor.*" *Discourses of Authority in Medieval and Renaissance Literature.* Eds. Kevin Brownlee and Walter Stephens. Hanover & London: UP of New England, 1989. 203-15.
———. *Desire Against the Law: The Juxtaposition of Contraries in Early Medieval Spanish Literature.* Stanford: Stanford UP, 1998.
———. "Frame and Structure in the *Conde Lucanor.*" *Revista Canadiense de Estudios Hispánicos* 8 (1983-84): 263-274.
Capmany y Montpalau, Antonio. *Teatro histórico-crítico de la eloquencia española.* Vol. 1. Madrid, 1786.

Carruthers, Mary. *The Book of Memory: A Study of Memory in Medieval Culture.* Cambridge: Cambridge UP, 1990.

Catalán, Diego. "Don Juan Manuel ante el modelo alfonsí." *Juan Manuel Studies.* Ed. Ian Macpherson. London: Tamesis, 1977. 17-51.

Cerquiglini, Bernard. *In Praise of the Variant: A Critical History of Philosophy.* Trans. Betsy Wing. Baltimore & London: Johns Hopkins UP, 1999.

Chartier, Roger. Forward. *The Color of Melancholy: The Uses of Books in the Fourteenth Century.* By Jacqueline Cerquiglini-Toulet. Baltimore: Johns Hopkins UP, 1997.

Cherchi, Paolo. "*Brevedad, oscuredad,* synchysis in *El Conde Lucanor* (Parts II-IV)." *Medioevo romanzo* 9 (1984): 361-374.

Crane, Thomas Frederick, ed. *The Exempla or Illustrative Stories from the Sermones Vulgares of Jacques de Vitry.* London: David Nutt, for the Folk-Lore Society, 1890.

Dagenais, John. "That Bothersome Residue: Toward a Theory of the Physical Text." *Vox intexta. Orality and Textuality.* Ed. A.N. Doane and Carol Braun Pasternack. Madison: U of Wisconsin P, 1991.

———. *The Ethics of Reading in Manuscript Culture: Glossing the* Libro de Buen Amor. Princeton, NJ: Princeton UP, 1994.

Degiovanni, Fernando. "Retórica de la predicación e ideología dominica en la quinta parte de *El Conde Lucanor.*" *Bulletin Hispanique* 101 (1999): 5-18.

Devoto, Daniel. "Cuatro notas sobre la materia tradicional en don Juan Manuel." *Bulletin Hispanique* 68 (1966): 187-215.

———. *Introducción al estudio de Don Juan Manuel y en particular de* El Conde Lucanor: *una bibliografía.* Madrid: Castalia, 1972.

Deyermond, Alan. "Cuentística y política en Juan Manuel: *El Conde Lucanor.*" *Studia in Honorem Germán Orduna.* Eds. Leonardo Funes and José Luis Moure. Alcalá de Henares [Spain]: Universidad de Alcalá, 2001. 225-239.

———. "Editors, Critics and *El Conde Lucanor.*" *Romance Philology* 31 (1977-1978): 618-630.

———. "The Sermon and Its Uses in Medieval Castilian Literature." *La corónica* 8 (1980-1981): 127-145.

Diz, Marta Ana. *Patronio y Lucanor: la lectura inteligente 'en el tiempo que es turbio'.* Potomac, MD: Scripta Humanistica, 1984.

Dunn, Peter N. "Don Juan Manuel: The World as Text." *Modern Language Notes* 106.2 (1991): 223-40.

———. "The Structures of Didacticism: Private Myths and Public Fictions." *Juan Manuel Studies.* Ed. Ian Macpherson. London: Tamesis, 1977. 53-67.

England, John. "'¿Et non el día del lodo?': The Structure of the Short Story in *El Conde Lucanor.*" *Juan Manuel Studies.* Ed. Ian Macpherson. London: Tamesis, 1977. 69-86.

———. "*Exemplo* 51 of *El Conde Lucanor*: The Problem of Authorship." *Bulletin of Hispanic Studies* 51 (1974): 16-27.

———. "'*Los que son muy cuerdos entienden la cosa por algunas sennales*': Learning the Lessons of *El Conde Lucanor.*" *Bulletin of Hispanic Studies* 76 (1999): 345-364.

Evans, Murray J. *Rereading Middle English Romance: Manuscript Layout, Decoration, and the Rhetoric of Composite Structure.* Montreal: McGill-Queen's UP, 1995.

Flory, David. "A Suggested Emendation of *El Conde Lucanor,* Parts I and III." *Juan Manuel Studies.* Ed. Ian Macpherson. London: Tamesis, 1977. 87-99.

Foucault, Michel. "What is an Author?" *Language, Counter-Memory, Practice: Selected Essays and Interviews.* Ed. Donald F. Bouchard. Trans. Donald F. Bourchard and Sherry Simon. Ithaca: Cornell UP, 1977. 113-138.

Funes, Leonardo R. "La capitulación del *Libro de los estados*: consecuencias de un problema textual." *Incipit* 4 (1984): 71-82.

———. "Las *palabras maestradas* de don Iohán: peculiaridad del didacticismo de don Juan Manuel." *Studia in Honorem Germán Orduna*. Eds. Leonardo Funes and José Luis Moure. Alcalá de Henares [Spain]: Universidad de Alcalá, 2001. 261-270.

———. "Ruptura e integración en la escritura didáctico-narrativa de don Juan Manuel." 20 March 2006. http://200.16.86.50/digital/8/Jornadas/Lit.%20Medieval/Funes1-1.pdf.

Genette, Gérard. *Palimpsests: Literature in the Second Degree*. Trans. Channa Newman and Claude Doubinsky. Lincoln and London: U of Nebraska P, 1997.

———. *Paratexts: Thresholds of Interpretation*. Trans. Jane E. Lewin. New York: Cambridge UP, 1997.

Gerli, Michael. "*Recta voluntas est bonus amor*: St. Augustine and the Didactic Structure of the *Libro de buen amor*." *Romance Philology* 35.3 (1982): 500-508.

Giménez Soler, Andrés. *Don Juan Manuel: Biografía y estudio crítico*. Zaragoza: Academia Española, 1932.

Gimeno Casalduero, Joaquín. *La creación literaria de la Edad Media y del Renacimiento (Su forma y su significado)*. Madrid: José Porrúa Turanzas, 1977.

Gómez Redondo, Fernando, *Historia de la prosa medieval castellana*. 3 vols. Madrid: Cátedra, 1998, 1999, 2002.

Groupe d'Anthropologie Historique de l'Occident Médiéval. 23 June 2006. http://gahom.ehess.fr/document.php?id=513.

Hammer, Michael Floyd. *Framing the Reader: Exemplarity and Ethics in the Manuscripts of the* Conde Lucanor. Diss. U of California, Los Angeles, 2003.

Hanna III, Ralph. "Miscellaneity and Vernacularity: Conditions of Literary Production in Late Medieval England." *The Whole Book: Cultural Perspectives on the Medieval Miscellany*. Eds. Stephen G. Nichols and Siegfried Wenzel. Ann Arbor: U of Michigan P, 1996. 37-51.

Huot, Sylvia. "A Book Made for a Queen: The Shaping of a Late Medieval Anthology Manuscript." *The Whole Book: Cultural Perspectives on the Medieval Miscellany*. Eds. Stephen G. Nichols and Siegfried Wenzel. Ann Arbor: U of Michigan P, 1996. 123-143.

Iser, Wolfgang. *The Act of Reading: A Theory of Aesthetic Response*. Baltimore and London: The Johns Hopkins UP, 1978. Trans. of *Der Akt des Lesens. Theorie ästhetischer Wirkung*. Munich: Wilhelm Fink, 1976.

Jameson, Fredric. *The Political Unconscious: Narrative as a Socially Symbolic Act*. Ithaca: Cornell UP, 1982.

Jauss, Hans Robert. *Toward an Aesthetic of Reception*. Trans. Timothy Bahti. Theory and History of Literature 2. Minneapolis: U of Minnesota P, 1982.

———. "The Alterity and Modernity of Medieval Literature." Trans. Timothy Bahti. *New Literary History* 10.2 (1979): 181-229.

Keller, John Esten. *El libro de los engaños*. University of North Carolina Studies in the Romance Languages and Literatures 20. Chapel Hill: U of North Carolina P, 1953.

———, ed. *Motif-Index of Mediaeval Spanish Exempla*. Knoxville: U of Tennessee P, 1949.

———, trans. *The Book of the Wiles of Women*. University of North Carolina Studies in the Romance Languages and Literatures 27. MLA Translation Series 2. Chapel Hill: U of North Carolina P, 1956.

Kemmler, Fritz. *'Exempla' in Context: A Historical and Critical Study of Robert of Mannyng of Brunne's 'Handlyng Synne'*. Studies & Texts in English 6. Tübingen: Gunter Narr Verlag, 1984.

Kinkade, Richard. *Los 'Lucidarios' españoles*. Madrid: Gredos, 1968.
———. "Sancho IV: Puente literario entre Alfonso el Sabio y Juan Manuel." *PMLA* 87 (1972): 1039-51.
Knust, Hermann, ed. *Dos obras didácticas y dos leyendas sacadas de manuscritos de la biblioteca del Escorial*. Madrid: La Sociedad de Bibliófilos Españoles, 1878.
Krappe, Alexander H. "Le Faucon de l'Infant dans *El conde Lucanor*." *Bulletin Hispanique* 35 (1933): 294-297.
Lacarra, María Jesús. *Cuentística medieval en España: Los orígenes*. Publicaciones del Departamento de Literatura Española 1. Zaragoza: U de Zaragoza, 1979.
———, ed. *Cuento y novela corta en España*. Vol. 1, Edad Media. Barcelona: Crítica, 1999.
———. "La mujer en la narrativa breve medieval." *Actas de las IV Jornadas de Investigación Interdisciplinaria*. Zaragoza: U de Zaragoza, 1987. 101-108.
Lawrance, J. N. H. "On Fifteenth-Century Spanish Vernacular Humanism." *Medieval and Renaissance Studies in Honour of Robert Brian Tate*. Eds. Ian Michael and Richard A. Cardwell. Oxford: Dolphin Book Co., 1986. 63-79.
Lida de Malkiel, María Rosa. "Tres notas sobre don Juan Manuel." *Romance Philology* 4 (1950-51): 155-194.
Lomax, Derek W. "The Lateran Reforms and Spanish Literature." *Iberoromania* 1 (1969): 299-313.
Looze, Laurence de. "*El Conde Lucanor*, Part V, and the Goals of the Manueline Text." *La corónica* 28 (2000): 129-54.
———. "Subversion of Meaning in Part I of *El Conde Lucanor*." *Revista Canadiense de Estudios Hispánicos* 19.2 (1995): 341-55.
———. "The 'Nonsensical' Proverbs of Juan Manuel's *El Conde Lucanor*, Part IV: A Reassessment." *Revista Canadiense de Estudios Hispánicos* 25.2 (2001): 199-221.
López-Estrada, Francisco. *Introducción a la literatura española*. 2nd ed. Madrid: Gredos, 1962.
Lucía Megías, José Manuel. "Los castigos del rey de Mentón a la luz de *Flores de filosofía*: Límites y posibilidades del uso del modelo subyacente." *La corónica* 27 (1999): 145-165.
Lyons, John D. *Exemplum: The Rhetoric of Example in Early Modern France and Italy*. Princeton: Princeton UP, 1989.
Machan, Tim William. "Scribal Role, Authorial Intention, and Chaucer's *Boece*." *The Chaucer Review* 24.2 (1989): 150-162.
Macpherson, Ian. "Amor and Don Juan Manuel." *Hispanic Review* 39 (1971): 167-182.
———. "*Dios y el mundo*–the Didacticism of *El Conde Lucanor*." *Romance Philology* 24.1 (1970-71): 26-38.
Maravall, José Antonio. "La sociedad estamental castellana y la obra de Don Juan Manuel." *Cuadernos Hispanoamericanos*. 201 (1966): 751-768.
Marichal, Juan. *Teoría e historia del ensayismo hispánico*. Madrid: Alianza, 1984.
Martin, Henri-Jean. *The History and Power of Writing*. Trans. Lydia G. Cochrane. Chicago & London: U of Chicago P, 1994.
Maurer, Armand A. *Medieval Philosophy*. 2nd ed. Toronto: Pontifical Institute of Mediaeval Studies, 1982.
Menéndez Pelayo, Marcelino. *Orígenes de la novela*. Vol. 1. Buenos Aires: Espasa-Calpe Argentina, 1946.
Menéndez Pidal, Ramón. *Poesía juglaresca y juglares: Aspectos de la historia literaria y cultura de España*. 6th ed. Colección Austral 300. Madrid: Espasa-Calpe, 1969.
———. "Poesía popular y poesía tradicional en la literatura española." *Estudios sobre el Romancero*. Madrid: Espasa-Calpe, 1973. 325-356.

Menocal, María Rosa. "Life Itself: Storytelling as the Tradition of Openness in the *Conde Lucanor*." *Oral Tradition and Hispanic Literature: Essays in Honor of Samuel G. Armistead*. Ed. Michael M. Caspi. The Albert Bates Lord Studies in Oral Tradition 15. New York: Garland, 1995. 469-95.

Michael, Ian. "The Function of the Popular Tale in the *Libro de buen amor*." *Libro de buen amor Studies*. Ed. G. B. Gybbon-Monypenny. London: Tamesis, 1970. 177-218.

Millares Carlo, Agustín. *Paleografía española: Ensayo de una historia de la escritura en España desde el siglo VIII al XVII*. Vol. 1. Colección Labor, Sección VI: Ciencias Históricas 192. Barcelona: Editorial Labor, 1929.

Mosher, Joseph Albert. *The Exemplum in the Early Religious and Didactic Literature of England*. New York: Columbia UP, 1911.

Mujica, Bárbara, ed. *Texto y vida: Introducción a la literatura española*. Fort Worth: Harcourt Brace College Publishers, 1990.

Murphy, James J. *Rhetoric in the Middle Ages: A History of Rhetorical Theory from Saint Augustine to the Renaissance*. Berkeley: U of California P, 1974.

Nieto, María Dolores. *Estructura y función de los relatos medievales*. Madrid: Consejo Superior de Investigaciones Científicas, 1993.

Orduna, Germán. "El exemplo en la obra literaria de don Juan Manuel." *Juan Manuel Studies*. Ed. Ian Macpherson. London: Tamesis, 1977. 119-142.

———. "La autobiografía literaria de Don Juan Manuel." *Don Juan Manuel: VII Centenario*. Murcia: U de Murcia, Academia Alfonso X el Sabio, 1982. 245-58.

———. "La élite intelectual de la escuela catedralicia de Toledo y la literatura en época de Sancho IV." *Actas del congreso internacional 'La literatura en la época de Sancho IV'*. Alcalá de Henares [Spain]: Universidad de Alcalá de Henares, 1996. 53-62.

Pabst, Walter. *La novela corta en la teoría y en la creación literaria*. Trans. Rafael de la Vega. Madrid: Gredos, 1972.

Palafox, Eloísa. *Las éticas del* exemplum: *Los* Castigos del rey don Sancho IV, El Conde Lucanor *y el* Libro de buen amor. México, D. F.: UNAM, 1998.

Paredes Núñez, Juan. *Formas narrativas breves en la literatura románica medieval: problemas de terminología*. Colección Propuesta 11. Granada [Spain]: Servicio de Publicaciones, Campus Universitario Cartuja, 1986.

Parkes, Malcolm Beckwith. *Pause and Effect: An Introduction to the History of Punctuation in the West*. Berkeley and Los Angeles: U of California P, 1993.

———. "The Influence of the Concepts of *Ordinatio* and *Compilatio* on the Development of the Book." *Medieval Learning and Literature: Essays Presented to Richard William Hunt*. Ed. J. J. G. Alexander and M. T. Gibson. Oxford: Clarendon P, 1976. 115-141.

Pego Puigbó, Armando. *El renacimiento espiritual: Introducción literaria a los tratados de oración españoles (1520-1566)*. Madrid: Consejo Superior de Investigaciones Científicas, 2004.

Prince, Gerald. *Dictionary of Narratology*. Lincoln and London: U of Nebraska P, 1987.

Reiss, Edmund. "Ambiguous Signs and Authorial Deception in Fourteenth-Century Fictions." *Signs, Sentence, Discourse: Language in Medieval Thought and Literature*. Eds. Julian N. Wasserman and Lois Roney. New York: Syracuse UP, 1989. 113-137.

Rico, Francisco. *Predicación y literatura en la España medieval*. Cádiz [Spain]: Universidad Nacional de Educación a Distancia, 1977.

Rimmon, Shlomith. *The Concept of Ambiguity–the Example of James*. Chicago and London: U of Chicago P, 1977.

Rodríguez-Puértolas, Julio. "Juan Manuel y la crisis castellana del siglo XIV." *Literatura, historia, alienación*. Barcelona: Labor, 1976. 45-69.

Romero, José Luis. *La revolución burguesa en el mundo feudal.* Buenos Aires: Sudamericana, 1967.
Sánchez-Albornoz, Claudio. *España: Un enigma histórico.* 2 vols. Buenos Aires: Sudamericana, 1956.
Scanlon, Larry. *Narrative, Authority, and Power: The Medieval Exemplum and the Chaucerian Tradition.* Cambridge: Cambridge UP, 1994.
Scholberg, Kenneth. "Figurative Language in Juan Manuel." *Juan Manuel Studies.* Ed. Ian Macpherson. London: Tamesis, 1977. 143-155.
Seidenspinner-Núñez, Dayle. "On 'Dios y el mundo': Author and Reader Response in Juan Ruiz and Juan Manuel." *Romance Philology* 42 (1988-89): 251-66.
Rimmon, Shlomith. *The Concept of Ambiguity–the Example of James.* Chicago and London: U of Chicago P, 1977.
Stéfano, Luciana de. "La sociedad estamental en las obras de Don Juan Manuel." *Nueva Revista de Filología Hispánica* 16 (1962): 329-354.
———. "Don Juan Manuel y el pensamiento medieval." *Don Juan Manuel: VII Centenario.* U de Murcia. Academia Alfonso X el Sabio, 1982. 337-351.
Stemmler, Theo. "Miscellany or Anthology? The Structure of Medieval Manuscripts: MS. Harley 2253, for Example." *Zeitschrift für Anglistik und Amerikanistik* 39 (1991): 231-37.
Sturcken, H. Tracy. *Don Juan Manuel.* New York: Twayne, 1974.
Tate, Robert Brian. "The Infante Don Juan of Aragón and Don Juan Manuel." *Juan Manuel Studies.* Ed. Ian Macpherson. London: Tamesis Books, 1977. 169-179.
Taylor, Barry. "Juan Manuel's Cipher in the *Libro de los estados.*" *La corónica* 12 (1983): 32-45.
———. "Old Spanish Wisdom Texts: Some Relationships." *La corónica* 14 (1985): 71-85.
Tobar, María Luisa. "Codice Puñonrostro. Descrizione e Storia." *Helikon* 17 (1977): 312-21.
Tubach, Frederic C. *Index Exemplorum: A Handbook of Medieval Religious Tales.* Helsinki: Akademia Scientiarum Fennica, 1969.
Valdeón Baruque, Julio. "Las tensiones sociales en Castilla en tiempos de don Juan Manuel." *Juan Manuel Studies.* Ed. Ian Macpherson. London: Tamesis Books, 1977. 180-90.
Weiss, Julian. *The Poet's Art: Literary Theory in Castile c. 1400-60.* Medium Aevum Monographs New Series 14. Oxford: The Society for the Study of Mediaeval Languages and Literature, 1990.
Welter, J.-Th. *L'Exemplum dans la Littérature Religieuse et Didactique du Moyen Age.* Paris & Toulouse: Occitania, 1927.
Wenzel, Siegfried. "Introduction." *The Whole Book: Cultural Perspectives on the Medieval Miscellany.* Eds. Stephen G. Nichols and Siegfried Wenzel. Ann Arbor: U of Michigan P, 1996. 1-6.
———. "Sermon Collections and Their Taxonomy." *The Whole Book: Cultural Perspectives on the Medieval Miscellany.* Eds. Stephen Nichols and Siegfried Wenzel. Ann Arbor: U of Michigan P, 1996. 7-21.
Zumthor, Paul. *Essai de poétique médiévale.* Paris: Editions du Seuil, 1972.
———. "Intertextualité et mouvance." *Litterature* 41 (1981): 8-16.
———. "The Text and the Voice." *New Literary History* 16.1 (1984): 67-92.
———. *Toward a Medieval Poetics.* Trans. Philip Bennett. Minneapolis and Oxford: U of Minnesota P, 1992.

INDEX

Abdon, King of Syria, 174
Agudeza, y arte de ingenio, 10n5
Alfonso X, "El Sabio", 22, 24, 27n22
Alfonso XI, 25n20, 42, 51, 105
Allegatio pro praecedentia regum Castellae prae regibus Angliae, 171
allegory: and allegorical reading in *exemplo* 48, 137-138, 144; in *exemplo* 26, 55-56; in *exemplo* 33, 106; of Good and Evil, 64-65
Allen, Judson Boyce, 18, 38, 39, 179n5
Althusser, Louis, 53
Alvar, Carlos, 23, 48n7, 172n4
Alvar, Manuel, 24
Amador de los Ríos, José, 127, 142
ambiguity: in *CL*, 14, 48, 53; disjunctive ethical, 63n19; of language, 80
Anticlaudianus, 180
Apólogo del filósofo que fue a una huerta a cortar verduras, 172n4, 173, 177, 178, 213, 214
aporia: in *CL*, 14, 53
Argote de Molina, 9, 10, 155, 183, 197n2; edition of *CL*, 122, 191, 196, 197n1, 201, 204; Juan Manuel as poet in, 197; print layout of *CL*, 199-200, 201; review of *CL* in, 198
artes praedicandi, 28
Articles of Faith, 129
Ashby, Alexander of, 38n7, 40, 41
auctor: Juan Manuel as, 104
Augustine, Saint: and Augustinian sign theory, 79; and Augustinian thought in *exemplo* 21, 94, 95, 98.
authorial intention: of Juan Manuel, 49-50; in *CL*, 142-143; in prologue, 73

autobiography: in *exemplo* 33, 105
Ayerbe-Chaux, Reinaldo, 23n15, 29, 37, 38, 125, 146n13, 157, 162n28, 190, 191; edition of *CL* 69n21, 122n5, 150n18

Baquero Goyanes, Mariano, 54n15
Barcia, Pedro, 38n6, 199, 200
Barlaam e Josaphat, 25
Battaglia, Salvatore, 22
Battle of the Río Salado, 51n12
Bennett, William, 20
Bernaldo, San, 125
Biblioteca Nacional, MS 17788: Pascual Gayangos' transcription of *CL*, 200
Biblioteca Nacional, MS 19426: copy of proverbs from *CL*, 183-184
Biglieri, Aníbal, 15, 105, 106, 107, 108, 112
Binario de virtudes, see *Libro binario*
Bizzarri, Hugo, 25, 156
Blecua, Alberto, 109n6, 120, 122n5-6, 125, 146, 151, 154, 155, 162n28, 165, 166, 167n29, 171
Blecua, José Manuel: edition of *CL*, 10n3, 25n20, 59, 69n21, 122n5, 146n13, 147n15, 150n18, 161n27
Bocados de oro, 156
Boccaccio, Giovanni, 22n12, 30, 83n8, 206, 207
Bonilla y San Martín, Adolfo, 214n1
Book of Count Lucanor and Patronio, 10n3, 24n16
Book of the Treasure, see also *Li livres dou trésor* and *Libro del tesoro*, 24n18

Book of the Wiles of Women, see also Libro de los engaños, 127
Bremond, Claude, 18, 19n9, 22
Buceta, Erasmo, 10n5
Burke, James, 49, 57n16, 75, 82, 83, 109, 116, 178

Calderón de la Barca, Pedro, 10, 134
Calila e Dimna, 25
Capmany y Montpalau, Antonio, 204
caritas, 91n14
Carruthers, Mary, 170
Cartagena, Alonso de, 171, 176, 182, 187, 188
Casalduero, Joaquín, 49
Castigos del rey Mentón, 25, 156
Castigos e documentos del rey don Sancho IV, 22, 24, 25, 90n13, 206
Catalán, Diego, 24
Cerquiglini, Bernard, 120n2, 121
Cerquiglini-Toulet, Jacqueline, 21
Cervantes, Miguel de, 10
Chartier, Roger, 21, 22
Chaucer, Geoffrey, 11, 22n12, 29
Cherchi, Paolo, 9n1, 23, 29, 30
compilatio, 133, 142, 172-173
Conde Lucanor: and *exemplo 2*, 88; and counselors, 89; and teaching, 86; as contribution to Spanish letters, 204-205; as didactic work, 13, 127-128, 196, 203, 204, 205; as doctrine, 17, 195; as entertainment, 40; as medicine, 40; as moral philosophy, 203, 207; as open or closed work, 14-15; as referential to Juan Manuel's life, 13, 15, 203; as representative of philosophical environment, 14; audience of, 167-168, 177-178, 205-206; criticism on, 49; cohesion of narrative parts in, 67; compared with *Decameron*, 207; compared with *Castigos e documentos*, 25, 26, 206; compared with *Libro de buen amor*, 14; comparison of *viessos* in, 61-62; conflict of Good and Evil in, 64; contradictory ethical behaviors in, 59, 61, 67; deceit and lying in, 56-59; discursive structure in, 181; early audience, 9-10n2; feudal estate society in, 49; friendship in, 57-58; God's blessings in, 68; God's will in, 69-70; good advice in, 70, 71; historical context in, 51; homiletic influence in, 29, 39; ideologemes in, 62; in the Golden Age, 10n4; literary sources in, 23n15, 26; manuscripts of, 122-123; meditation on language in, 83; offers instruction on the use of *exempla*, 11; oral component in, 35; orthodox reading of, 141, 195, 208; Parts II-IV, 9n1; realism in, 28; reception of, 13-16, 142, 161; programs behavior, 53; second print edition, 10; theological subject-matter in, 77-78
Corral, Pedro de, 172
Costanza: daughter of Juan Manuel, 105
Council of Basel, 171
Crane, Fredrick Thomas, 21
Crónica abreviada, 24
Crónica sarracina, 172
Cuenca, Alonso de, 125, 130
Cuestión sobre el acto de cavallería, 171, 176, 182, 185, 187, 188n8, 189, 196

Dagenais, John, 17, 32, 52, 119, 133, 134, 170, 178, 179, 181
Dante Alighieri, 30, 83n8
dark language: in *CL*, 80-81; in *Libro de los estados*, 80; and fallen state of language in *Libro de los estados*, 78-79
De commo la onrra deste mundo non es sinon commo sueño que pasa (*Capítulo LIIII* of *CL* in manuscript P), 211
De la emaginaçión que puede sacar a omne de entendimiento (*Capítulo LIII* of *CL* in manuscript P), 209
De Magistro, 79
De Modo Praedicandi, 40, 41
De Regimine Principum, 25, 42n2
Decameron, 206, 207
Degiovani, Fernando, 23, 29
Descripción de Mérida, 172, 173, 176, 213
Devoto, Daniel, 9n2, 49, 105n4
Deyermond, Alan, 15n8, 27n22, 28, 122n5
Dios y el Mundo (God and World): as *carreras* or paths, 50, 71, 72, 74, 110, 116, 164, 165, 185; as dilemma, 71-73, 161; as ethical conflict in *CL*, 52, 59-60; as paradox, 30, 104; in *Libro binario*, 176
Disciplina Clericalis, 25, 128
divisio (and *divisio textus*): 32, 38n7, 116; as critical reading practice, 11, 39, 170, 180; in manuscript M, 181-182

Diz, Marta Ana, 49, 108n5, 116n12
doctrine: and *Castigos del rey Mentón*, 25; *CL* as, 17, 117; Church, 78, 80, 104, 105; in manuscript P, 183; mediated, 96; orthodox, 44
Dominican Order, 11, 23, 27n21, 39, 84
Don Juan, "El Tuerto", 51
Don Jaime, Señor de Xérica, 81
Don Remón, "Knight of the Castle of San Ambrosio", 125, 130
Dunn, Peter, 49, 55, 75, 114n9, 205

education: of Juan Manuel, 23n16-25, 84; of youth, 86
Eiximenis, Francesc, 171, 174
England, John: 19, 35n5, 49, 75, 77, 83; edition and translation of *CL*, 64n20, 69n21, 86n11, 90n12, 92n15, 93, 109, 164, 165, 167
Enrique II, 187
entendimiento(s), 15, 40, 79, 80, 84, 86, 88, 89, 91, 116
Erasmus, Desiderius of Rotterdam, 20
estado(s), 45n5, 46n6, 53, 76, 102, 115, 153, 154
Estoria de españa, 25
Evans, Murray, 136
exemplo 51, *see also* S manuscript of *CL*: authorship of, 162-167
exemplum: as narrative sign, 11, 30, 76, 84, 94, 96, 109, 114, 136; as models of behavior, 53; association with orthodoxy, 72, 127; authority of, 11, 20n11, 29, 30, 53, 73, 74, 100-101, 105, 115; definition of, 19-20n9; for edification of reader, 21; for moral education, 20; for private reading, 22; hidden in *exemplo* 21, 92; in Part V of *CL*, 12; in preaching and sermons, 11, 18, 27n22-28, 40, 48n7, 76, 77n3, 143; influence on lay authors, 11n6, 18, 28; Juan Manuel's use of, 30, 94, 98; Latin and vernacular, 22; literary and homiletic traditons, 28; literary history of, 19n9-10-21; mediated meaning of, 96; negatively charged, 135; power to coerce, 98; relative meaning of, 95-97, 136; rhetorical use of, 15, 41, 52n14, 60, 69, 73, 74, 77, 84, 94, 114, 115, 203; secular and religious, 127; semiotics of, 96

fazienda: in *exemplos* 2 and 21, 94
Flores de filosofía: 25; in manuscript G, 155n21, 156n22-157, 160, 216n4

Flory, David, 164, 165
forma tractatus, 38, 179, 202
formulaic language: in *CL*, 35, 37
Fourth Lateran Council, 23, 111
Fradejas Rueda, José Manuel, 208
France, Marie de, 115n11
Franciscan Order, 11
Funes, Leonardo, 24n19, 95n18

G manuscript of *CL*: five-part *CL* in, 123, 155; *Flores de filosofía* in, 156-157; scribal authorship in, 158-159; *usus scribendi* in, 161, 168
García, Diego, 51n12
García de Castrojeriz, Juan, 24n20
García Gudiel, Gonzalo, 25
Gayangos, Pascual, 123, 200, 204, 205, 206n7, 216n1, 217n5-6, 218n7-8, 219n9-11, 221n12
Genesis, 56
Genette, Gérard, 33n4, 145n12
Gerli, Michael, 94, 95
Giles of Rome, 25, 42n2
Giménez Soler, Andrés, 49, 205n6
Gloeckner, Nydia, 170
Glosa del Pater Noster, 125
good works: 47; and salvation discussed in *CL*, 101-102, 111-112; in manuscript G, 159
Gómez Redondo, Fernando, 15, 24n19, 156
Gracián, Baltasar, 10n5, 203n5
Gran crónica de Alfonso XI, 51n11
Gran crónica de ultramar, 100
Greeks and Romans: debate in *Libro de buen amor*, 94-95
Greenia, George, 42n1
Groupe d'Anthropologie Historique de l'Occident Médiéval, 22n13

H manuscript of *CL*: as source of wisdom, 144, 145; doodles in, 145, 149; ideological reading of, 151n19; marginalia in, 147, 151; proverbs in, 145-146; reader's interest in *enxienplos*, 151, 152; reader's notes, 148, 150-151; scribal authorship in, 153-155; scribal corrections in, 151; *usus scribendi* in, 161, 168
Hammer, Michael, 122n5, 172
Hanna III, Ralph, 119
Heredia, Doctor of The Holy Inquisition, 16, 198
Holy Scripture: contradictions in, 78, 105

Holy Trinity: discussed in *Lucidario*, 131
Holy War: and Crusade, 101, 104
homiletic tradition: influence on lay authors, 28-29; in *CL*, 39
horizon of expectation, 32, 122
Huot, Sylvia, 115n11, 119, 130

ideology: and ideological tension in *CL*, 63; and ideologically bound reading, 133; and political in manuscript M, 189; and shaping of in *CL*, 151; as practice, 53; feudal, 44; medieval estate, 50; reactionary of 15th century Spain, 196
implied reader, 32n1, 97n22
Infante Don Manuel: father of Juan Manuel, 105, 106
Insulis, Alanus de, 180
Iser, Wolfgang, 32

Jameson, Fredric, 62n18
Jauss, Hans Robert, 16, 17, 32, 195
Juliá, Eduardo: 208; edition of *CL*, 122n5

Kasin, Abdul, 190
Keating, L. Clark and John E. Keller: edition and translation of *CL*, 10n3, 19n10, 24n16, 25, 59, 62n17, 64n20, 69n21, 90n13, 93-94, 96n19, 146, 147n15, 183n6
Keller, John E., 23, 127
Kemmler, Fritz, 18, 20
King Richard, "The Lionheart", 101, 153
Kinkade, Richard, 24n18, 131
Knust, Herman, 156, 216n4, 219n9
Krapf, Eugenio, 125, 209n2, 210n3
Krappe, Alexander, 105n4

Lacarra, María Jesús, 23n14, 49, 96n20, 127
language: fallen state of, 78
Latini, Brunetto, 24
Lawrence, Jeremy, 172
Le Goff, Jacques, 18, 19n9, 22
Li livres dou trésor, 24
Liber de exemplis naturalibus, 23
Libro binario, 171, 175, 176
Libro de las armas, 197n1
Libro de buen amor, 14, 28, 32, 94, 95, 170

Libro del caballero Zifar, 22, 25, 142n9, 156
Libro del cavallero et del escudero, 49
Libro de la caza, 24
Libro de los cien capítulos, 25, 156
Libro de los estados, 27, 39, 43n4, 49, 50, 52, 54, 72, 76, 78, 80, 111, 115, 141, 142n9
Libro de los engaños, 25, 124, 125, 127, 128, 129, 141
Libro de los enxiemplos del Conde Lucanor et de Patronio, 9
Libro de Patronio, 125
Libro de los proverbios, 128
Libro del tesoro, 24n18
Libro de los treinta sabios, 156
Libro infinido, 24n16, 25, 42n3, 43n4, 47, 50, 52, 54, 72, 77, 91n14, 110
Lida de Malkiel, María Rosa, 10n4, 23, 27n21, 49n9, 127
litany: Juan Manuel's use of, 37
Lomax, Derek, 11n6, 23, 76, 127
Longchamp, Raoul de, 180
Looze, Laurence de, 32, 40, 54n15, 75, 76, 82, 83, 109, 116, 120, 205
López de Mendoza, Íñigo, Marqués de Santillana, 171, 182, 188n8
López Estrada, Francisco, 10n4
Lord's Prayer, *see also Pater Noster*, 125, 129
Louis IX, Saint, 187
Lucía Megías, José Manuel, 156n23, 172n4
Lucidario: 24, 124, 125, 130, 131, 138, 143; as source of orthodox instruction, 132, 195
Lyons, John, 20

M manuscript of *CL*: and *compilatio*, 173; and mirror for princes, 176-177; as anthology, 172-173; audience of, 177, 196; contents of, 171-172; evidence of reading in, 121, 182-183, 190; marginalia in, 170, 180; page layout in, 35; proverbial wisdom in, 183; reader's notes in, 185-190, 196; reading aids in, 32-34, 35, 38, 169-170, 179, 181; studied for political doctrine, 185, 189; *viessos* in, 61
Machan, Tim William, 133, 135
Macpherson, Ian, 31, 49, 53, 57, 58, 80n5, 91n14, 99, 102, 105, 116n12, 127, 202, 203, 205n6

man: as God's creation discussed in *CL*, 109-110
Manuel, Pedro, 197
Manuel de Villena, Doña María, 191
Manuel Figueroa, Doña María, 191
Maravall, José Antonio, 49, 52n13
Marichal, Juan, 171
Masquefa, Fray Ramón, 22n21
materialist philology, 12, 119, 126
Mauser, Armand, 14n7
Menéndez-Pelayo, Marcelino, 162, 206
Menéndez Pidal, Ramón, 121
Menocal, María Rosa, 13, 15, 54n15, 114n9, 134n6, 141, 196
Michael, Ian, 197n2
Milá y Fontanals, Manuel, 204
miscellany: 18, 119, 143, 173; organizing principles of, 119, 126, 127, 136, 142, 183, 190, 195
modus legendi, 12
Molina, Doña María de, 24, 51
molinismo, 24n18-25
moral relativism, 115
mouvance, 120n1
Mosher, Joseph, 18, 19, 176
Mujica, Bárbara, 200
Murphy, James, 27, 38n7, 40, 41n9, 77n3, 79

Nieto, María Dolores, 49
novelas: 10; and *fábulas* compared to *CL* in Argote de Molina edition, 197-198, 199
Novelas ejemplares, 10

open / closed dichotomy: 13-14; and open text, 60, 133; and openness, 85, 133, 136; and openness of medieval book, 172
ordinatio, 132, 196
Orduna, Germán, 23, 25, 26, 38n6, 49

P manuscript of *CL*: as expression of manuscript culture, 124; as source of doctrine, 128, 141, 144, 195; authorial intentions in, 135-136; *compilatio* in, 126; compiler's criteria in, 130; contents of, 125; evidence of reading in, 121, 132; ideological reading in, 133, 142-143; organizing principles in, 126; pedagogical use of, 143, 144; reading process in, 126, 132, 143-144; scribal authorship in, 133, 134, 137-138, 139, 151; scribal deletions and emendations in, 128; thematic ties in, 130, 132; *usus scribendi* in, 168
palabras maestradas: as deceit, 97, 142; in *exemplo* 21 and *Libro de los estados*, 93n17, 141-142; in manuscript H, 151; scribal correction of, 139-141
Palafox, Eloísa, 23, 29, 52n14, 96
paradox: in *CL*, 15, 43, 48, 52, 53, 71, 72; in *exemplo* 2, 86n11, 87; in *Libro de los estados*, 45, 46-47; in *Libro infinido*, 43, 45, 47
paratext, 33n4
Paredes Núñez, Juan, 23n14, 127
Parkes, Malcolm, 136, 172
Pascual, San Pedro, 125, 129
Pater Noster, 129
Patrañuelo, 10
Pego Puigbó, Armando, 129
Poema de mio Cid, 25
political unrest: in Juan Manuel's time, 24, 50-51
Poridat de las poridades, 128
prayer: stories that end with, 103n1, 104n2
Prince, Gerald, 97n22
Proposición contra los ingleses, 171, 176, 182, 185, 187, 196
proverb(s): and maxims in *CL* Parts II-IV, 81-82, 87, 109; paradoxical, 82; tongue-twister, 81

reading, *see also divisio*: and *modus legendi*, 12, aids, 11, 12, 33; binary, 175; ethical, 17, 52; fix(-ed, -ing), 12, 161; ideological, 13, 133, 151, 155; in *CL* Parts II-IV, 109; in pieces, 199, 202; medieval, 31, 39, 74; orthodox, 13, 15, 17; retrospective, 53; right, 12, 13, 117, 196, 202, 203, 207
Reconquista, 153
Reiss, Edmond, 83n8, 84n9, 205
Rhetorica ad Herenium, 19n9
Rico, Francisco, 23
Rimmon, Shlomith, 63n19
Rodríguez-Puértolas, Julio, 49
Romero, José Luis, 51-52n13
Ruiz, Juan, 14, 80n4, 83n8, 84n9, 94

S manuscript of *CL*: as an anthology, 122n3; as best text, 37, 124; *emendar* in, 80; *exemplo* 51 in, *see also exemplo* 51, 73n22, 75n2, 161-162, 163;

five-part *CL* in, 122; Part V of *CL* based on, 158-159; possible patron of, 190-191; reading of, 191; scribal note in, 190
Sacrament(s): 105, 111, 129; of Confirmation, 78; of Reconciliation, 101
Saint Victor, Hugh of, 39n8
Salisbury, Thomas of, 38n7
Sánchez Albornoz, Claudio, 51n13
Sánchez Cantón, F.J., 208
Sancho IV, 22, 23n16, 24, 25, 90n13, 131
Santo Oficio, 198
Sasoferrato, Bartolo de, 186n7
Scanlon, Larry, 11, 18, 29, 30, 77n3, 101, 104
Schmitt, Jean-Claude, 18, 19n9
Scholberg, Kenneth R., 43n4
Seidenspinner-Nuñez, Dayle, 14, 54n15, 104n3, 177
Serés, Guillermo: 74n1; edition of *CL*, 69n21, 122n5, 146n13, 150n18
Servasanctus, 23
Seven Virtues, 175, 182
sign(s): ambiguous, 84n9, 116; contingency of meaning in *exemplo* 21, 95
sin(s): in *exemplo* 33, 109; in Part V of *CL*, 113, 114; in *Libro binario*, 175; in *Vida de Jesucrist*, 174; of Count Lucanor, 97, 99-100
Stéfano, Luciana de, 45n5, 49
Stemmler, Theo, 126, 127, 173

Sturcken, H. Tracy, 51n12
Suárez de Figueroa, Lorenzo, 191n9
Suer Alfonso: proverb in *CL*, 146n13

Tate, Robert: edition of *Libro de los estados*, 80n5, 99, 105
tautological argument: in *CL*, 48n8
Taylor, Barry, 80n6, 104n3, 156n24, 145, 177
Testamento del maestro Alfonso de Cuenca, 125
Ten Commandments, 129
thema: in sermons, 38
Thetford, Richard of, 38n7
Timoneda, Juan de, 10
tradicionalidad escrita, 121
Tubach, Frederic, 19n9, 96, 143n11
tyrant: compared with king in *Libro infinido*, 43-44

Valdeón Baruque, Julio, 50n10
variance, 119-121
Vida de Jesucrist, 171, 174, 176
Vitry, Jacques de, 21

Weiss, Julian, 39n8
Welter, Jean, 18, 19n9
Wenzel, Siegfried, 12, 119, 126, 143, 173
wisdom literature, 145, 147

Zumthor, Paul, 35, 37, 120n1, 121

NORTH CAROLINA STUDIES IN THE ROMANCE LANGUAGES AND LITERATURES

I.S.B.N. Prefix 0-8078-

Recent Titles

RECLAIMING THE BODY: MARÍA DE ZAYA'S EARLY MODERN FEMINISM, by Lisa Vollendorf. 2001. (No. 270). -9274-2.

FORGED GENEALOGIES: SAINT-JOHN PERSE'S CONVERSATIONS WITH CULTURE, by Carol Rigolot. 2001. (No. 271). -9275-0.

VISIONES DE ESTEREOSCOPIO (PARADIGMA DE HIBRIDACIÓN EN EL ARTE Y LA NARRATIVA DE LA VANGUARDIA ESPAÑOLA), por María Soledad Fernández Utrera. 2001. (No. 272). -9276-9.

TRANSPOSING ART INTO TEXTS IN FRENCH ROMANTIC LITERATURE, by Henry F. Majewski. 2002. (No. 273). -9277-7.

IMAGES IN MIND: LOVESICKNESS, SPANISH SENTIMENTAL FICTION AND *DON QUIJOTE*, by Robert Folger. 2002. (No. 274). -9278-5.

INDISCERNIBLE COUNTERPARTS: THE INVENTION OF THE TEXT IN FRENCH CLASSICAL DRAMA, by Christopher Braider. 2002. (No. 275). -9279-3.

SAVAGE SIGHT/CONSTRUCTED NOISE. POETIC ADAPTATIONS OF PAINTERLY TECHNIQUES IN THE FRENCH AND AMERICAN AVANT-GARDES, by David LeHardy Sweet. 2003. (No. 276). -9281-5.

AN EARLY BOURGEOIS LITERATURE IN GOLDEN AGE SPAIN. *LAZARILLO DE TORMES, GUZMÁN DE ALFARACHE* AND BALTASAR GRACIÁN, by Francisco J. Sánchez. 2003. (No. 277). -9280-7.

METAFACT: ESSAYISTIC SCIENCE IN EIGHTEENTH-CENTURY FRANCE, by Lars O. Erickson. 2004. (No. 278). -9282-3.

THE INVENTION OF THE EYEWITNESS. A HISTORY OF TESTIMONY IN FRANCE, by Andrea Frisch. 2004. (No. 279). -9283-1.

SUBJECT TO CHANGE: THE LESSONS OF LATIN AMERICAN WOMEN'S *TESTIMONIO* FOR TRUTH, FICTION, AND THEORY, by Joanna R. Bartow. 2005. (No. 280). -9284-X.

QUESTIONING RACINIAN TRAGEDY, by John Campbell. 2005. (No. 281). -9285-8.

THE POLITICS OF FARCE IN CONTEMPORARY SPANISH AMERICAN THEATRE, by Priscilla Meléndez. 2006. (No. 282). -9286-6.

MODERATING MASCULINITY IN EARLY MODERN CULTURE, by Todd W. Reeser. 2006. (No. 283). -9287-4.

PORNOBOSCODIDASCALUS LATINUS (1624). KASPAR BARTH'S NEO-LATIN TRANSLATION OF *CELESTINA*, by Enrique Fernández. 2006. (No. 284). -9288-2.

JACQUES ROUBAUD AND THE INVENTION OF MEMORY, by Jean-Jacques F. Poucel. 2006. (No. 285). -9289-0.

THE "I" OF HISTORY. SELF-FASHIONING AND NATIONAL CONSCIOUSNESS IN JULES MICHELET, by Vivian Kogan. 2006. (No. 286). -9290-4.

BUCOLIC METAPHORS: HISTORY, SUBJECTIVITY, AND GENDER IN THE EARLY MODERN SPANISH PASTORAL, by Rosilie Hernández-Pecoraro. 2006. (No. 287). -9291-2.

UNA ARMONÍA DE CAPRICHOS: EL DISCURSO DE RESPUESTA EN LA PROSA DE RUBÉN DARÍO, por Francisco Solares-Larrare. 2007. (No. 288). -9292-0.

READING THE *EXEMPLUM* RIGHT: FIXING THE MEANING OF *EL CONDE LUCANOR*, by Jonathan Burgoyne. 2007. (No. 289). -9293-9.

When ordering please cite the *ISBN Prefix* plus the last four digits for each title.

Send orders to: University of North Carolina Press
P.O. Box 2288
Chapel Hill, NC 27515-2288
U.S.A.
www.uncpress.unc.edu
FAX: 919 966-3829

The Department of Romance Studies Digital Arts and Collaboration Lab at the University of North Carolina at Chapel Hill is proud to support the digitization of the North Carolina Studies in the Romance Languages and Literatures series.

DEPARTMENT OF
Romance Studies
Digital Arts and Collaboration Lab

www.ingramcontent.com/pod-product-compliance
Lightning Source LLC
Chambersburg PA
CBHW030647230426
43665CB00011B/987